Dylan Thomas
The Code of Night

By the same author:

DAVID HOLBROOK

Dylan Thomas
The Code of Night

UNIVERSITY OF LONDON
THE ATHLONE PRESS
1972

Published by
THE ATHLONE PRESS
UNIVERSITY OF LONDON
at 4 *Gower Street London* W C I

Distributed by
Tiptree Book Services Ltd
Tiptree, Essex

© *David Holbrook* 1972

0 485 11135 7

Printed in Great Britain by
WESTERN PRINTING SERVICES LTD
Bristol

For Harry Guntrip

in gratitude for his immense work
in claryfying object-relations theory
and in promoting insights into
the problem of being human

ACKNOWLEDGEMENTS

Extracts from Dylan Thomas's *Collected Poems 1934–1952* and *Selected Letters* (arranged by Constantine Fitzgibbon) are reprinted with the permission of the Dylan Thomas Estate and J. M. Dent & Sons Ltd.

ACKNOWLEDGEMENTS

Extracts from Dylan Thomas's *Collected Poems 1934–1952* and *Selected Letters* (arranged by Constantine Fitzgibbon) are reprinted with the permission of the Dylan Thomas Estate and J. M. Dent & Sons Ltd.

For Harry Guntrip

in gratitude for his immense work
in claryfying object-relations theory
and in promoting insights into
the problem of being human

Introduction
The Genesis of Identity

Dylan Thomas's *Vision and Prayer* begins:
                    Who
                Are you . . .
and ends with a verse which focuses its shape on the word 'I':
                    I
                Am found . . .

The present work is an attempt to show that Dylan Thomas's poetry was an anguished attempt to ask and to answer the question, which is King Lear's question, 'Who is it that can tell me who I am?' He suffered a profound confusion of identity and what R. D. Laing has called 'ontological insecurity'. He was, in fact, a schizoid individual—one of those persons, suffering from a dreadful feeling of never having been born, psychically, into whose plight we are now gaining important new insights. These, I believe, will help us to understand Dylan Thomas's confused behaviour, his incoherence, his alcoholism, his impulse to project a public image, reactions to him ranging from religious adulation to angry rejection, his sexual behaviour, his maddening unreliability, his wit, his solemnity, his hate. But they also help us to understand his poetry.

The critical question will remain, of course, as to how much his poetry has to offer as creative art. As will be seen, however, the 'schizoid diagnosis' enables us to approach this question from a different perspective. It does not absolve us from value judgements but it makes the essential question about a work of art this: 'Does the work convey to us something insightful of the nature of being human?' If we ask this, then I believe we shall conclude that Dylan Thomas did communicate some very fresh insights into strange aspects of human make-up and inward experience. But here we shall need to try to distinguish between his genuine insights, his more chaotic comments on life and certain other anti-human energies in his work. We are enabled to do so, I believe, by certain psychoanalytical explorations of some of the more uncanny aspects of the earliest stages in the formation of the human identity. The phrase 'schizoid diagnosis' is taken from the work of H. Guntrip, whose two fundamental works on psychoanalytical theory will be invoked in this book.[1] Guntrip demonstrates how, in seeking the origins of mental disorders, psychoanalysis has penetrated deeper and deeper into the primary stages of the formation of the human personality. Since they have come to work increasingly with psychotic patients, psycho-therapists find themselves faced with having to help individuals to find answers to the question, 'What is it to be human?' Unless they can draw out answers in such patients, these can never become autonomous human beings. Here, we who have to do with poetry cannot but be interested, because the creative artist is driven by the same need—to question the very basis of one's being and existence. So, as I believe, and as I have argued in other works, the psychoanalyst and the literary critic are beginning to talk the same language in a new way, which helps us to understand poetry better.

Happily, because of other works I have written on the subject, I can leave many of the questions which will immediately spring to the reader's mind, for discussion elsewhere. Here I feel free to take some ideas from recent psychoanalytical thought and see if they can help us to understand the poetry of Dylan Thomas as we have not done before.

I will however insist that it is no part of my intention to 'explain away' Thomas's poetry in terms of the 'sublimation' of other, more 'real', impulses, or as the mere symptoms of a 'sickness'. As Viktor Frankl has pointed out, the capacity to question the nature and point of our existence is that which makes us man. To suffer from existential frustration and despair is not to be 'sick', but to be human. This attitude, found today in 'existential' psycho-analysis, completely reverses the attitude of classical Freudian

[1] *Personality Structure and Human Interaction* (1961) and *Schizoid Phenomena Object-relations, and the Self* (1968).

psychoanalysis, which tended, in a reductionist way, to reduce spiritual anxieties to problems of neurotic complexes or whatever, as though cathedrals were compensations for guilt, or symphonies were the cloaked expressions of sexual aggression. This reductive approach to culture has been one of the worst legacies of Freud's metapsychology and his attempt to base his theory on naturalistic biological science.

Nor is it my intention to 'explain away' cultural activities in 'biological' terms of the expression of, for example, 'unsatisfied desires'. Here the work of the phenomenologists has emphasised that we must pay attention to the meaning, here and now, of symbols and signs in the consciousness of an individual, if we are to understand the way in which he creates himself and his world. It is to reduce the spiritual capacities of a human being to imply that these must be explained in terms of his biological functioning. This attitude accords, too, with the growing recognition in 'object-relations' psychoanalysis, that Freud 'never found a place for culture' and that now it is of the greatest importance to put culture at the centre of man's life, in our attitude to his nature. This revision of perspective has been achieved in recent years by some of the most important 'Freudians'—such as the late D. W. Winnicott. In his paper *The Location of Culture* (in *Playing and Reality*) Winnicott says that 'when we speak of a man we speak of him along with the summation of his cultural experiences', and he notes that when faced with the psychotic the questions a psychotherapist must help him to answer are 'What is it to be human?' and 'What is the point of life?'

The artist may have a disturbed personality, and the disturbances may be at the root of his existential anguish. But it does not dispose of the existential anguish to explain the personality problem. However, if we examine the nature of the psychological disorder, it may help us to understand the meanings of the artist's utterance, as we could not before. Moreover, it may help us to have more compassion, so that as 'participant observers' we do not respond to his torment in inappropriate ways. Problems of personality are acute with Dylan Thomas, as I shall try to show.

There are other dangers in establishing links between an individual's life, his make-up as a 'person', and his art. However, I believe the dangers are less, now it is accepted in existentialist, phenomenological and 'object-relations' psychoanalysis, that culture and symbolism are to be seen in terms of the 'strategy of survival', or, to put this in a more positive way, as ways of developing and sustaining a human identity and a sense of meaning in life.[2] What I shall boldly do, at any rate, is to place my interpretations side by side with fragments of the history of my subject and with conjectures about his life experience derived from the internal evidence of the poetry, leaving the reader to judge whether one illuminates the other or not. The conjectures will be about his experience of psychic parturition.

Many philosophical anthropologists today link the earliest 'encounter' with the mother with the formation of the identity, and see it as the basis of perception. So, our whole attitude to the world is linked with our capacity to love and be loved. When an individual has never been helped to feel real in a real world, this makes it very difficult for us to respond appropriately to him, in any kind of 'encounter'. We tend to project our own problems over him, identify with him, and try to supply him with a role. This itself explains many strange aspects of Dylan Thomas's effect on the world as a literary figure.

The point is that because he had not been sufficiently 'confirmed' in that first 'meeting', by the 'creative reflection' of the mother, he forever after sought to enlist others in confirming his confused identity, by getting them to supply him with some kind of self. The American poet Richard Eberhart confessed to being drawn into a maternal role with Thomas: 'I had to (and was delighted to) get him up in the morning by plugging his mouth with a bottle of beer, this wonderful baby . . .' Many remarks used of him are the kind we use about a baby or infant. Some saw him as an 'elemental clown' (Augustus John) or a 'splendid clown' (Laurence Durrell). Others saw him as a 'fabulous, aging cherub' (Theodore Roethke). Most of those who responded to him note the ambivalence of an infantile vitality combined with destructiveness: 'Many of his poems are concerned with death or the darker forces, yet they all have the joy of life in them . . .' (Louis MacNeice).

[2] Cf. 'Existential analysis . . . attempts to understand the particular world of experience to which (pathological expressions) point and how this world is formed and how it falls apart', Manfred Bleuler quoted in *Existence: A New Dimension in Psychiatry*, ed. Rollo May (1958).

As a man, it is evident that Dylan Thomas had a 'hypersensitive reaction to society' (Glyn Lewis) and a weak reality sense. As some observers say, he showed a 'deliberate avoidance of the complexities (which exist on the active level of moral choice and psychological discrimination) of adult, mature experience' (D. S. Savage). Some saw him as 'a poet of genius unable to face life' (Karl Shapiro). Yet at the same time he seemed to be ruthless in his self-analysis. Suzanne Roussillat observes 'His ruthless self-analysis and pitiless searching bring him face to face with problems which, consciously and unconsciously, beset all men.' Here arose a strange dichotomy, not unlike that found in Dostoevsky's Idiot. Thomas could not 'cope' with life, yet saw more deeply than others into it. He faced deep human problems—yet disguised these in his poems so well that no-one could say what these problems were about: 'Thomas sometimes attempted to keep people from understanding his poems' (Karl Shapiro).

Thomas worked very hard:

He wrote slowly, I found to my surprise, and with difficulty in that small square hand . . . He also mutated adjectives and nouns until he squeezed them into the right shape to suit his theme. He went on worrying at them for ages before he was satisfied. I saw one phrase which filled a whole exercise book, repeated over and over again in various ways . . . (Laurence Durrell)

but the end-product was often incomprehensible:

What I honestly want to know is why, as a scholar, as one who is not unacquainted practically with the intricacies and ardours of verse-composition, and after a week of evening readings with a headache at the end, and not a single line of this volume left memorably ringing in my mind, I can get more sense out of an Anglo-Saxon riddle . . . (Geoffrey Johnson).

At the same time Thomas himself spoke of seeking a deeper awareness of inner problems than ever Freud had provided:

Yes. Whatever is hidden should be made naked. To be stripped of darkness is to be clean, to strip of darkness is to make clean. Poetry, recording the stripping of the individual darkness, must, inevitably, cast light upon what has been hidden for too long, and, by so doing, make clean the naked exposure. Freud cast light on a little of the darkness he had exposed. Benefitting by the sight of the light and the knowledge of the hidden nakedness, poetry must drag further into the clean nakedness of light more of the hidden causes than Freud could realise.

(*New Verse*, October 1939)

I believe Thomas meant what he said here. And I believe that to this extent he knew what he was doing—which was to express the schizoid plight of needing to be born psychically to the 'first nakedness', by coming into the light. I believe other poets, such as Sylvia Plath, learnt from him how to express deeper aspects of this plight. I believe Thomas devised a 'code of night' to express the urge to 'strip off darkness' and 'make clean' the heart of being —to be born in the being for the first time.

But there are also dangers, as we shall see. For the study of schizoid processes by Fairbairn, Winnicott, Guntrip and Laing shows that the 'strategies' of such individuals may well take on a 'widdershins' character—and involve them in what we must call 'false solutions'. This falsity may have its own heroic quality but it can be perverse in a number of ways because it is based on hate rather than love, and on negative rather than positive modes. One such 'solution' with Dylan Thomas was that at times he seems deliberately to have sought to create and preserve chaos in his work. And, as is obvious, he sought at times to involve the reader in the inversion of values, in vindications of hate, and even in his 'death-circuit' delusions about the nature and goals of self-destruction. That is, he shows a joyful attachment to the impulse to schizoid suicide—the joy being an expression of the delusion that suicide was the path to a new birth. So, strangely, like Sylvia Plath, while he poignantly wanted to live, he wanted to destroy himself too.

In unravelling the problem of our response to the appeal of such a schizoid individual we need ourselves to go back to the very start of the human identity—for it is a re-enactment of what happens there to which we are responding. Here we are fortunate, because a number of disciplines are increasingly concerning themselves with these origins of the human person—philosophy (of the existentialist kind), philosophical biology (especially the phenomenologists) and psychoanalysis. With their aid we may explore some of the earliest states of being, such as the strange telepathy that happens between adult and baby—a state occasionally explored in literature. Winnicott called it 'primary maternal preoccupation', and, for example, Coleridge in his poem *Frost at Midnight* virtually takes us into this state. The poet is sitting in the silent night beside the cot of his sleeping infant. His own identity, going over to merge with the undifferentiated baby, seems to grow as tenuous as the blue flame on the grate, and seems also, like the 'film' on the grate bars, as likely, with its *'puny flaps* and *freaks'*, to be about to go out of existence with no more than a flutter:

> The thin blue flame
> Lies on my low-burnt fire, and quivers not;
> Only that film, which fluttered on the grate,
> Still flutters there, the sole unquiet thing.
> Methinks its motion in this hush of nature
> Gives it dim sympathies with me who live,
> Making it a companionable form,
> Whose puny flaps and freaks the idling Spirit
> By its own moods interprets everywhere
> Mirror or echo seeking of itself,
> And makes a toy of Thought . . .

The rest of this poem explores the nature of perception, as it develops in the infant, and ways in which it is possible to feel real, by having a vivid sense of meaning in one's surroundings. One way to confirm one's own reality is by identifying to an exceptional degree with another, and feeling into what one imagines the other to be feeling, or to be likely to feel. By intensely identifying with his sleeping infant, in a kind of *couvade*,[3] Coleridge seems to attain a conviction of being alive, and secure again in his identity, through intense sense-memories which he 'gives' the baby:

> The nigh thatch
> Smokes in the sun thaw . . .

The way in which perception of a meaningful world is created by such forms of 'encounter' is now being recognised by many observers. Winnicott's concept of 'creative reflection' is endorsed by the work on 'encounter' by F. J. J. Buytendijk, and by certain reflections of Jacques Lacan. The origins of a positive sense of

---

[3] *Couvade* is the male equivalent of 'primary maternal preoccupation'. In anthropology it is used of the father's experience of actual birth pangs. Here I mean identifying with the baby as the mother does.

meaning in life in these processes is being explored by existential philosophy (Buber–Binswanger).[4]

The schizoid individual is one to whom this development of the sense of I AM, a secure reality sense, and a sense of meaning, have never been given by the processes of psychic parturition and by 'creative reflection' by the mother in her 'mirror-role'. What he still urgently needs is confirmation of identity, at the heart of being, such as the mother gives.

As psychoanalytical thought develops it seeks to explain not only how we are 'confirmed' by our ego-relationships with others (e.g. family, social situation, occupation, church, etc.), but how we develop in our 'inner world' a secure sense of our own existence, even when we are alone, round the internalisation of our experience of 'the significant other'—and others. This way of thinking about identity and perception now unites the scientist (see Marjorie Grene's *Approaches to a Philosophical Biology*) with the philosopher and the literary critic. Inevitably, this approach to man's inward life involves us, too, in different modes of thinking about man. We can see this in a passage from Buber:

> The I-Thou relation consists in confronting a being external to oneself, i.e. one which is radically other, and to recognise it as such. This recognition of otherness, however, is not to be confused with the *idea* of otherness. To have an idea of something is appropriate to the I-It relation. What is important is not thinking *about* the other, even *as* an other, but of directly confronting it and saying Thou to it. Hence a real access to the otherness of the other does not consist in a perception but in thou-saying, and this is at once an immediate contact and an appeal which does not posit an object, but of which the object-relation is, in fact, a distortion. This does not mean that the Thou is some unknown sort of object but rather *that the movement which relates the Thou is not like one that sets any theme of discourse.*

The I-Thou relation, therefore, escapes the gravitational field of the I-It in which the externalised object remains imprisoned.[5]

---

[4] See the article 'Stade du Miroir' in *Vocabulaire de le Psychanalyse*, J. Laplanche and J. B. Pontalis; also *New Left Review*, 51, p. 63 ff., and J. Lacan, *Ecrits* (Paris, 1966). See also F. J. J. Buytendijk on play, smiles and 'encounter' in Marjorie Grene, *op. cit.* (1965).

[5] Quoted in 'Martin Buber and the Theory of Knowledge', Emmanuel

This perception opens up a whole area of experience and knowledge which our intellectual world has too long ignored.

We cannot satisfactorily account for the poetry of a writer like Dylan Thomas unless we escape from that kind of thinking which belongs to the I-It, and enter into explorations of this kind of 'confronting', nor can we respond to it properly without going more deeply into problems of existence and meaning. Dylan Thomas was speaking of experiences which are 'new' in the sense that they have never before been made communicable in just his way and cannot be made communicable in the 'I-It' way, because to try to do so is to threaten 'imprisonment'—and a reduction of live to dead objects. His work perhaps has as its parallel the contemporary investigations of the growth of the foetus in the womb, or the study of the 'nursing couple'—areas of human truth which, for unconscious reasons largely, have remained more or less unexplored until recently. This penetration to the realm of the start of life in medical science has its complement in the progress of psychoanalytical thought to the study of psychic parturition—as when 'object-relations' psychology explores the internalisation of the I-Thou as a 'confrontation', out of which a 'Thou-saying' may come.

This progress towards beginnings, however, also has a philosophical significance and this in turn has a bearing upon creative expression and symbolism. It has import that philosophers such as Sartre, Merleau-Ponty, and Martin Buber have concerned themselves with aspects of being and existence; that psychoanalytical thought has come to focus on the primary mother-child relationship, while poetry such as that of Dylan Thomas centres round images of mother and child, birth, extinction and beginning. Our problems of meaning in life can no longer be solved easily by secure references to a transcendental reality: 'God is dead'—at least as an object 'out there' to be apprehended beyond ourselves. Even where there is belief in a spiritual reality, emphasis has turned, in theologians such as Teilhard de Chardin, Buber and Tillich, to finding it within the given reality of this world and in the substance of our human existence. So, where we need to discover 'ontological security' in a sense of being, we inevitably

Levinas, *The Philosophy of Martin Buber*, ed. Schlipp and Friedmann (1968), p. 138. My italics.

turn to the origins of that sense—or the origins of our lack of such a sense—in primary experiences from which the individual identity springs. Thus, to explore contemporary writing, or to make up one's mind about conflicting attitudes to life, one is inevitably brought to need to explore accounts of human origins, the ontology of being.

The fact that philosophers and those concerned with the cultural record of experience are turning to psychology to tell them what it is to be human has in part provoked the crisis in psychology. This discipline is in consequence being forced to see the limitations of 'objectivity' and to concern itself with man's inner life. So, the literary critic who turns from poetry to enquire into the truth of human nature, finds himself involved in that crisis. He cannot make his decisions and evaluations about contemporary writing until he has made up his mind where he stands in the quest for a unifying concept of man's reality.

* * *

A major problem here, however, is how we can find terms in which to discuss the problems we encounter. As soon as we explore the earliest processes of psychic growth, the relation between what Winnicott called 'the maturational processes and the facilitating environment', we enter into regions of which it is almost impossible to speak. The problem is even more acute when these processes do not go right, for articulate expression itself grows out of them—they create an 'I' which can say 'I AM' and speak of the world. If these processes themselves go chaotic and leave a chaotic self as their product—how can we speak of this formlessness and disintegration clearly, when it cannot speak of itself or find communication with a meaningful world? This problem was tackled superbly by R. D. Laing in *The Divided Self*—in which he led us into an investigation of the meaning of such chaos, phenomenologically.

But let me take one of the essential problems, and see how we may explore it, as we find it in psychology and in poetry—the question raised above, of success or failure in 'psychic parturition'.

We can only develop the capacity to speak of this area of experience, I believe, if we approach it with the help of those who have been courageous enough to live through forms of committed contact with individuals who are re-living formative processes in face-to-face 'encounter', like Winnicott. Such a psychoanalyst has the advantage of communicating, in a close and sometimes desperate relationship, with individuals in regression for whom, for some reason, these earliest experiences have failed to complete themselves. Having studied in particular the problems of mothers and infants and of patients in regression, Winnicott came to believe he had discovered a special state of extension of identity in the mother already referred to, which 'deserved a name', so he called it 'primary maternal preoccupation'. This concept is of the greatest importance to my study here. It describes the capacity of the mother to 'forego her self-interest', and to more or less lose her own identity, or let it go 'fluid', so that the new human being can 'make use of it'. At first the infant believes he 'is' the mother, and makes the mother his 'subjective object'. As the mother 'recovers her self-interest' she 'disillusions' the baby about this primitive identification, and enables him to make her his 'objective object'. This is a positive and creative process whereby the new child discovers reality and the reality of himself, of the *me* and the *not-me*. But no human infant can become himself until he has gone through this process of intense primary identification, in the realm of 'being'. If it fails he may become a 'schizoid individual'.

But there is a degree to which we all suffer the schizoid problem because neither we nor our mothers were perfect: and the complex processes of life never complete themselves perfectly. So, the 'schizoid person' who has identity problems of a severe kind, speaks, in a sense, for us all. What he utters will always find an echo in us.

The way in which the mother creates the new human individual is through 'being for' the infant. This is a female capacity. If she cannot 'be' for him, and allow him to make use of her in those mysterious, intuitive, ghostly ways of primary maternal preoccupation, then she will try to make do by a substitute 'bustling' activity. But this will be a *male* activity, and even 'pseudo-male'. The male capacities are necessary for our dealings with the world: but they are not good enough to provide 'psychic parturition' for the very start of the human identity. The baby, needing love and psychic nurture, but only getting an empty and mechanical (male) 'doing for' will feel this kind of unimaginative handling as an 'impingement'. It doesn't feel right: and it doesn't feel like 'feminine element being'. The child then has to try to put himself together, consequently, on the basis of experiences which don't feel right, and feel 'false', and on male activities, when female modes were needed: a self is established by 'doing' rather than 'being', and by thinking rather than feeling. This theory Winnicott extends into a theory of human bisexuality, of great significance for the understanding of problems of identity, as we shall see later.

The adequate human identity is composed of a core of 'being' established by the mother's 'female element' capacity to 'be' for the infant, to let him make use of her emotional and spiritual capacities as a woman. This establishes a core of being, which Winnicott calls the 'True Self', and which is drawn out first in the female element of 'being'. Later from this core can develop all those capacities to deal with the world which belong to the 'male element' of activity. But the female element of 'being' comes first. The mother at first is enabled to 'go over' into primary maternal preoccupation by 'forfeiting her self-interest' while her man takes care of the external world on her behalf. Later, as she 'recovers', she recovers also her 'male element' capacities to deal with the outside world. Many of us have observed this in a woman who has had a baby. At first she finds it very difficult to cope with the outer world at all, and is completely involved with her infant. Here the father can help her to 'return' to the world, as if by holding on to the rope while she is at the bottom of the well. Gradually she returns to 'self-interest' which is also an interest in the world around her, and in doing so she begins to offer the baby 'male element' aspects of herself in a normal way. The baby thus takes in both female element and male element, into an integrated personality, in touch with the 'True Self'.

Where, however, the baby has had to establish a sense of self from his mother's 'male activity' when it is a substitute for female 'being', this inevitably has a false quality. Her inadequate handling is experienced as hate: it feels like 'being done to'. What is established may be a 'False Self' based on pseudo-male 'doing' (and this can include very active *thinking* and also compulsive '*bad*' *thinking*). Since the infant struggled to continue to exist by falling in with the mother's pseudo-male activity, his False Self has a 'conformity basis', and is maintained by doing what is expected of him, rather than what feels exactly and inwardly 'right'. At the centre of his being, however, such an individual may be left with a sense of hollowness, of a conformity that does not belong to the true life pattern of the self, and a sense of having never been born, in the realm of being, into his essential inheritance.

Moreover, the situation is more desperate than this, because the structure of the self based on conformity to pseudo-male 'impingement' feels insecure and ramshackle. At the heart of being there remains a deep hunger to 'be', and, since the child's ego is a mouth-ego, this hunger to exist fully feels like a voracious mouth. It feels so powerful that it threatens to eat up the object, and devour any objects of love. It feels so hungry that it threatens thus to destroy all objects, and to leave the self bereft, so that it would perish.

Furthermore, since the infant offered love in trying to establish an 'I-Thou' relationship with the mother, and since this love feels as if it has been rejected by her 'impingement' response which is experienced as hate, the infant feels that what he has inside him must be 'bad'. By infantile logic he concludes that to love is dangerous not least because his ego is a 'mouth ego', and his hunger to love and be loved feels so voracious that it threatens from within to eat up his love objects, and even himself. He thus develops a complexity of confused and conflicting energies within the personality, which reduce his living power and threaten his sense of meaningful existence.

Only in such terms can we begin to discuss the bodily and psychic origins of the tragic schizoid predicament. Individuals who suffer such schizoid problems in an acute way experience severe feelings of weakness of identity as feelings of hollowness at the core; fears of being full of 'bad stuff'; fears of being confused with others or actually becoming them; feelings of not being 'in' the body (i.e. feelings of depersonalisation); fears that relationship will 'empty' them, or fill them with harm, or eat them up; fears of coming 'unstuck' or being petrified—all of which are discussed with great understanding in the early works of R. D. Laing on problems of 'the divided self'. But since it is essentially in the area of 'female element being' that the trouble lies, there is in such individuals a yearning to feel strength at the heart of identity, combined with a terrifying feeling of having never been born at that heart—as if there were a (psychic) baby in them which *had never been born*. They yearn for this 'regressed libidinal ego' to be born. Yet, since they fear their own weakness, part of them also turns in hate against this weak self. In Fairbairnian terms, the 'anti-libidinal ego' turns on the 'regressed libidinal ego' and crushes it.[6]

Such explorations of infant feelings explain the powerful psychic energies at work behind identity problems such as we encounter in poetry at times. There is no more compelling demand than that made by a very young child, that you confirm his identity by reflecting him. Indeed, so compelling is the power of this demand that it even seems at times to the young parent when the demand is first experienced that he or she will lose their own identity in the process. Indeed, to some extent a mother has to forfeit her self-interest and be, psychically speaking, 'eaten' in order to bring up a child, and this fear of going out of existence is a continual theme in nursery rhyme and fairy story. It underlies our fascination with cannibalism. Such strong feelings to do with loss of identity are not confined to women, of course. A man can feel them, too, with his 'female' element, as we have seen from Coleridge's poem.

The individual with severe existential problems continues to want to be born—though, of course, the birth he yearns for is a psychic birth. His yearnings, however, often become expressed in symbols of birth, or of having not been born, or of being thwarted from birth, or in some symbolism of the difference between the desire for birth of the True Self and the substitute nature of the False Self which is, in the meantime, acting as 'caretaker'. 'Return to the womb' phantasies may thus express a desire to return to 'psychic parturition', and as many have observed this is one of Dylan Thomas's recurrent images. Discovery of the 'me' in relation to the real world, with all the connected problems of perception and interaction with one's environment, are seen by object-relations psychology as originating in that positive kind of mothering which establishes our creative relation-

[6] The above paragraphs summarise theories from Melanie Klein, D. W. Winnicott, W. R. D. Fairbairn and others. See a more thorough summary in Guntrip's *Schizoid Phenomena, Object-relations and the Self* and in my own *Human Hope and the Death Instinct* (1971). See also *Playing and Reality*, D. W. Winnicott (1971) and *Psychoanalytical Studies of the Personality*, W. R. D. Fairbairn (1948).

ship with the world as object. This is seen by Coleridge who desires an environment for his son in which the natural world shall confirm the infant like a creative mother, as a manifestation of God, who shall 'By giving make it ask'. What is established by such successful reflection is a dynamic of 'intentionality'—what Winnicott calls 'creative looking'.

In Yeats's poem *Among School Children* I believe we may also find a reference to the problems of the experience of being mothered. Reflecting on the children in the classroom before him, the poet meditates on childhood experience in general. He seems to be speaking of his own sometime 'ideal object' Maud Gonne as he knew her as a child, but we can say, I believe, that Yeats's problems of object-relations were so severe that they can be traced to earlier origins at the start of identity, so that we would be justified in linking his attitude to Maud Gonne as a child to his experience of his own mother when he was a child. Thus, when he speaks of the extreme closeness between himself and Maud, he is surely also speaking of the infant's primary identification with the mother?

> it seemed that our two natures blent
> Into a sphere from youthful sympathy,
> Or else, to alter Plato's parable,
> Into the yolk and white of the one shell . . .

Maud has now been 'emptied' by Time:

> Hollow of cheek as though it drank the wind . . .

From the point of view of object-relations psychology this expresses feelings not only about mutability but also primitive feelings about the 'emptying' of the mother. So, before long, the mother appears, in the extraordinary verse:

> What youthful mother, a shape upon her lap
> Honey of generation had betrayed,
> And that must sleep, shriek, struggle to escape
> As recollection or the drug decide,
> Would think her son, did she but see that shape
> With sixty or more winters on its head,
> A compensation for the pang of his birth,
> Or the uncertainty of his setting forth?

Is not this the expression of a sense of schizoid futility—of a feeling of existential meaninglessness which nothing can overcome? He speaks as if the infant has been thrust on the mother by the temptation of the urge to procreate: she can only reject it. The infant can only feel its own birth as an impingement—its reactions are only to 'sleep, shriek, struggle to escape/As recollection or the drug decide'. The baby can be put to sleep by anodynes: insofar as it is awake and aware, through reflection, of its existence, it shrieks or struggles to escape, because being born into life is too terrible. Yeats seems here to regard birth as entering into a kind of imprisonment—an attitude to the original emergence of oneself also found in Sartre—and in Dylan Thomas ('Time held me green and dying—'). The 'imprisonment' is the experience of 'impingement'—felt as hate. From this unwilling entry the rest of life proceeds in mere futility—supposing it to be regarded so by the mother, who is incapable of the 'creative reflection' such as Coleridge wishes his child, in *Frost at Midnight*.

From the 'schizoid diagnosis' I believe we can reinterpret Yeats's poem as recording a glimpse in memory of psychic parturition at the hands of a mother who cannot convey a hopeful and creative sense of being a human 'going concern' to her baby, and convey joy in his creative potentialities for the future, by her intuitive response to his smiles and gestures. She rejects him and can only give him a sense of 'uncertainty' in his setting forth—that is, a profound 'ontological insecurity'. So, nature can seem like a 'spume that plays/Upon a ghostly paradigm of things': reality can seem but a projection on to a ghostly scheme, without real substance. Apperception and perception are confused. Even artefacts are 'old clothes upon old sticks to scare a bird'. Except insofar as he can exist in the intellectual constructions of the mind, Yeats does not feel real or secure. He feels a bitter contrast between the idealism of a mother who cannot 'be' for her child, the non-human images of religion, and the actual individual with human needs:

> Both nuns and mothers worship images,
> But those the candles light are not as those
> That animate a mother's reveries . . .

Out of this poignant quest for what is 'real', in such lines, Yeats seeks that which gives meaning to human existence. It is somewhere between bodily vitality in existence and the creations of the mind and its symbolism:

O chestnut tree, great rooted blossomer,
Are you the leaf, the blossom, or the bole?

But in the background is the schizoid feeling to which Laing draws our attention: 'life, without feeling alive'. The poetry is spun out of a lack of confidence in distinguishing between *me* and *not-me*, and the 'inner contents' of the mind and 'inner contents' of the body, which have no confirmed substance established by the mother's creative reflection. Because time wrecks the physical body, Yeats can find no secure significance in being in the body (and was not given enough in infancy by loving handling). The mind, which feels the body tied to it like something to a dog's tail, can too easily yield only 'blear-eyed wisdom out of midnight oil'. Between the physical existence and mental aridity there is a third dimension—that of the 'body swayed to music' and the blossoming tree, in which all the parts become a whole whose significance transcends mere existence. In culture, which symbolises the space between union and separateness, a man can exist, and his symbolic culture links his consciousness with his bodily existence, since it is from the latter that symbols emerge. In this can be found a sense of 'being alive' as a human creature, which is neither mere bodily existence, nor mind-spun paradigm, but something else which does not 'bruise' body to 'pleasure' soul.

This exploration of the question of 'the point of life' has its origins, as I have tried to suggest, in a reminiscence of the earliest environment, where the problems began of the need to integrate the 'ideal' (the phantasy) and the 'real' (the body-feelings)—a problem Yeats himself seems never to have satisfactorily solved. This tendency to 'split' experience itself had its origins in psychic parturition, and can be related to the problems of 'primary maternal preoccupation'. A mother who cannot 'be' for her infant is forced to 'impinge' and this feels like *hate:* so, she leaves him in doubt about his 'inner contents', and because she has not been able to 'receive' his love gifts, these feel 'bad'. This is associated with the rejection of love, and from it follows the strange inversion of values noted by W. R. D. Fairbairn in schizoid individuals who substitute hate for love because the latter is too dangerous.[7] The infant is dependent on the mother, however, and

[7] See the next chapter for a discussion of this topic.

is presented with an acute problem of existence by the ambivalence of which he becomes aware in her: her rejecting side and his bad elements cannot be relied on. She has not been able to make him feel whole and valued for his own sake, for what *he is*. Unable to say I AM with confidence he develops intense problems, both about accepting her and accepting himself.

Yeats's answers to these problems tend to result from the psychological processes called introjection, splitting and projection. He takes the threatening aspects of his mother into himself as 'bad object' to deal with them there, while the object itself, recognised only through 'male element doing', becomes something of an intellectual construct and, since the subject depends upon it, is made into an 'ideal' object which is totally dependable. It is pure and perfect: it must not be spoilt by contact with any of the rejecting elements of hate and impurity which belong to the real mother, or which lurk as 'bad' within oneself. For such individuals, obviously, there are great difficulties in adult life in relating to an actual woman and combining their libidinal and ideal sides into the capacity to relate in an integrated way with the ideal and the libidinal in the object. As subject they are divided and find it difficult to accept the ambivalence in themselves, in case the bad 'spoils' the good. They also find it difficult to integrate male and female elements in themselves, since the female element has proved so dangerous and threatening, while the sensitive core of the True Self is weak and empty. The female element therefore tends to become split off and projected over others (here over ideal objects (Maud Gonne) or bad objects ('love has pitched his mansion in the place of excrement')), while they cope with life in terms of 'pseudo male doing', on the one hand, and tormented idealism on the other. All these problems of finding the 'other' we find in Yeats, as in many other poets, from Heine to Sylvia Plath. In Dylan Thomas we find many problems arising from difficulties in 'finding' and relating to one 'whole' woman, in the acceptance of her as a real 'other' person, and not a paradigm spun out of his idealism.

My exegesis on psychic parturition and the problem of finding the 'other' as it occurs in poetry indicates, I believe, that there are some literary subjects which are impossible to elucidate satisfactorily unless we make use of the insights of psychotherapy.

Dylan Thomas I believe to be such a subject: there was surely never a poet to whom so great attention was given without yielding more than a pinch of meaning? The difficulty of understanding what yet fascinates explains, I suggest, this immense industry of attention to Dylan Thomas. There are only a few poems in his oeuvre which yield an immediate clear meaning: so, we have to try to meet him halfway. I recognise I am part of this industry myself. But I believe that the nature of Thomas's critical reception is an aspect of the whole problem. For some reason Thomas seeks to draw us into a certain kind of relationship to him. This may be hostile, like my own earlier response. Or it may be an attempt to give his work far more than the benefit of the doubt. Whatever our reaction, I believe it is impelled by something like *couvade*: our response is a form of 'primary maternal preoccupation' itself.

Such a statement will no doubt make many literary critics and scholars uncomfortable. How is a literary critic like a gravid mother? But it is a conclusion to which all my studies point. Thomas lures us into the role of mother, therapist, or other reflecting participant, who can supply completeness to an identity which is incomplete, and supply confirmation to an identity which does not feel real in itself. To leave such an individual in anguished need of 'reflection' unconfirmed would feel too dreadful, and would expose *us*—the potential reflectors—to threats of annihilation ourselves. For where we cannot confirm, since 'all life is meeting' (Martin Buber), we feel unconfirmed ourselves: like Coleridge in *Frost at Midnight* we become evanescent. His unconscious invitation to us to help him *complete* an incomplete personality explains the appeal which has created the Dylan Thomas industry as a world-wide phenomenon, and the passionate partisanship that focuses on him and his work.

My thesis here will be based on an assumption that Thomas was confused in some way at the very start of his identity by his mother's handling and so was dogged all his life by a sense of having to cope with a ghost of a self, or of being in competition with a ghost of a self as well as having a self. The True Self remained unborn,

> Crouched in the natural doorway
> Sewing a shroud for a journey . . .

Birth was for him a kind of death—being born into life to exist
(like Laing's patients) without feeling alive:

>Since the first womb spat forth a baby's corpse . . .

Moreover, not only do we have a problem of True and False
Self, and a confusion of selves in Dylan Thomas—but we also have
the kind of need which Laing found among schizoid patients, to
preserve chaos in self-defence against the dangers of integration. The
schizoid individual can feel so afraid of human contact that he
feels he can only prevent himself being taken over by others if he
preserves himself as a loose and chaotic assemblage of selves. To be
in such a condition obviously affects the capacity to use symbols,
since symbolism can be used only by a self which is capable of
relating to others, to the external world, and to the inner psychic
reality of the self. The schizophrenic cannot symbolise, and the
schizoid individual cannot get on 'good terms with himself',
because he failed to be on good terms with his mother in the first
place, who is the origin of the first symbol and all symbols.

Thus, as a poet, Dylan Thomas presents acute problems because
he had to preserve chaos in his work. This was a 'strategy of
survival', maintaining his own division:

>And let my hero show his double strength
>And all his laughter hidden up his sleeve . . .

What he preserved by such hard work is a dissociation so frightening that we are drawn to attempt to supply meaning because
we cannot bear to leave no meaning, or incomplete meaning, or
chaos. His need to preserve chaos even involved him in killing the
life in his own work and in mechanical methods of composition.
These negative impulses parallel his impulse in life to destroy
himself. Here it is interesting to note that Professor Ralph Maud's
study *The Notebooks of Dylan Thomas* indicates that many of the
poems on which Thomas's reputation rests were in fact written
by the age of nineteen and worked over again and again until
they were published. When one studies these it is often disappoint-
ing to find that the end product has less life than the original, so
that (for instance)

>And heaven was a cloudy hole, and hell
>A burning stick across the bum of space
>>('In the beginning', *Notebooks*, p. 240)

written at nineteen, becomes

> And, burning ciphers on the round of space
> Heaven and hell mixed as they spun . . .
> ('In the beginning', *Collected Poems*, p. 22)

My evidence here, for my psychological analysis, is almost entirely based on interpretation of the poetry. But I shall refer to biographical material occasionally. For instance, it is of very great interest to me that Dylan Thomas's mother had an earlier child die in her womb, and that he himself had a difficult birth. I know from observing those close to me how intense a woman's memory of her dead child can be and how it can become a major element in her attitude to experience throughout her life—perhaps from some unconscious desire to restore that original baby to life, symbolically. Inevitably, such intense needs can confuse others. I shall also discuss Thomas's alcoholism, and link it with the oral aggressiveness of his poetry.

One of the most debatable aspects of the present work, however, is that at times I have been obliged to embark upon *sheer conjecture* about my subject. This might seem to invalidate the work altogether, from the point of view of the professional biographer. It is, of course, no excuse to say that many works of biographers and critics also exhibit conjecture. I must try to vindicate my own processes here.

The difficulty arises, I believe, out of the nature of the schizoid predicament itself. My primary concern is to *make accessible the meaning of the poetry*. One of the problems, as I have suggested, is that with the schizoid individual communication itself tends to be incomplete. As is recognised in therapy, the psychotherapist treating a schizoid patient has to strive extremely hard to find some way of establishing communication. This is at one with the problem of seeking to confirm the patient's identity by a creative reflective response to his potentialities.

Inevitably this establishing of communication involves the psychotherapist in the imaginative attempt to postulate the meaning of what the patient is saying. There is an occupational hazard in this, which is brilliantly discussed by Leslie H. Farber in *The Ways of the Will* in a chapter called 'Schizophrenia and the Mad Psychotherapist'. The problem is deciding whether the 'poet' which the therapist 'finds' in his schizophrenic patient is in his own head or the patient's. Where a schizoid patient is comprehensible

to his therapist but to no-one else, we may suppose that if the
therapist is enthusiastic about his utterances and believes them
to be poetry, then the 'poet' may only be in the therapist's
head. But Laing has also shown that the poetry of schizoid
patients can become meaningful to us, if we are given a little
help through insight into their symbolism to complete its meaning. In the work of Dylan Thomas of course we have some poetry
already found meaningful by many people, and he was a practising
poet as most schizophrenic patients are not.

A great deal of Dylan Thomas's poetry, though it is fascinating,
eludes us and is not meaningful by itself. In some way it is not
complete: and the critic's task is to complete it, so that the meaning
can be found. This involves us in attempting to decode the 'code
of night', and I believe an understanding of the problems of
symbolising found in schizoid patients can help us. But we first
have to decide *what kind of meaning this poetry could possibly have.*
Here we need to introduce various possible patterns of human
experience like Cinderella's slipper, to see if they fit. Many have
applied the patterns of Christian symbolism to Dylan Thomas,
and they have found that in the light of them his poetry makes a
kind of sense. I have seldom found such explanations convincing.
After studying object-relations psychology I came to believe that
the feelings of identification with Christ, of wanting to be born
again, and of arrested birth in Thomas's work are symbols to
which a better key is the deeper pattern of the schizoid predicament, and the dynamics of the schizoid individual wanting to
become a person and find meaning in his life. Insofar as these are
Christian they are symbols belonging to elements in Christian
mythology itself which express man's universal need to overcome
despair and find a meaning in his existence.

So we need to conjecture possible patterns of meaning and this
involves us in wondering what, in the man's experience, is the
fundamental 'position' (to use a Kleinian term).[8] Though a
biographer normally sticks to the facts of relics and records—
things that can be shown to have happened—he will often be

---

[8] Melanie Klein speaks of the 'schizoid position' and the 'depressive position'
meaning not only a stage in growth, but a stage whose complex features remain
within an individual's psychic tissue all his life and lie beneath the phenomena of
his consciousness.

found to depart from fact, and to make conjectural deductions which belong to the area of those 'human facts' of the psychic life—as, for instance, by discussing the influence of his mother on a subject. Here we are usually willing to accept patterns of cause and effect at the surface level of human interaction. So-and-so's mother was a dominant woman and left little room for other women in his life: this kind of causal connection would seem to us acceptable conjecture.

Trouble arises, however, when one approaches emotional or identity problems whose origins are very early in personal development and belong to the 'schizoid position'. Intense resistance occurs because to even see these involves the recognition of the 'regressed libidinal ego', the weak and infantile core of the self—and all our fears of loss of existence. So we are in difficulties if we try to explore the meaning of a poem and to complete its meaning we have to encounter the expression of the experience (say) of being so much 'let down' by the mother that the identity itself is in jeopardy. Yet, as I have suggested, poems such as Yeats's *Among School Children*, and Coleridge's *Frost at Midnight* do pursue problems of existence related to this earliest experience of being 'put together' (or perhaps 'not being put together') by the mother's physical and psychic care. Is it legitimate to make such a conjecture about the earliest of experiences?

Now the literary public obviously finds it acceptable to say of Dylan Thomas, 'his mother pampered and coddled him . . . in part because such was her nature, but also in part because she regarded him as a semi-invalid, a role he accepted easily'[9]—though obviously in this there is much conjecture. Publisher and reader have no doubt about such a subjective conjecture over cause and effect. Yet the publisher perhaps hesitated to allow the biographer to reveal that, on one occasion at least, Dylan Thomas the man defecated in his clothes like a baby, and at times required maternal attention like a child still untrained. We can, that is, tolerate the explicit recognition of regression to a degree—but there is a limit, beyond which we become too alarmed to go. My conjectures are intended to pursue considerations into this dangerous territory.

Of course, nothing of the life of a baby who became a poet can

[9] Constantine Fitzgibbon, *Life*, p. 24.

ever be known as biographical *fact*. There are ancillary facts, such as Thomas's incapacity to take the top off an egg himself in adolescence and his slow suicide by alcohol. *But there is plenty of evidence of a schizoid predicament in the poetry.* I ask for the validity of my conjectures to be judged from this evidence in his symbolism (and sometimes symbolic failure). Having made my conjectures, by applying the 'schizoid diagnosis' to the poetry and then analysing the symbolism as schizoid symbolism—does the poetry make better sense? And do the postulated 'events' seem likely? If they do, then we can forget them, take down the scaffolding of the schizoid diagnosis—and see the poetry for the first time as an artefact, expressing deep problems of existence which are universal ones. The poetry can then be seen as an heroic attempt to solve existential problems, by one whose existence was always in doubt, in a way we find it hard to bear even to understand.

I

Ethical Problems of the Schizoid Individual

With schizoid individuals the normal processes of development, towards being able to relate to a whole world from a whole self, have been disrupted, because of an early failure to be assured of an inner entity of the self. The disruption takes the form of divisions within the self: Fairbairn sees this splitting of identity having its origins in the 'early oral phase' of infant development. Here Fairbairn explores the links between incorporation, love and hate which we shall find of great importance in dealing with Dylan Thomas. And from his insights we can see how specific moral problems arise from the schizoid condition.

'The ego of the infant', Fairbairn says, 'may be described as a "mouth ego".'

So far as the infant is concerned, the mouth is the chief organ of desire, the chief instrument of activity, the chief medium of satisfaction and frustration, the chief channel of love and hate, and, most important of all, the first means of intimate social contact. The first social relationship established by the individual is that between himself and his mother; and the focus of this relationship is the suckling situation, in which his mother's breast provides the focal point of his own libidinal attitude.

(*Psychoanalytical Studies of the Personality*, p. 11)

To Fairbairn the characteristic difficulties of the schizoid individual in dealing between inner and outer reality belong to what Abraham called the 'early oral stage' and centre round a '*libidinal attitude of oral incorporation*'. As Guntrip says:

The schizoid phase has its own characteristic form of aggression.

The frustrated hungry infant does not *aim* to destroy the breast but to possess it. He may however . . . in phantasy see himself destroying it in the act of seeking to possess it . . . One of my schizoid patients woke up in terror one night feeling herself nothing but one big hungry devouring mouth swallowing up everyone and everything . . . (*Personality Structure*, p. 342)

The essential problem of the schizoid individual is that he has not established a developing sense of a relationship between himself as a person and his mother as a person. The phantasies of the frustrated 'mouth ego' predominate over the realities of individual human beings. These are of the kind described by Melanie Klein:

The phantasied onslaughts . . . follow two main lines: one is the predominantly oral impulse to suck dry, bite up, scoop out and rob the mother's body of its good contents . . . the other line of attack derives from the anal and urethral impulses, and implies expelling dangerous substance . . . out of the self and into the mother. Together with these harmful excrements, expelled in hatred, split-off parts of the ego are also projected . . . *into* the mother . . . (*Developments in Psychoanalysis*, p. 300)

As we know, this projection of the self into the mother becomes complicated by the child's curiosity later about the siblings inside the mother, and his envy of them. Here we may note in passing that with Dylan Thomas the curiosity and hate directed at the inside of the mother, associated with his schizoid hunger and its urge to empty her, was almost certainly complicated by other significant factors. We shall certainly find it to be so in his poems, where visceral imagery predominates. Indeed, nearly all the tendencies of the schizoid individual discussed in Fairbairn's classical essay 'Schizoid Factors in the Personality' in *Psychoanalytic Studies of the Personality*, may be found strikingly evident in the verse of Dylan Thomas.

Schizoid individuals, Fairbairn says, are introvert and often have *uncanny insights:*

Schizoid individuals who have not regressed too far are capable of greater psychological insight than any other class of people, normal or abnormal—a fact due, in part at least, to their being so introverted (i.e. preoccupied with inner reality) and so familiar with their own deeper psychological processes

(processes which, although not absent in individuals who would ordinarily be classed as simply 'psychoneurotic', are nevertheless excluded from the consciousness of such individuals by the most obstinate defences and stubborn resistance).

(op. cit., p. 3)

This capacity to see into deeper psychological processes is found startlingly in Dylan Thomas. His uncanny perceptions here are both a major element in his writing *and* also one reason why so many individuals (who were psychoneurotic rather than schizoid) rejected him by their own defence mechanisms—as the present writer has done in the past, while still being fascinated by him.

Intellectual pursuits have a special attraction for schizoid individuals because they are so much concerned with 'inner contents'. They are concerned with 'inner contents' because they were never convinced of their own value as persons in infancy and so are much preoccupied by 'what is inside them' (if there is anything at all). Of course, such problems are but an exacerbated form of the common existence problems of us all. As Fairbairn points out, we all have schizoid feelings at times, and to some degree, and this makes the utterance of schizoid individuals so fascinating to us, however much we are unable to share their whole point of view, or accept it as 'sane'.

The consequences for the schizoid individual of being 'fixated in the early oral situation' by deprivation are, Fairbairn says, as follows:

(1) A tendency for the breast (rather than a person) to become the libidinal object (and so the object of libidinal capacities comes to be regarded as a kind of breast rather than a person).

(2) The libidinal attitude is one in which *taking* predominates over *giving*.

(3) The libidinal attitude is one in which there is not only taking but incorporating and internalising.

(4) There is a tremendous significance in fullness and emptiness.

We shall find these tendencies recurring in the work of Dylan Thomas. Fairbairn also gives as main characteristics of schizoid persons: (1) an attitude of omnipotence; (2) an attitude of isolation and detachment; (3) a preoccupation with inner reality. Such characteristics may be conscious and overt, or unconscious, and they may be masked, as the attitude of isolation and detachment may be masked, by a 'façade of sociability'. The relevance of these points does not have to be laboured—take the omnipotence of Thomas's 'tumultuous world of my own being', or 'I call all the seas to service'.

The schizoid finds a 'tremendous significance' in 'fullness and emptiness' because

> he has emptied his mother—particularly since deprivation has the effect of not only intensifying his oral need, but also of imparting an aggressive quality to it. Deprivation also enlarges the field of his incorporative need . . . and so . . . the anxiety which he experiences over emptying the breast . . . gives rise to *anxiety over destroying his libidinal object.*

> (Fairbairn, op. cit., p. 11)

These anxieties are obvious in such a poem as *I make this in a warring absence* as we shall see.[1]

Failure on the part of the mother to convince the child that she really loves him as a person

> renders it difficult for him to sustain an emotional relationship with her on a personal basis: and the result is that, in order to simplify the situation, he tends regressively to restore the relationship to its earlier and simpler form and revive his relationship to his mother's breast as a partial object.

> (Fairbairn, op. cit., p. 13)

As we have seen, the incapacity to develop a full relationship with a person means that for the person the schizoid individual substitutes a 'partial object'. This means depersonalising other people. Here the classical instance is the schizophrenic youth who was a patient of Fairbairn's and who had the bitterest antagonism towards his actual mother, while dreaming of lying in bed in a room from the ceiling of which poured a stream of milk (the ceiling being the floor of his mother's room). The stream of milk was a symbol of his need for love, which he could only conceive in terms of a *depersonalised* source of nourishment. Depersonalisation of the love-object, in terms of disembodied breasts of one kind and another, symbolised in various ways, is frequent in the poetry of Dylan Thomas: 'the pale nippled air', 'in the cloud's

---

[1] 'He sees his love walk in the world, bearing none of the murderous wounds he gave her . . . but he sees and knows that all that has happened will happen again, tomorrow and tomorrow.' Dylan Thomas on the poem in *Letters*, p. 186.

breasts'—in life the women whom he 'cuddled up to', and the bottle.

Obviously, the depersonalised image of a breast suggests that finding another whole person in love is intolerable to the schizoid individual. It thus belongs to the problem of not being able to find value in others, because one has never been given a feeling of value in oneself. This failure to find human value in others, as we shall see, is what makes a poem such as Dylan Thomas's *Lament* express a fundamental contempt for others, because in it other people are regarded 'only as a means of satisfying . . . requirements'. Because they assert their independent reality they so challenge this partial object need that they become the butt of hate. This fundamental problem colours Thomas's attitudes to some of the characters in *Under Milk Wood*, when he must deny this kind of schizoid hate and the contempt for others it involves. His attitude can often be seen as the schizoid one of 'taking' rather than giving, which because it is over-dependent can easily become one of hatred and anger whenever a love-object insists on being herself, and so exposes his over-dependency and fear of dependence. Woman, in his work, is often hated because she reminds him of his dependency, and his vulnerable area of 'female element being'.

And here our exploration of schizoid characteristics approaches the problem of creativity, as a form of giving. The schizoid individual wants to give, but is inhibited by his problem of preoccupation with 'inner stuff'. Since his love has been rejected or met by hate, he comes to the conclusion that what he tried to give from within himself was *harmful and bad*. Yet it is his substance: and so he is in a profound dilemma, if he is a creative worker, for to create and give clearly and to enter that kind of sharing is full of dangers of emptying and being emptied. The end of creativity itself threatens doom, especially as it is associated with the 'female element'.

Fairbairn explains the origins of this dilemma thus. Excreting to the child is at first a creative activity—the (internal) things belonging to himself he gives. He takes in what he values through the mouth from the breast. He gives to his mother what he excretes—which is what he devalues or rejects; yet this is a valued giving, too. If the mother does not give and receive in her handling of the baby, then this giving and taking may become confused. The individual may feel that giving will mean that the virtue will go out of him.[2] So he will substitute exhibitionism or role-playing for genuine relationship, which is too dangerous.

Another important aspect of schizoid attitudes is the equation which develops in such individuals between creative activity, internal contents, and the problem of giving: 'at a deep mental level, taking is emotionally equivalent to amassing bodily contents, and giving is emotionally equivalent to parting with bodily contents'. Associated problems are the difficulty the schizoid person has in 'expressing emotion in a social context', and his feeling that, after any form of giving (such as creativity), he needs a period of quiet and solitude 'in order that the inner storehouse of emotion may have an opportunity to be replenished'.

Defence against emotional loss gives rise to attitudes of detachment and to forms of behaviour which seem cold and inhuman. With Dylan Thomas there was a marked contrast between what seemed to be generosity (as in public exhibitionism) and private meannesses. He was often cruel to his family and would reward friends who lent him houses by stealing from them, while often alienating those who offered him love and friendship in deliberate petty ways. Perhaps his role-playing and exhibitionism (and even the poetry) can be seen as substitutes for actual relationship, actual contact, which Dylan Thomas felt too dangerous, because it might 'empty' him. For related reasons perhaps he could not eat in the same room with his children, because in such a situation his own fears of loss of inner contents would be aroused by his children's strong emotions around the subject of taking in nourishment. His alcoholism perhaps related to the same problem.

The incorporative problem in the schizoid individual is bedevilled by his sense that *he has had to steal love*: he therefore becomes paranoic, self-preservative, and narcissistic. Fairbairn explains this logic thus. As we have seen;

If a child feels (a) he is not really loved for himself as a person by his mother and (b) that his own love for his mother is not accepted by her, he may be traumatised, and feel:

[2] A woman may find it difficult to part with her children, and either lose interest in them or be over possessive after they are born because they are still part of her. As we now know, Dylan Thomas's birth was a difficult one and his mother subjected him to severe maternal overprotection—both of which may have been schizoid manifestations in her. See pp. 42–3 below.

(a) the mother is a bad object insofar as she does not seem to love him.

(b) the outward expression of his own love is bad . . . so he tries to keep his love as 'good' as possible by retaining it inside himself.

(c) love relationships with external objects are bad, or at least precarious . . . (op. cit., p. 18).

It has proved impossible for the schizoid individual to develop his own identity by taking into himself aspects of his object as a whole: he has instead taken 'partial objects' by stealing love into himself, in order to survive, by having *something* in his inner world. Consequently, there occurs in Fairbairn's words: 'a narcissistic inflation of the ego arising out of *secret* possession of, and considerable identification with, internalised libidinal objects (e.g., the maternal breast and the paternal penis)'. The 'precariousness of relationships with external objects' Fairbairn speaks of is surely the essence of Dylan Thomas's poetry, while the conflict between the love kept as 'good' as possible within himself and his internal bad objects is its driving power. The 'precariousness' impels his existential quest.

Dylan Thomas's concepts of relationship are very much those of relationship with 'part objects': from Fairbairn's comment above we may expect to find that much of Thomas's phallic and mammary imagery is in fact an expression of his secret possession of and identification with 'internalised libidinal objects'. These, because they are substitutes for normal fruits of introjection (in one who has an incorporative urge to take and devour), feel as if they have been 'stolen'. Thus a need for secrecy arises because the individual feels he has 'emptied' others: this, according to Fairbairn, is an especial characteristic of markedly schizoid individuals. Thomas speaks of 'the secret child in me' and in a way his own 'code of night' is itself secretive in this way.

Thomas's inward secret cosmos which is also 'the tumultuous world of my own being' seems to have meant more to him, in terms of libidinal attachment, than his real life. He shows in this the 'schizoid infatuation' of 'being in love with' the system (or private phantasy 'world') he has created, as in *Fern Hill*. In his poetry we certainly find a sense of this secret inner value and a 'sense of inner superiority' ('I was lordly . . .'). Because of this sense of being special, he is the odd man out, a feeling he perhaps had in his early life (cf. his satisfaction in excelling in cross-country running.)

We can also see the connections here between paranoia, hypochondria, and the fear of dependence. As Fairbairn points out, because schizoid individuals feel they have not been loved as persons in their own right by the mother, they remain profoundly fixated upon the mother. 'The libidinal attitude accompanying this (mother) fixation . . . is . . . not only characterised by extreme dependence, but also rendered highly self-preservative and narcissistic by anxiety over a situation which presented itself as representing a threat to the ego.' To continue to be over-dependent upon a not-good-enough mother can thus have terrifying implications for a schizoid person. So too can dependence on a woman, for reasons on which we have touched. With Dylan Thomas his own experience of being mothered filled him full of fears of inner badness and outer threats.[3] He never manages to express a fully committed, warm-hearted, finding-and-giving love relationship.

The over-valuation of thought processes goes with a fear of and disgust at inner contents—of the bodily stuff of existence, which is felt to be full of harm, especially when giving is involved. This explains much of the imagery of disgust in Dylan Thomas's poetry, as it does much disgust in contemporary writing (cf. Sartre's *espèce d'écoeurement douceâtre* which is *la nausée* itself).

Fairbairn's final points are concerned with explaining the strange inversion of values in the schizoid individual. His experience of the failure of his mother to love him feels to him as if he has destroyed his mother's affection and made it disappear. 'At the same time he feels that the reason for her apparent refusal to accept his love is that his own love is destructive and bad' (op. cit., p. 25). He concludes that *his love is bad*, and this problem 'provides many of the great tragedies of literature'. Because they feel their love is bad, schizoid individuals experience great difficulty in giving, and have obvious motives for 'keeping their love inside them'— Dylan Thomas eminently did. It is too precious because it is too

---

[3] 'He sees her as a woman . . . who, out of a weak coldness, reduces to nothing the great sexual strength, heats and prides of the world . . .' Thomas on *I make this in a warring absence* in *Letters*, p. 186.

dangerous to release upon his objects. 'Thus (the schizoid individual) not only keeps his love in a safe, but also keeps it in a cage' (Fairbairn, op. cit., p. 25). The schizoid individual not only keeps his own love within himself: he also erects defences against the love of others for him. (A patient of Fairbairn's said to him, 'Whatever you do, you must never love me'.) So, a schizoid individual feels he must neither love nor be loved, and will draw on the resources of his hate, to alienate people, by quarrelling with them—to keep his libidinal objects at a distance. He can only permit himself to be loved from afar off.

This is the second great tragedy to which individuals with a schizoid tendency are liable. The first is, as we have seen, that he feels his love to be destructive of those he loves. The second arises when he becomes subject to a compulsion to hate and be hated, while all the time *he longs deep down to love and be loved*.

(Fairbairn, op. cit., p. 26)

Because of these perplexities the schizoid individual comes to be impelled towards 'an amazing reversal of moral values'. He has an immoral motive to hate, since the joy of loving is hopelessly barred to him, and so 'he may as well deliver himself over to the joy of hating and obtain what satisfaction he can out of that'. 'He thus makes a pact with the Devil and says "Evil be Thou my good" and "Good be Thou my evil" '. It is this abandon to the pleasures of destructive hate Thomas expresses in *Lament*

And all the deadly virtues plague my death . . .

and in his delight in alcoholism—'What'll you have?' 'Too much . . .'

The 'moral motive' is 'determined by the consideration that, if loving involves destroying, it is better to destroy by hate, which is overtly destructive and bad, than to destroy by love, which is by rights creative and good'. The feeling 'I may as well hate' is expressed (and caricatured) in Dylan Thomas's comic portrayal of Mr Pugh, whose intentions to poison his wife are almost pure, so total is the hate Thomas caricatures in him.

By such strange moral inversions, as we shall see, the hunger in the schizoid individual's inner world can become such a force of primitive hate that the individual takes to self-destruction, in a last desperate attempt to love and be loved: both Dylan Thomas and Sylvia Plath, for example, identify intensely with Christ, the embodiment of God's greatest love, even at the moment of suicide.

Thomas, in *Vision and Prayer* says,

> Now I am lost in the blinding
> One . . .

and, as we shall see, his fascination with both Christ and Houdini symbolises the urge to be reborn out of the stifling sack of the self into a new freedom of spirit, because, as Fairbairn says, 'the schizoid individual, deep down, longs to love and be loved'.

2
Dylan the Sea Son

With Dylan Thomas we encounter problems of identity whose origins can never be explored, as a biographer might wish to explore them, in terms of personal data in which their causes might be found. They are too 'early', and they involve unconscious factors which are too deep. Even the persons concerned—Thomas, if he were still alive; his mother and father—could tell us nothing. We are left to deduce from internal evidence—as from the poetry. In his biography, however, Constantine Fitzgibbon notes that:

> Dylan Thomas was born in his parents' home as was customary in those days. It was not an easy birth, nor was an easy birth anticipated. Nancy, then eight, was not a healthy child *and the Thomases' second baby had died within its mother's womb.*
>
> (*Life*, p. 22)

In the words I have italicised I believe we have the most significant fact about Dylan Thomas's life-history. The note that follows, a few pages further on, is second only in importance to this:

> What is quite clear is that his mother pampered and coddled him throughout his whole childhood to her, and his, heart's content—in part because such was her nature, but also in part because she regarded him as a semi-invalid, *a role he accepted easily* ... (*Life*, p. 24, my italics)

Later the significance of being *given a role* in Thomas's life will appear. His upbringing obviously involved the experience of being inhibited in independence:

> At the age of seventeen, when having high tea at a friend's house, he did not know how to deal with a boiled egg: his mother had always taken the tops off for him. Nor does his rather remote father appear to have objected to this upbringing.
>
> (*Life*, p. 24)

Dylan was 'spoiled'. But in order to understand the consequences
we have to go much deeper than conventional attitudes, which
characterise Dylan Thomas as a 'mother's darling'. In accounts
given by Pamela Hansford Johnson and Edith Sitwell we can see
that his appeal to them was precisely that of the 'mother's darling'
and, interestingly enough, it was as this that Augustus John
painted him.

But this conventional attitude is sentimental and tends to be
blind to the underlying hate involved in this phenomenon, of a
family pattern inhibiting the growth of an individual, and of
sacrificing him to the needs of others to feel real by making use of
him. Of course, I am here using the word hate in a special sense,
a sense which interprets hate not as the opposite of love (which
would be indifference)[1] but as the expression of a need to survive,
whose voracious element is *fear of loss of identity*. Where a mother
clings on to her child, suffocates him or prevents him achieving
independence, this failure manifests her extreme dependence upon
him—in order to prevent *herself* going out of existence. Her own
infantile 'mouth ego' is in play—and so we can speak of this as
hate. And behind it we can deduce an inability of the mother to
'be' for her child: Winnicott points out that the consequent
'impingement' of 'pseudo male doing' activity *is experienced by
the infant as hate*.

As Guntrip points out, discussing 'primary maternal preoccupation', where the mother is ill, psychically speaking, she may fail
to wean her child psychically:

[she] cannot let him grow to an increasing strength and security
so that he can become independent of her, because either she
has not been able to give him the primary necessity for his
security, the state of identification and intuitive understanding
—'her infant has never had her and so weaning has no meaning'
—or else she weans him too suddenly to free herself from him
'without regard for the gradually developing need of the infant
to be weaned'. (*Schizoid Phenomena*, pp. 223–4)

What we do know of Dylan Thomas is that his development
towards self-reliant independence was inhibited. This information, combined with our knowledge of other aspects of his life,
would seem to indicate that something of this kind of failure

[1] See M. Balint, *On Primary Love and Psychoanalytical Technique*, London (1952).

accounted for both his inability to deal with reality and his sense
of inward emptiness and danger. (Similarly, with Sylvia Plath,
we gain a sense that 'weaning had no meaning' because the
regressed ego seems still unborn, as symbolised in her verse and
its recurrent return to images of immense mouth-ego hunger or
hate.)

With Thomas, I shall go further, to conjecture from Winnicott's paper on male and female elements and its implications.[2]
This paper discusses the problems of identity in a patient which
resulted from his being handled as a girl in infancy. The question
I want to raise in connection with it is—if a man can suffer because
in early infancy he was handled as if he were a girl, is it not possible
for an individual to be confused in his identity by *being handled as
if he were another sibling who had died earlier*? The second child in
the Thomas family had died within the mother's womb: Dylan
Thomas's was a long, painful and difficult birth. These experiences could have their bearing on one another. Winnicott records
how a boy of eight was found to be suffering from an 'unbearable
sense of guilt because of the death of a sibling that took place some
years *prior to his own birth*'. This was a 'displacement from the
Oedipus complex' but 'it could have deeper repercussions, if it
was *in some way conveyed by his earliest handling*' (my italics).
I propose to conjecture here that Thomas's problems of identity
were the consequence of his being handled by his mother in such a
way as to convey to him some sense of being confused with a dead
sibling, as if he were a ghost, or a dead baby resurrected, or as a
baby which, in the place of that baby, must never be allowed to
become independent but remain the lost but resurrected baby
forever alive, 'for as long as forever is'. Because he was not treated
as himself, loved for himself in his own right, his mother never
allowed him to make her his 'subjective object'—'he never had
her', so 'weaning had no meaning'. Moreover, she did not want
to wean him, but to keep him as a *ghost*-child. These conjectures,
of course, have no point as a diagnosis of the condition of the
person Thomas: but we can at least see if they help to supply
meaning to his more chaotic poetry.

Winnicott says of his patient who had a 'girl' within himself,

---

[2] 'Creativity and Its Origins' in *Playing and Reality*. See H. Guntrip's discussion
in *Schizoid Phenomena*, pp. 249 ff.

> This man had to fit into [his mother's] idea of a girl [he was the
> second child, the first being a boy] . . . she dealt with him in all
> sorts of ways as if he were a girl . . .

Perhaps we could re-phrase this, with reference to Dylan Thomas's
primary experience:

> This man had to fit into her idea of a dead baby brought to
> life . . . he was the child that followed the death of another
> child in the womb . . . She dealt with him in all sorts of ways
> as if he were that 'other' child . . .

This could feel like the most terrible 'impingement' or experience of 'hate', in place of that love which should confirm being—
with consequent confusion of identity and a more than ordinary
sense of being in 'life without being alive', and of being a
self which could not feel 'I AM', but suspect it was some other
self.

Since, as I have suggested, 'impingement' and an unwillingness
to 'let another creature go' into independence are manifestations
of hate—that is, of an excessive need to incorporate another, or
exploit him for one's own needs, we can conjecture that Mrs
Thomas's hate was the attempt to turn her son into something
other than he was because of her excessive dependence upon him.
The power of 'primary maternal preoccupation' is intense, and
would be experienced as strong magic—the oral-phantasy magic
of the infantile mouth-ego, with all its feelings of omnipotence
and its intentions to 'eat the world'. Exerted against an infant such
psychic power could deeply affect his whole identity and his
dealings with reality. A child could become deeply confused by
the effects of his mother's confusion and predatory need.

Where such forces operate, they tend to operate in a whole
family set-up, and the Thomas family seems no exception. We
have glimpses of a strange relationship between mother and
father, and of forms of intense identifying. So, perhaps, the
Thomas family was a 'schizophrenogenic'[3] family, pervaded by
the magic and hate, and consisting of identities merging with or
threatening one another.

Something of this magic and hate seems to be symbolised in the
mythology of the family. Dylan's father, for instance, chose

[3] Likely to produce schizophrenia in its members. See the work of R. D. Laing
and D. Cooper.

Dylan's name from a significant episode in the *Mabinogion*. There it is written of Math, son of Mathonwy, the magician king:

> She was brought unto him. The maiden entered. 'Maiden,' asked he, 'art thou a virgin?' 'So far as I know, I am,' said she. He took his magic wand, and bent it—'Step over my wand,' said he, 'and if thou art a virgin I shall know.' She stepped over the wand, and as she did so she dropped a fine he-child with golden-yellow hair. The boy gave a loud cry, . . . And Math son of Mathonwy said: 'I shall name this child, and the name I shall give him is Dylan.' Thus was the golden-haired boy named, and straightaway he made for the sea . . .
>
> (Quoted in *Life*, pp. 24–5)

Fitzgibbon admits that the choice is an odd one and quotes Dylan Thomas later as having said in error that his name meant 'prince of darkness'—which 'sounds like the echo of a dismissive reply on his father's part'. What Fitzgibbon fails to see is the unconscious symbolism of the choice. He asks 'why the Son of the Sea name?'—but answers only in terms of a mundane discussion of 'the sea' in English poetry. He does, however, perceive that 'D. J. Thomas was determined that his son should be the poet he had failed to be himself'. In this desire that the son should be willed into a role we may suspect impinging hate on the father's part, too. He wanted to coerce Dylan into the role of being a poet who did not fail because of his alcoholism—into being him, and a pure or ideal image of himself at that. Such a need in a father to make his child live his own life out would add to the confusion already created by the mother.

The passage from the *Mabinogion* is full of magic, and the magic symbolism strangely persists in the mythology of Dylan Thomas, as in a shot of the Christ-child fading into the sea in a biographical film—into Thalassa, the universal mother. The father's choice of the name 'Dylan' reveals, surely, that the passage quoted had a particular significance for him and so reveals unconscious motives. The father here phantasies an ideal object, which he was no doubt capable of projecting over his wife—seeing her as the ideal 'maiden' of mythology, when in truth Mrs Thomas was simply a rather foolish and garrulous woman. Dylan Thomas's predicament may have thus been affected by his father's inability to find the reality of the actual woman, substituting an unreal ideal in his private myths. We are told by Fitzgibbon that Mrs Thomas was 'a sweet, gentle and *rather childish woman*' (who gave her son a '*measureless and uncritical love*') and who was said to have '*nothing in common with the father at all*' (my italics). When she had women visitors the father would ignore them and walk through the room to his study. This glimpse of a non-relationship seems a long way from the relationship between Math and the maiden.

From the fragments we have in the biography concerning Dylan Thomas's parents, we gather a sense of individuals who were not very real to one another. Certainly they do not seem to have regarded one another with mutual respect or to have enjoyed one another's company much. This lack of real relationship is perhaps symbolised by D. J. Thomas's choice of the passage about the magician Math. It could be that he identified with this character who, not by his penis, but by a bent magic wand, causes the *maiden* to have a child. This implicitly denies actual physical contact. Why did this myth appeal so to D. J.? It may perhaps have been because the father suffered guilt at the painful feeling that his libidinousness had caused the death of the previous child in the womb. That is, his bodily love had caused death and must be denied—as it is beautifully denied in the *Mabinogion* episode. The pain of a birth such as Dylan's is a disturbing reminder of mortal reality. Wishing to magic this away D. J. prefers a mythical case of parturition—'she dropped a fine he-child'. By naming Dylan Thomas 'Dylan' D. J. perhaps sought to escape the distress of guilt and fear in him, caused by the child's painful birth, for which he felt responsible. He sought to believe that Dylan was not born in pain from a wife with whom he had nothing in common. Dylan was born in magic from the sea and was to 'partake of its nature'. He was to be the father's own ideal self. These super-human idealisations suggest a deep threat to the infant, who implicitly is not loved in his own right for his own sake.

So, by very extravagant conjecture, we can postulate that D. J. Thomas called Dylan Thomas 'Dylan' because he wished to mould him into something other than himself—even as his mother wished him (as I believe) to be her dead baby brought to life again. D. J. Thomas wanted Dylan to be himself, born again, so that he could fulfil his own ideal role, as he could not himself. If we accept this account of certain aspects of his infantile environment it will then seem obvious why Dylan Thomas so often felt that the environment was malignant and full of hate, and why he communicates a sense of confusion of identity. This problem of hate reappears, as we shall see, in his feelings about his own children.

Nearly all of what I have said above is conjecture. But the conjecture is developed from a great deal of study of Dylan Thomas's writing, and from accounts of his life and behaviour. His anguish can, I believe, only be explained if we penetrate deeply beyond the conventional and sentimental accounts of his origins. Constantine Fitzgibbon's account is, of course, far too conventional to help us understand the springs of Thomas's creativity. He merely says, 'it was from his Thomas forbears that Dylan inherited his literary talent and his brains', while 'It was perhaps from his mother that he inherited the gaiety, sweetness and generosity that were such an essential part of his personality'.

Whence, then, came the self-destructiveness, the relational incapacities, the cheating, lying and lack of self-discipline, the anguished contest between the true and false self, the combination of poetic deadness and life—and the ultimate desire to die?

The answer would seem to be that, because of inadequacies of identity in his parents, at a very deep level, Dylan Thomas was exposed so long and so profoundly to their unconscious hate that his own identity and reality sense—the very foundations of his psychic tissue—were gravely damaged in the formative years. As readers of his poetry, we are fascinated by the way in which he is driven to pursue existential problems and by his tortured pursuit of the need to feel real. We are also perplexed by the recurrent failure of the creative impulse, except for a few remarkable achievements.

Mrs Thomas later came to sign her letters 'Dylan's Mam': her earlier behaviour suggests a weakness of identity that made her identify to a dangerous extent with her son—dangerous because this meant that she was living at his expense and was unable to 'disillusion' him in a positive and creative way towards independence. It was not that, like D. H. Lawrence's mother, she turned to a kind of sexual relationship with her son in the absence of love for the father, though the experience of impingement, the intensity of her over-dependence, and the experience of not having one's love received, not being 'loved for one's own sake', account for the schizoid fear of sex we can find in Dylan Thomas's writing. He was, I have suggested, dealt with as if he *should not be himself*, and so was urged towards non-being by those who should have confirmed his being. This would have established a fear of 'female element being' and a fear of woman at the deepest level in such an individual: and this we find in his poetry.

Associated with this failure in the realm of 'being' behind the schizoid problem in Thomas's life, is his preoccupation with 'inner contents'. The mother's incapacity to 'let him go' to be himself in life could belong to the same symbolism as that of a birth which is difficult because the mother refuses to let the child out of her body. She may have identified with him out of an 'overvaluation of inner contents'. He was so excessively important to her, *because he came out of her body*: there was after all another child which did not come out alive. We may even say that both the mother and father sought to incorporate him psychically, and keep him in their minds. At the same time the mother handled him in a 'pseudo-male' way which failed to convince him of the goodness and security of his 'inner contents'.

This schizoid 'bind' transferred to Thomas by the whole context of his infancy, could explain his hypochondria which could then appear as a fear of 'badness within': 'For him a cold in the head was pleurisy; 'flu pneumonia, and every hangover incipient D.T.s.' Thomas told Fitzgibbon that he had had cirrhosis of the liver and tuberculosis; he believed he would not live long. He suffered from asthma and a stark medical note (*Life*, p. 23 footnote) indicates that Thomas's lungs were not in good condition at his death. He had lung haemorrhage as a boy, and often coughed until he vomited as a man. Yet his liver did not seem to be damaged, despite his fears. I mention these points here to indicate that whatever their origins, Dylan Thomas had several problems suggestively symbolic of a schizoid predicament: (*a*) Thomas was much concerned with the dangers of 'inner badness'; (*b*) there was some physical confirmation of this; yet (*c*) much of his anxiety was groundless and would seem to have a symbolic meaning (of the kind Freud saw in hysteric illnesses); (*d*) where there was fear (as of a 'bad' liver) the heavy drinking would seem to be a strange kind of attempt at self-cure (to put 'something good there') or to punish the libidinal ego for its weakness. We may add (*e*) that the autopsy and the detailed footnotes in the biography are themselves perhaps forms of unconscious collaboration of others with Dylan Thomas's intense psychic preoccupation with what is 'within the self' and its badness or danger.

We may even deduce from the fact that his mother had a baby die in her womb and that his was a difficult birth the possibility that Dylan Thomas's mother was herself a schizoid person for whom birth represented a dangerous 'giving'—parting with 'inner contents'—which she was able to resist in a catastrophic way. Guntrip, in discussing regression as an attempt at rebirth, gives some instances:

A markedly schizoid woman patient dreamed of watching a baby being born and said: 'They couldn't get the baby out. Its head came but then it stuck . . . The baby could not be got out.' Two schizoid wives who had babies while under treatment, both reported that the birth was very prolonged and difficult and they had been told that at one point *they had drawn the baby back inside.* Evidently they identified their baby with their own Regressed Ego. Winnicott stresses the secret hope of one day finding conditions in which the True Self can be reborn . . . (*Personality Structure and Human Interaction,* p. 439)

The fear of being 'drawn back inside' as Guntrip points out, prompts a good deal of 'visceral' phantasy in patients; I believe this to explain the predominance of visceral imagery in Dylan Thomas's poetry.

I want to assume, then, for the purposes of this book that Dylan Thomas's mother was a schizoid woman who identified him as a baby with her own 'regressed libidinal ego', and confused him with herself and the dead baby once within herself, so that he came to stand both for her unborn true self and for the stillborn sibling. In him the hope that her 'true self' might be reborn came true whereas the previous baby died by being 'drawn back into the womb'. So intensely did she feel this that she handled Dylan as if he were (*a*) herself or part of herself (her own regressed ego), (*b*) the dead baby resurrected, (*c*) not himself but another whom she dearly wanted him to be. Insofar as the regressed ego is the 'true self' still unborn, it belongs to the female element of vulnerable 'being'. Where this core of the self is weak there would often

seem to be a confusion of male and female elements in an individual, and a deep fear of the female element. Since the female
element is the feeling and creative aspect of our make-up, this can
mean a fear of the poetic in oneself. Such fears could be 'deepened'
when the creative powers become the focus of the father's will.

These conjectures may sound fantastic. They are, however,
based on much in Guntrip and Winnicott and others, and here
they will not seem irrelevant, I hope, by the end of this book. If
we assume something like this to be true, it follows that catastrophic failures of 'primary maternal preoccupation' and of later
family nurture could have led to intense problems of identity in
Thomas. The growing individual could feel himself almost
swamped by the hate in the situation. The mother was seeking to
make her child, which was an independent living thing, into part
of herself. She could never let him go, or let him grow into
independence because with him would go her own hope of ever
being born anew. The son is thus deprived of his capacity to find
'ontological security' or any strong sense of self in his own right.

This clinch or double-bind would be made worse by the father's
unconscious desire that Dylan Thomas should by magic become
his ideal self. The effect on identity would obviously be a sense of
terrifying oppression, against which the only possible response
could be hate exerted in return, in a desperate quest for a sense of
identity. Yet this hate- or false-self-activity could provide no
essential core of identity and it would be enormously difficult to
find the true self, for all the hate directed at the subject is a defence
against its discovery, by denial. As we shall see, the consequences
of the experience of such hate in infancy can include tremendously
anti-social modes of behaviour, such as Thomas displayed in his
alcoholism and in other ways, as he strove to feel real.

The connections between alcoholism and such problems of
early formative nurture are made plain by Karl Menninger, who
in discussing suicide describes the alcoholic as 'a spoiled child who
never grew up':

I doubt very much [he goes on] if any child is spoiled by too
much love. What passes for excessive 'love' on the part of the
parents is often only thinly disguised hate or guilt, and this fact
is perceived by the child, if not by the neighbours . . . For all
these aggressions against him the child will certainly, some day,

perhaps at great cost to himself, take full and terrible revenge.
(*Man Against Himself*, p. 150)

The 'terrible revenge' taken by Dylan Thomas (as also by Sylvia Plath) was a form of suicide. But yet that suicide was a desperate attempt to be reborn, out of the hate which in earliest infancy threatened independent existence, and out of an oppressive family situation which failed to provide them with ego-strength.

Schizoid suicide can be a manifestation of the 'regressed libidinal ego' seeking rebirth. Here it will be useful to summarize Guntrip's account of the origins of this:

> When the infant finds himself in a relationship to outer reality
> which imposes on him greater strains than he is capable of
> bearing, he mentally withdraws from the outer world into his
> inner psychic life. (*Personality Structure*, p. 430)

We may look at the processes involved in two ways. To Fairbairn the problem is to be seen in terms of the ego's need for the object. The infant's needs become so intensified that they seem to be dangerous to love-objects: 'the schizoid withdrawal from object-relations is motivated by *the fear that one's love is destructive*' (my italics). But the object is also needed to confirm the subject's identity, and we can also see the problem in terms of the ego's need to preserve itself. Winnicott looks at the matter in such terms. 'He regards good mothering', says Guntrip, 'as consisting of *adjustment* to the infant without *impingement*.'

> The mother must supply the baby's needs at a time when he
> feels them, but not force attentions on him when he does not
> want them. If she does the latter, she impinges on the baby's
> sensitive psyche . . . Fairbairn has also recently stressed . . . the
> pressure of the parents' needs and problems on the child . . .
> (ibid., p. 430)

So, when he feels intolerable impingement, the child withdraws from the outer world into himself, and 'the first move towards the creation of the schizoid position has been made'. If the breaking off of object-relations were complete, it would be followed by a collapse of the ego, so that the child could hardly be kept alive. 'He must therefore detach a part of himself to remain in touch with a reality from which he retreats' (ibid., p. 430). Here we have a division which may be observed both in the life and poetry of Dylan Thomas (and in the poetry of Sylvia Plath):

What Fairbairn calls the Central Ego, Winnicott the False Self, and Freud the 'reality-ego' is left with depleted energies, like a forward screen of front-line troops 'in touch with the enemy' and struggling to hold its position by whatever manoeuvres seem useful. *The emotional heart of the personality has drawn back inside out of reach of being hurt* . . . (ibid., p. 430, my italics).

Guntrip believes that a split in the psyche occurs so that a libidinal self draws back, leaving a de-emotionalised self to maintain a 'somewhat mechanical touch with the outer world'.

If, however, the withdrawn ego remained without objects it would become depersonalised and no doubt undermine the Outer Reality Ego as well. To ward off this danger a world of internal objects has to be set up and an inner world created . . . Here, as Fairbairn says, the ego tries to master its bad objects (in their duplicate psychic version) since it could not master them in outer reality, but only to find itself tied to a fifth column of persecutors secretly attacking it inside the inner world where safety had been sought in retreat. The world of internal bad objects is set up. (ibid., p. 431)

Guntrip quotes a patient:

'I don't know that I want to come to terms with this blasted world of daily life. It's better to keep my own fairy story going. Better not see people or things as they really are. Retire into your fairy-story of wicked witches and bad dragons. Why the hell should I go into the outer world? Why should I have any further dealings with my impossible father? Why go out and meet strange people I probably won't like? Better to go to a theatre and read a book. But my troubled dream world is my real fairy-story world.' (ibid., p. 431)

In Dylan Thomas we often find a preference for a private world of phantasy above the 'blasted world of daily life'—a distinct dissociation between a 'mechanical touch with the outer world' and 'an inner world of internal objects': but yet a striving for touch, too—because he intuitively knows that in such touch is life. In Dylan Thomas's response to the death of Ann Jones we have an indication of a deep de-emotionalisation and a mechanical schizoid response to human reality (see below, p. 195). In his *Fern Hill* we have beautifully expressed the anguish of having to forfeit a 'real fairy story world'.

As Guntrip says, the psychotherapist can find his patients too *imprisoned* in a world of internal bad objects

Having had to grow up, not on the basis of feeling safely in touch and secure in a reliable good relationship with the mother, but on the basis of feeling that his inner self is not understood by anyone and he must work hard to organise himself to keep himself mentally alive and functioning, it seems impossible to the patient to reverse this situation. To give up operating one's own ego-maintenance system seems like inviting collapse and extinction ... (*Schizoid Phenomena*, p. 235)

Guntrip is speaking here of the problem of offering therapy to the schizoid individual: fear of relationship and the experience of trust let down makes the individual feel 'what if the therapist should prove in the end to be of no more use than mother was?' But from this observation we can see how irrelevant it is to accuse such an individual of being unwilling to relinquish this withdrawal, and this inner world, and to come into the world of ordinary life, and normal values. It is a life and death matter to cling to the inner one. As Guntrip says:

The entire world of internal bad objects is a colossal defence against loss of the ego by depersonalisation. The one issue that is much worse than the choice between good and bad objects is the choice between any sort of objects and no objects at all. Persecution is preferred to depersonalisation.

(*Personality Structure*, p. 432, my italics)

This predicament of clinging to something within by hate is poignantly illustrated in Sylvia Plath's poems about her dead father, one of which is significantly called *The Colossus*: the father she sticks together, petrified and grotesque, is a 'colossal defence' against 'loss of the ego by depersonalisation.' In *Daddy* she reveals how she hates him. He is an internalised object to which she strives to relate. But he is also in his grave. She attempts suicide to 'find' him and in this desperate quest she prefers a physical extinction to 'loss of the ego by depersonalisation', which seems infinitely more terrible ('I do it so it feels real': *Lady Lazarus*). Dylan Thomas's 'old ramrod' epitomises his attachment to a similar bad construct in himself. In his case a cure for this internal world of bad objects is sought by drinking. We have thus a complex mixture in Dylan Thomas—of the search for self-cure;

the impulse to slow suicide; his destructiveness, of which he was aware, and his wish at the end to be 'forever unconscious'. As Guntrip points out, 'the ultimate unconscious infantile weak ego is very clearly experienced consciously as a fear of dying, when its threat to the stability of the personality is felt.' This can be associated with 'a wish to die'.

This is felt as 'a longing to regress, to escape from life, to go to sleep for an indefinite period, or a wish to get out of things and evade responsibility.' We find all these expressed in various ways by Dylan Thomas. The most poignant aspect of these conse-quences of profound ego-weakness is that the 'life-tiredness' expressed in the withdrawal from life and even in suicide attempts is aimed at rebirth. Guntrip quotes several instances of patients who made suicide attempts with loopholes left, and quotes others who said

'I've often felt it would be lovely to put my head in the gas oven and go unconscious. But I couldn't do it, because I couldn't be sure of being able to turn the gas off at the right time, before it killed me.' Another patient . . . on several occasions went downstairs . . . and lay down beside the gas oven and turned on the gas . . . (*Personality Structure*, p. 238)

Guntrip comments:

Schizoid suicide is not really a wish for death as such, except in cases where the patient has utterly lost all hope of being under-stood and helped. Even then there is a deep unconscious secret wish that death should prove to be a pathway to rebirth. One patient in the middle of a paranoid-schizophrenic episode had a vivid compelling phantasy of slipping into the local river and drifting downstream to re-emerge at some point out of the waters as a new creature . . . What is the mental condition which drives a human being into such a dilemma as needing to stop living while not wanting to die? (ibid., p. 239)

Here it would seem likely that Dylan Thomas (like Sylvia Plath after him) was an individual with a deep attachment to life, but with such a fear of the terrors of reality and inner vacancy that he wished to 'stop living' and yet, far from wanting to die, really wished to be reborn. The terrible truth is that by the logic of this schizoid pattern, and because of the dissociation between his 'mechanical' dealings with the world and his withdrawal into an inner world of internalised objects (the world of his poetry), his attempts at re-birth killed him.

With Dylan Thomas we can see that his drinking manifests the impulse to withdraw combined with the attempt at self-cure. Karl Menninger includes alcoholism as a form of suicide:

the victim of alcohol addiction knows what most of his critics do not know, namely, that alcoholism is not a disease, or at least the principle disease from which he suffers; furthermore, *he knows that he does not know* the origin or nature of the dreadful pain and fear within him which impel him blindly to alcoholic self-destruction . . . we frequently see patients who start out with *conscious* suicidal intentions and end up by getting drunk (or who get drunk first in order to make a suicide attempt), as if this was (as it is!) a less certain death than shooting. (*Man Against Himself*, pp. 150 ff.)

Alcohol addiction is therefore somewhat akin to lying beside the gas stove—an attempt at self-destruction so arranged that it should misfire, or that others should come to the rescue. But fundamentally it is an attempt at finding a way *to be*: 'alcohol addiction can be thought of not as a disease, but as a suicidal *flight from disease*, a disastrous attempt at the self-cure of an unseen inner conflict' (ibid., pp. 150 ff.). Menninger usefully relates alcoholism both to ambivalence over love objects and to revenge for impingement in ways closely relevant to Dylan Thomas's predicament. The poetry can be looked at, as an oral activity, and, in a related light, as an attempt to withdraw, to be reborn, to cure oneself. Thomas said, 'I want to go to the Garden of Eden': but the Garden of Eden was where man began.

If we turn to medical studies of maternal overprotection, and link this with alcoholism in relation to weaning, we can see that many further characteristics of Dylan Thomas as a person are explained. Moreover, such overprotection itself we find to be an indication that the mother was too ill to give her child security of being, and so we can see how it gives rise to problems of identity with which the symbolism both in poetry and behaviour in life are attempts to deal.

Some of Dylan Thomas's characteristics fit the text-book account of this syndrome exactly, as we see, if we examine such a study as that made by David M. Levy in *Maternal Overprotection*.

One aspect of this situation of the over-protected child is that the mother 'won't let him grow up', with consequent 'infantilisation', and 'prevention of independent behaviour'. The picture is well portrayed 'by a mother who holds her child tightly with one hand and makes the gesture of pushing away the rest of the world with the other. Her energies are directed to preserving her infant as infant for all time, preserving it from all harm and from contact with the rest of humanity' (p. 38). This is a failure of psychic weaning, of necessary disillusion. Since such an unreal situation can only be preserved by hate—that is, by denial, by willing things to be other than they are—aggression plays a significant role on both sides:

> For her child she will fight hard, make every sacrifice, and aggressively prevent interference with her social monopoly. Her aggression, directed so strangely against the intruder, yields however before the child. Towards him she is submissive, her discipline falters when he becomes assertive in the latter half of infancy, and is gradually destroyed. (ibid., p. 58)

This aggression directed at the mother can become a characteristic of the adult brought up in this way, and we find such aggression directed at the 'object' in Dylan Thomas's poetry:

> I make a weapon of an ass's skeleton
> And walk the warring sands by the dead town,
> Cudgel great air, wreck east, and topple sundown,
> Storm her sped heart, hang with beheaded veins
> Its wringing shell, and let her eyelids fasten.
> Destruction, picked by birds, brays through the jaw-bone,
>
> And, for that murder's sake, dark with contagion
> Like an approaching wave I sprawl to ruin.
> (*I make this in a warring absence*, Collected Poems, p. 79)

This rage against an adult object is obviously linked with feelings towards his mother and her devouring capacities ('his mother's womb had a tongue that lapped up mud').[4] In the same poem there is an image of the unborn 'regressed ego', as if it were a sibling dead forever in the womb:

[4] See Sylvia Plath, 'Mother, you are the one mouth/I would be tongue to. Mother of otherness/Eat me ...', *Poem for a Birthday* (*The Colossus*, p. 81). See also D. H. Lawrence on Frieda as 'the devouring mother' in his letters.

'See,' drummed the taut masks, 'how the dead ascend:
In the groin's endless coil a man is tangled.'

This could also be a symbol of the threat of annihilation by an 'impinging' mother. There is an intense feeling that the world-as-object threatens a death such as destroyed this tangled man, the 'other' self who is terribly vulnerable:

The terrible world my brother bares his skin.

This fear of annihilation is countered by an aggressive urge to force the alienated object, by cosmic aggression, to suckle him.

Now in the cloud's big breast lie quiet countries...

The aggressive feelings towards *all* objects in the poem are exaggerated and intense: we may find in them a symbolisation of the aggression of the over-protected child:

infantile aggression is manifested in having one's own way, dominating every situation, manipulating the scene in order to be the central figure, displaying temper when crossed. The overprotection may be described as a process in which infantile power, unmodified, expands into a monstrous growth that tends to subjugate the parents.

(K. Menninger, *Man Against Himself*, p. 39)

We may link this observation with the associated problems of identification we have discussed in Dylan Thomas's life and his inability to find independence. Dylan Thomas could not develop beyond infantile states of primary identification with the object. So his demands on the object (any woman who became his object) were total and felt to be matter of life and death.

Thomas's characteristic energy of 'merging', his failure to distinguish between 'me' and 'not-me', his birth imagery, his unreal omnipotence are all illuminated by Fairbairn's account of the compulsiveness of schizoid persons:

The infant ... has no alternative but to accept or to reject his object—an alternative which is liable to present itself to him as a choice between life and death. His psychological dependence is further accentuated by the very nature of his object-relationship; for, as we have seen, this is based essentially upon identification. Dependence is exhibited in its most extreme form in the intra-uterine state, and we may legitimately infer that, on its psychological side, this state is characterised by an absolute degree of identification and absence of differentiation. Identification may thus be regarded as representing the persistence into extra-uterine life of a relationship existing before birth. In so far as identification persists after birth, the individual's object constitutes not only his world, but also himself; and it is to this fact, as has already been pointed out, that we must attribute the compulsive attitude of many schizoid and depressive individuals towards their objects. (*Psychoanalytical Studies*, p. 47)

The compulsiveness may also be linked with the problem of sexual disgust. The chapter of Menninger from which I have been quoting gives a number of cases of suicide and alcoholism in which it seems that where there is a 'previously conditioned over-protective attitude' the problem is made worse if a child is sickly, or if a child is likely to die. This may 'reinforce the overprotection' and the birth of a dead previous child could surely cause this to happen. There is also evidence that over-protection often goes with an excessive need for physical contact on the mother's part which leaves the child with a 'revulsion from sexual contact'.

Sometimes mothers who are guilty or hostile extend the period of breastfeeding, or over-compensate for their lack of true love for the infant in other ways of handling, which 'impinge' and are experienced as hate as Winnicott has also pointed out. Menninger says

There are mothers frankly hostile to the infant, for whom breast-feeding is a pleasurable experience. On the other hand, an over-protecting mother may regard the act as a loathsome ordeal . . . the emotions of disgust experienced while suckling a child ordinarily are attended by feelings of guilt . . . the disgust [has] its roots in sexual conflicts involving the sucking act . . . and in a strong and bitter hostility to the passive feminine role. (*Man Against Himself*, pp. 61-2)

If we combine Winnicott's insights with Menninger's we can see how maternal failure can perhaps generate conflicting feelings of hunger and disgust in adult sexuality, combined with deep fears of annihilation in physical contact. These feelings, as Menninger indicates, can lead to forms of aggressive delinquency. The underlying hostility in the overprotection is responded to later by a monstrous tyranny of the child over the mother: and this child becomes an adult who can become at worst an egocentric psychopath, except insofar as this development is stemmed by 'reality experiences'—i.e. such discovery as he can make of the 'not-me'.

As we have seen, Fairbairn said, 'The child's ego is a mouth ego'. This indicates the link between problems of identity and aggressive oral ways of expressing them. The 'being' that should have been taken in by identification at the breast, and the subsequent psychic suckling and weaning, all fail to be satisfactorily accomplished in such an individual as Dylan Thomas. Therefore in his adult life he resorts to schizoid oral 'taking' and other incorporative ways of behaviour, to seek to obtain the psychic satisfactions which were denied him in infancy, as a means to feeling real and feeling his identity confirmed. He is left in a state of needing to exert a 'sucking' attitude to the world.

Thomas, as we know, had a 'taking' attitude to women, whom he treated as partial objects (i.e. breasts) purely for his own gratification. This can be seen as an extension into adult life of the attempt of the over-protected infant to tyrannise over his mother. He seeks to reduce her to 'maternal obeisance': 'the child's merest wish becomes the mother's absolute command . . . the child represents a deity on whose altar the mother willingly sacrifices her life.' While all the other women Thomas wanted to take were 'all Caitlin really' to him, he expected his wife to 'sacrifice her life on his altar' (so that when he dies she feels she only has a *Leftover Life to Kill*). For the same reason Thomas identifies with the Christ-child, and the image of the Virgin and Child fading out over the sea at the end of the film about him is an image of the 'infant deity' on whose altar *all women as mother* would 'willingly sacrifice' their lives. This attitude to women is essentially one of aggressive and egocentric primitive hate.

Thus it is of course the grossest sentimentality for Constantine Fitzgibbon to seek to pass off Thomas's promiscuity by saying, 'He simply liked women'—and for Thomas himself to say, 'I am a lover of the human race, especially women', since his behaviour with women is essentially prompted by hate—the hate he suffered from his own mother, countered by an aggressive 'taking' attitude by which alone he can feel alive.

An important aspect of Thomas's alcoholic self-destruction was its oral element of primitive hate. In Menninger's terms, it was a 'typical infantile revenge reaction':

It is performed with the mouth; in the second place it places a fictitiously high value upon the magical virtues of the substance desired; more important still, its practical aggressive values are indirect . . . the alcoholic cannot risk giving up the love objects to which he clings, angry and resentful as he may feel towards them, consciously or unconsciously . . . the alcoholic suffers at the same time from the wish to destroy his love-objects and the fear that he will lose them. He also fears the consequences of the aggressions which he is constantly impelled to make against them and from which he deters himself only by fierce internal restraint which in time accumulates to the point of leading him to seek a form of anaesthetisation which indirectly achieves the very aggressions and other consequences which he so feared he would succumb to. (*Man Against Himself*, p. 149)

Menninger speaks of the 'great disappointment' in infancy for which alcoholism is a compensation. He gives cases of over-maternal protection as the origin of alcoholism. The combination of overcompensation for hate, prolongation of breast-feeding, and associated guilt and disgust even led one alcoholic's mother, who nursed him until he was three years old, to paint her breasts with stove-blacking, to frighten and repel him. Again we may glimpse the immense energies which lie behind such 'spoiling' as seems evident in Thomas's case:

The mother of another alcoholic made of her child a pet and darling, almost ignoring the other children . . . The inconsistency in attitude toward the child bespeaks an ambivalence on the parents' part and explains why these patients are so often described by their friends and relatives as 'spoiled': 'a spoiled child that never grew up' . . . (op. cit., p. 150)

The alcoholism is a 'terrible revenge' for the disguised hate of the spoiling. There is much else in Menninger that can help us to understand Thomas and his poetry. Not everything can be discussed here, but there is one further important oral feature: Dylan Thomas's father was both an alcoholic and a poet and wanted Dylan to 'be' himself. As he learned to be a poet from his father, so too he learned his alcoholism. As Menninger says: 'Alcoholism cannot possibly be a hereditary trait, but for a father to be alcoholic is an easy way for the son to learn *how* to effect the retaliation he later feels compelled to inflict' (op. cit., p. 155).

Alcoholism is an oral activity whose excitement reproduces the excitement of suckling, and so is erotic. This eroticism interestingly enough tends to take a homosexual path. We have suggested that Thomas had to build an identity on 'male doing' because of a failure of 'female element being'. The failure of 'being' leads to a fear of the female element in oneself and others—so, such an individual also fears woman, and develops a deep attraction to the father. Menninger finds this attachment to the father in the alcoholic and finds a 'conflict between his wish for passive erotic dependence on him, and the rejection of this wish'.

It is almost axiomatic that alcoholics in spite of a great show of heterosexual activity, have secretly a great fear of women and heterosexuality in general, apparently regarding it as fraught with much danger. They often realise that they do not possess normal sexual powers or interests, frankly avowing that it is not sexual gratification they seek from women as much as affection, care, love—by which they mean maternal solicitude . . . (op. cit., p. 157)

Dylan Thomas, Constantine Fitzgibbon tells us, sought women so that he could 'cuddle up to' them. Menninger notes also how

ultimately, the normal wife rebels against giving to a grown man supposedly her protector and master. The outcome is inevitable. The patient then assumes a grieved or contemptuous or utilitarian or even consciously hostile attitude toward her and all women . . . and turns towards men with a mixture of friendly and provocative behaviour, with temporary jollity and popularity but ultimate misery and personal loss. At the same time that he is drinking with boon companions who appear to be substitutes for his father he is defying and grieving his real father and rejecting his real mother or her substitute. This, in turn, gives rise to remorse which leads to self-depreciation and self-injury. Meanwhile the exasperated wife considers or applies for a divorce. Immediately, the little-boy husband rushes back to her with tears, prayers, and promises to which she very likely succumbs and the whole cycle begins again.

(op. cit., p. 158)

In Dylan Thomas's alcoholism we have the same kind of expression of hate, unconsciously directed at the mother, and displaced on to the father, that we have in Sylvia Plath's *Daddy* poems—and in her desire to plunge into her father's grave in search for him, in search for being. The 'sulking, skulking, coal black soul' in *Lament* bears a significant relationship to her internalised 'black' father image, to which she is attached by hate.

Alcoholism, Menninger says moreover, is a defence against 'internal dangers':

As soon as these internal dangers threaten the destruction of the individual by his own impulses, alcoholism is chosen or sub- stituted as a kind of lesser self-destruction serving to arrest a greater self-destruction. (op. cit., p. 158)

In all such manifestations, one finds the terrible closed-circuit logic of the schizoid individual whose 'self-destruction is accom- plished *in spite of* and at the same time *by means of* the very device used by the sufferer to relieve his pain and avert this feared destruction.' What killed Dylan Thomas, as it killed Sylvia Plath, was a mode of (false male doing) behaviour resorted to in order to escape destruction from internal objects within and loss of identity, in order to be reborn.

We may, I believe, conclude that Dylan Thomas's mother was an '*ill* mother' who could not wean her baby—and even that he 'never had her, so that weaning has no meaning'. He was never disillusioned, towards maturity, independence, and 'the capacity to be alone', and never found a real sense of relationship between the me and the not-me. He never entered satisfactorily into this process of developing adequate powers of perception by being given support to the ego in terms of 'being' towards 'creative looking'. He could therefore seldom believe in a benign environ- ment, nor easily 'find' the outside environment. He had to sub- stitute for it an inner one full of 'bad objects'—and seek to impose his inner world on the outer. The outer world, time, growth, reality, the existence of others, seemed to him threats, because they required an independence he could never achieve: contact in relationship brought a threat of annihilation. In order to counter these paranoid fears he clung to absolute dependence, to a state before the not-me divided from the me. He sought to feel that the whole cosmos must be 'me'. So he existed in a perpetual inability to be 'disillusioned' to find true reality, while every other person he sought to make 'me' in the same way that the infant at first identifies with the breast-mother. His mother conveyed to him by her handling that she confused him with a ghost, and so he always felt unreal and confused in his identity, and lacking in a sense of being and ontological security. These dreadful aspects of his predicament were both the mainsprings of his poetry, and the causes of his self-defeat.

3
The Role of the Reader

Only by resorting to such psychological insights, I believe, is it possible to avoid inappropriate responses to Dylan Thomas, and see what it was he was trying to do. It is possible, of course, to reject him. We can try to say that he is 'the least intellectual of our poets' and imply furthermore that he sought to get away with unintelligently concocting poetry which only seems, by fabrication, to be profound. But it is obvious that Thomas was perceptive and intelligent. Is it that he couldn't write intelligibly? It is certainly true that the problems he wrote poems about didn't lend themselves to conscious intelligent reflection. We might then allow a 'poetry of the blood': but need this be so visceral, so chaotic, so cosmic in such a dissipated way?

Even if we allow that Thomas was trying to deal with primal or primitive experience, need that have involved us in being asked to accept his view of himself as of such uncircumscribed importance to the universe? Especially when we know how disastrously and tragically unable he was to deal with human reality? How can we equate this promiscuous alcoholic with Christ, as he seems to want us to do?

In responding to his work and his myth even more exhausting demands are made on us. For not only are there baffling poems and poems which seem, even after many attempts, still meaningless—but we may suspect that some of the chaos has been deliberately contrived.

But even if the poetry is chaotic the needs of Dylan Thomas are clear. He was, above all, one who urgently sought ontological security. Inevitably when we encounter him we at once feel impelled to try to supply it, and where it cannot be supplied by communication through symbolism, we feel, it must be supplied in terms of a persona. So, there is the film of Dylan Thomas's life in which he is spoken of with awe as if he were the Christchild, and which begins with a hushed shot of a light in his birth-chamber and ends with a 'fade' over the sea with the image of the Virgin and Child in the sunset. How shall this revered image be reconciled with the 'drunken lout' one critic has called him? Actually, both the shot of the birth-chamber and the image of Mother and Christchild fading into the sea are profoundly relevant as we have seen—they link the desire to be mothered with the desire to be crucified, and to merge like the Son of the Sea into some primal source, as by alcoholism—to be born again.

The 'schizoid diagnosis', I believe, thus explains much of the larger-than-life quality of responses to Dylan Thomas's persona—markedly different from, say, our responses to greater artists like James Joyce and D. H. Lawrence. There is a marked religiose quality, for example, in some writing about the poet—well illustrated by the publicity leaflet for the film about him.

An uncanny portrait of the poet comes off the screen—charming, gifted, beset by disquietude, driven to wild hilarity and clowning, burdened by the cares of living. Selections from his work, spoken by Dylan Thomas himself with his own Welsh magic, are alternately passionate, gentle, desperate, soaring. Together with the images of great beauty and revelation, the effect is a low-keyed, unremitting tension. Dylan Thomas is quite simply unforgettable.[1]

Even his most earnest supporters, however, feel a clash between his 'sacramentalising' of himself and nature, and the more dis-sociated behaviour of the worst episodes in his life. Aneirin Talfan Davies, for instance, in *Dylan: Druid of the Broken Body* says: 'It is only a misunderstanding of the role and function of the poet's vocation which could lead us to believe that a poet's public (or private) misdemeanours invalidate, in any real way, his poetic statements.' He admits, though, that Brinnin's *Dylan Thomas in America*, 'must have made, and still makes, it difficult for many readers to take seriously his claim to be, in any real sense, a religious poet.'

Our difficulties are increased by Thomas's evident irresponsi-bility at times as an artist:

[1] Contemporary Films Inc. leaflet advertising *The Days of Dylan Thomas*.

... The poet, like any other human being, can act in an ir-responsible way. Thomas was conscious of the dangers of conforming to the public image of the charm-poet; this would be the ultimate irresponsibility. He knew he could dazzle his audience with a display of verbal pyrotechnics—did he not possess a 'lovely gift of the gab'? But this would be a betrayal of his vocation as a poet through the partial acceptance of truths. (Aneurin Davies, op. cit., p. 9)

In biographical works about him a certain sentimentality, as I have already noted, suppresses the truth about Thomas's behaviour. Constantine Fitzgibbon, for instance, glosses over many disturbing aspects of Thomas's life, without taking which into account we cannot begin to understand him either as a person or a cultural phenomenon, as we shall see.[2]

I now believe that the reaction of everyone to Dylan Thomas (myself included) is marked by our unconscious recognition that he was very dangerous, because he evoked such hate and in-security in all around him. The very incompleteness of his identity evoked a response on the part of anyone he was with to complete it: they were forced into a role, and therefore forced into the anguish of his desperate (and self-destructive) 'attempt at self-cure'. They tried to give him a role, to save him from chaos—and to save themselves. Beside this, there was an unconscious realisa-tion in most that almost certainly *nothing could ever be done* to bring Dylan Thomas out of his worst dissociated states, because of the intensity of his death-circuit. This is a very terrifying perception, since it raises in each of us the harsh fact of the existence of an 'inner reality' with which we cannot perhaps ever come to terms: we cannot dictate to this inner structure, nor alter it at will. We too may be undermined by weakness, lack of integration, and self-destructive 'circuits'. Thus, when an individual presents himself and evokes these responses in us, our reaction is a *con-*

[2] There is a common tendency for biographers to seek to make their subjects larger than life, while concealing their deepest weaknesses. Dickens, for instance, has suffered from this. In truth his capacity for relationship was poignantly inept, while 'he felt that in reality his life, in spite of its triumphs and successes, was essentially a tragic failure' C. G. L. Du Cann, *The Love Lives of Charles Dickens* (1961), p. 253. An American reviewer said he found my implication that Mrs Thomas did not love her son 'offensive': yet he made no mention of Thomas's own remarks, 'my mother is a vulgar humbug' (*Letters*, p. 44); 'the pettiness of a mother I don't care for . . .' (*Letters*, p. 36) and elsewhere.

trolling response. This person threatens the core of our own being, and is therefore so dangerous that he must be controlled at all costs.

This reaction in others was itself exploited by Dylan Thomas as a means of establishing a (false) identity by role-playing and exhibitionism in lieu of true relationship. Some individuals fell into the role of mothering him: others sought to control him by annihilation, or by trying to beat him into normality. There are many ugly incidents in his life which disturb us, and tend to make us reject him even more. Such manifestations have to be 'forgotten', to preserve the sentimental account of his life. But even this suppression of memory is a form of attempt to control Dylan Thomas, to seek to make him 'safe' (and to make those who react to him feel 'safe' too).

I believe that Dylan Thomas was forced to accept many such 'controlled' roles in his life, because of a desperate uncertainty as to which self was his true self, and because he could not establish touch with his true self in an integrated way. A true core to himself, however, he did find from time to time in some of his poetry. Even so, the death circuit of the false self—or false systems as I shall later call them—was so powerful that there was a conflict between the true core of the self and the unwillingness to allow integration to develop—because of the anguished awareness this could bring. To be able to see his own predicament clearly was too terrible—so much so that the self-destructiveness often turned on the true creative quest itself. We therefore have the spectacle of a man lacerated by his own impulse to destroy even the only possible way of remaining alive—his thin true thread of continuity of identity, and the genuine creative voices by which he sought to work on this by symbolism.

Dylan Thomas was an alcoholic, caught up in all the self-deception of the sufferer who seeks by addiction to feel real, and to effect a self-cure, but whose worst symptoms are his duplicity and his need to disguise the aggressiveness of his self-destructive impulses by pretending that his lapses are really only 'jolly little occasions'. In personal relationships he was disastrously lacking in the capacity for object relations and he was liable to behave to others in a suddenly unreal or 'split' way. He combined over-dependence with the denial of dependence, and 'over-idealising of the love-object' with multiple object-behaviour, all of which indicate profound identity problems.

He found it exceptionally difficult to accept the paternal role, and, as we have seen, sometimes this aroused feelings with which he could not cope.[3] These feelings were almost certainly to do with strong emotions in himself caused by the children arousing the 'regressed libidinal ego' with its extravagant oral needs—hunger for love. Such forms of behaviour can be related to his alcoholism and his poetry and its content of oral aggressiveness. In the end, with a dreadful logic in the symbolism, he used a poetry prize to pay for his wife to abort their last child.

Thomas could deal realistically with neither money nor with property. I don't regard it necessarily as of supreme value in the personal life to deal efficiently with these things, but it is no good brushing aside the fact that a serious incapacity to deal with them is an indication of a weakness of the reality sense, if we want a biographical picture to be true. It is only sentimental to try to make out (as Anthony Burgess has done) that Dylan Thomas was 'killed by the Income Tax authorities'. Thomas was so little able to deal with the world because he had never been sufficiently 'disillusioned' in the way necessary for an individual to be able to find the real world. He could not relinquish his belief in his own magic, and his own intense need to impose his inner world on the outer.

What mattered in Dylan Thomas's world only mattered insofar as it affected him: even the War and bombing seem to him therefore chiefly inconveniences in *his* life, rather than de-structive manifestations in the outside world. The outer world was all him and he was the world: nothing mattered but the ruthless preservation of his own ego—which he was concerned to maintain if necessary at the expense of others.

In private life he was given to petty thieving, misrepresentation, and catastrophic 'letdowns'—followed by attempts to cover up the disaster by charm, elaborate contrition, an ironic self-criticism

---

[3] '... he had no patience with any nervous ailments or manifestations in his children' ... 'late lunch ... always eaten alone, apart from the children: and I can't blame him for that, as there is nothing worse than brawling children's meals.' 'It was not often we went anywhere *en masse* ... he even went so far as not travelling in the same carriage with them.' (Caitlin Thomas, *Leftover Life to Kill*, passim)

that sought to trivialise serious aggression, and remorse. He suffered from an inability to finish work and there was an extraordinary dichotomy between Thomas's best integrity as a working writer (as shown by his painstaking revision) and his irresponsibility in dealing with the world at large: between his responsibility to his true self and the fearfulness of real relationship which made him so dissociated in his dealings with the outside world. One consequence of this was the intellectual and conceptual incoherence manifest in some of his public statements and in some of his poems, by contrast with some of his earlier reviews which show him as intelligent and perceptive.

Two other characteristics relevant to mention here were his compliance—shown in his willingness to accept roles supplied by others: and his chronic hypochondria. Such a fragmentary and unreal life, with all its false beliefs about the world, and false modes of dealing with it, can only be preserved by a 'ruthless egoism', and a 'strategy of survival' of heroic proportions. His reputation is a tribute to this poignant heroism, while his best work is spun out of it. He wrote to preserve his identity—sometimes from moral motives, but sometimes from immoral ones. It is additionally difficult for us to 'place' his work and discriminate between poems because he also writes at times to seek to preserve a chaotic system within the self to which he is attached as if to life itself, despite its destructiveness.

So even in approaching his poetry we have to distinguish between genuine and false. For instance, is he a 'druid' and was he genuinely religious? He himself here makes the most facile statements, as in the prefatory note to *Collected Poems 1934-1952*. How much did he believe them? One consequence has been an intense endorsement of his work as devotional.

As will appear, I believe this has a deep unconscious symbolism: the problem is to take this identification with Christ in one who was both dissolute and suicidal, and a creative artist. I believe the link is provided by insights into schizoid suicide. But unconscious elements here generate an intense uncritical response in some Christians, who wish to enlist him as a prophet. For instance, in the journal of the American National Council of Teachers of English, appeared an article *The Wellspring of Dylan* by Sister Roberta Jones in which she says he breaks the bonds of ... death in the vital reality which he discovered in his poetry ... His virility is flourishing in his daughter's 'Almost Posthumous' letters from her mother, Caitlin. There is such abundant vitality in his works that it becomes almost articulate in its fullness at times, but this lifestream—full measure, pressed down, and overflowing— sometimes disciplines to the tension of true art. When it does, the vigor it holds becomes a fruitful lifestream ... For this we human workers, sometimes—searchers, must be eternally grateful. He has his place among those whose vitality could never be fully submerged; even when life overwhelmed them: they live ...

Of his 'own union with Christ' (in *Vision and Prayer*) she says: This blinding light of mystic insight, this realization of Christ's redemption is an affirmation out of nothingness of self, that He saves each one who admits Him, is perhaps the gift only of the creative genius or saint ...

(*The English Journal*, Vol. 55, no. 1, p. 82)

In the face of such acclaim it seems almost impossible to question a reputation which is based on the appearance of a vitality so 'tumultuous' that it could only at times achieve 'the tension of true art'—or only at times be coherent. Was Thomas a rogue and mad? Or was he a genius and saint? There is a spell here which transfixes critics. To unravel this spell of persuasion, and to discover the true core of it, is to unravel one of the most complex problems of the arts in the modern world.

We can best unravel it by concentrating our attention on the poems. Dylan Thomas's poems make us feel uneasy: sometimes they seem mad, and yet express a particular anguish behind them that communicates itself to us. They cry to us, with the character in *Adventures in the Skin Trade*, 'O God make me feel something, I must be impotent!' Moreover, they are like ghosts, howling to us to confirm an identity. They beckon to us, and demand that we shall adopt a role and complete them by our response.

Many of my readers will have experienced the feeling of being driven mad by a baby or infant—say, during a teething fit in which the child was beside itself with paranoia. This can be a very frightening experience, not least because of the insecurity and hate aroused in oneself, which evokes one's own regressed ego. There is something of this feeling in our response to some of

Dylan Thomas's poetry. It is not only that we are being asked to play a role. We have to supply a meaning and thereby to confirm an identity. In this we find ourselves in the predicament analysed by Farber, that of the therapist who, in treating schizophrenics, tends to become distorted in his own attitudes to life. The problem is to judge how far we can allow ourselves to be maddened by such poetry, and how many compensatory rewards and satisfactions we get that make up for this.

Even if we take a few comparatively easy poems by Dylan Thomas, we shall find, especially if we look at what other critics have written, that we become enlisted in a common struggle to contribute meaning where whole meaning is absent in the artefact itself, though a kind of meaning seems only a hair's breadth away, or a cloud of meaning seems hovering ready to congeal, or come into focus. Often, however, even in stretching towards the meaning it seems that we cannot grasp it without distorting our own view of experience. We are giving the benefit of the doubt, perhaps, to the expression of some problem of existence which we wish to share, whose expression we feel must be valuable—it will be a universal statement of despair or loneliness. But we can see that if we are to clench the expression of this by helping Thomas to a meaning, we shall have to swallow some other gloss on experience—such as a belief in omnipotence, or a revulsion from physical contact, or the rejection of time and reality as a loss of freedom. We are likely to begin by seeing ourselves looking in a mirror as if to confirm an identity, only to find ourselves drawn through the mirror into a world where our whole relationship with experience is threatened with inversion.

So, I have found in writing this book that in order to get anywhere at all I have sometimes had to write mad interpretations of mad poems: and then try to extricate myself as best I can. This may exhaust the reader as much as it has exhausted me. But in the end one does, I believe, experience a sympathy for Thomas, and an understanding of his plight, which puts a new light on much of the literature one afterwards comes into contact with.

A hostile reader may say that for me my critical role has become merely a mock therapeutic one, in which I can play at being a psychoanalyst. To this I could only retort that in discussing Dylan Thomas again I only began with the utmost reluctance, since I recognised that my point of view had completely changed since *Llareggub Revisited* and to face up to this would be awkward and embarrassing. But I was driven to write this second book because I wished to find good grounds for discriminating against the prevalent ethos of our fashionable literary world, and its concern to endorse schizoid false solutions, while neglecting the underlying problems of existence which the schizoid writer forces us to consider. I hoped to become able to 'hear' Dylan Thomas as he had not yet been 'heard'.

I have discussed the same problem in connection with Sylvia Plath, and in trying to 'hear' in this way (when the avant-garde hear something quite different) I believe I am trying to apply the kind of insights to literary criticism which D. W. Winnicott emphasises for psychotherapy.

Psychotherapy is not making clever and apt interpretations; by and large it is a long-term giving the patient back what the patient brings. It is a complex derivative of the face that reflects what there is to be seen. I like to think of my work this way, and to think that if I do this well enough the patient will find his or her own self, and will be able to exist and feel real. Feeling real is more than existing, it is finding a way to exist as oneself, and to have a self into which to retreat for relaxation.

But I would not like to give the impression that I think this task of reflecting what the patient brings is easy. It is not easy, and it is emotionally exhausting. But we get our rewards. Even when our patients do not get cured they are grateful to us for seeing them as they are, and this gives us a satisfaction of a deep kind. ('Mirror-role of Mother and Family' in *The Predicament of the Family*, ed. Peter Lomas, p. 32)

In literary criticism, of course, often, as with Sylvia Plath and Dylan Thomas, the 'patients'—the subjects—are dead. But to try to hear or see them as they are in their works is also a way to try to find 'a way to exist as oneself' and to share this quest with others. As Farber says, what we are here forced to concern ourselves with is the nature of humanness: and this can be both exhausting and satisfying.

The first problem, then, is to recognise that Dylan Thomas was sensitive, intelligent, and painstaking. The present writer acknowledges that it is very little credit to his former study that he tried to deny this. In writing about poetry at the age of twenty Thomas wrote well:

'The Death of the Ear' would be an apt subtitle for a book on the plight of modern poetry. Mr. West, writing in the June *Adelphi*, did not mention the fact—a fact that must be obvious to him—that most of the work of Mr. Pound, much of Mr. Auden and Mr. Day Lewis, and the entire output of Mr. Pound's disciples, Mr. Ronald Bottrall, Mr. Carlos Williams, etc., does sound abominable. It would be possible to explain this lack of aural value and this debasing of an art that is primarily dependent on the musical mingling of vowels and consonants by talking of the effect of a noisy, mechanical civilization on the delicate mechanism of the human ear. But the reason is deeper than that. Too much poetry to-day is flat on the page, a black and white thing of words created by intelligences that no longer think it necessary for a poem to be read and understood by anything but the eyes.

(*The Adelphi*, 1934)

Thomas conveys the poise of an educated literary man when he writes, about Lyle Donaghy and John Lehmann,

There is a shapeless promise in this ooze of words, and a pendulous romanticism of theme and texture, that contrast almost favourably with the pallid, the bogus 'modernisms' of Mr. Lehmann's lyrics and the only half disguised whimsicalities of his prose-pieces. Mr. Lehmann conveys the impression of a narrow but sensitive mentality seeking through poetry not, as he himself declares, 'the extreme attic of the mind,' but the nursery of half forgotten illusions . . . He superimposes a false vitality upon the body of a tired and a moded poetry, evading all the issues of the flesh or the spirit. (*The Adelphi*, 1934)

Reviews he wrote at this time show that Thomas was a perceptive reader. This, for instance, is from a notice of J. W. Tibble's edition of the poetry of John Clare:

He was an intimate poet, having little or none of the extasies and flourishes of an invalid romanticism; content with visible shapes and objective meanings, he did not question the natural world; he did not attempt to measure its mysteries by a hand-ruled philosophy, to work, through what would inevitably have been confused metaphysics, towards a solution of the unhappy state of mind that had shuttered him from society and forced upon him for companions the abstraction of a shadow and the inadequate concreteness of words. What is remarkable, under these conditions, is that the best of Clare becomes both social and universal poetry, and that, even at his worst, he had none of the private, masturbatory preoccupation of the compulsive egoist. (*The Adelphi*, 1935)

At twenty-one, Thomas was here writing in the manner of *The Calendar of Modern Letters*, meaningfully and well. Such intelligent comment contrasts startlingly with the note to *Collected Poems*:

I read somewhere of a shepherd who, when asked why he made, from within fairy rings, ritual observations to the moon to protect his flocks, replied: 'I'd be a damn fool if I didn't!' These poems, with all their crudities, doubts and confusions, are written for the love of Man and in praise of God, and I'd be a damn fool if they weren't.

This is a whimsical posture: the adoption of a false role. What happened to Thomas's intelligence between twenty-one and thirty-eight? The same young man who was writing the perceptive reviews above was also writing poems such as that from which came the lines quoted as a motto to this volume:

The Woman Speaks:
No food suffices but the food of death;
Sweet is the waxen blood, honey the falling flesh;
There is no fountain springing from the earth
Cool as the wax-red fountains of the veins;
No cradle's warmer than this perished breast,
And hid behind the fortress of the ribs
The heart lies ready for the raven's mouth,
And lustreless within the ruined face
The eyes remark the antics of the hawk . . .

. . . O sprinkle on my head
That dust you hold, O strew that little left;
Let what remains of that first miracle
Be sour in my hair. That I may learn
The mortal miracle, let that first dust
Tell me of him who feeds the raging birds.
(*The Adelphi*, 1934)

The same young man knew that his intelligent, and capable 'front' (such as he presents in his charming letters to Pamela Hansford Johnson) was at any moment likely to be undermined by catastrophe—not by the rebellious sensuality of a young James Joyce, but a capacity to defeat and humiliate himself, even as artist. In his poetry he began to explore the region of the origins of this internal threat—a region which could only be explored by uncanny symbolism, and which, as he drew near, involved him in chaos and vacancy.

The reader may not be convinced that my conjecture about Thomas's predicament is related to a confusion unconsciously made by his mother and an earlier dead sibling. But let us assume for the purposes of my exploration that at the heart of Dylan Thomas's dissociation is the problem of the 'regressed libidinal ego'—the unborn true self of being, with a desperate need to be born, or 'reborn' ('reborn' since at least the living body has been born already). Guntrip points out that this is our universal problem—our common problem of existence. But in order for us even to see this a 'major cultural revolution' will be necessary. We have to become able to accept our weakness and not find such acceptance humiliating. But in an individual, if there is hopelessness and despair, and no confidence that there ever can be help, so that no such acceptance is possible, there may develop a reckless abandon. The individual may then give himself up to hate and even a 'death-circuit' of flight from life.

Everyone supplied Dylan Thomas with roles when he approached them in such a way as to beseech them to help him become himself, but few seemed to have understood him and their responses were on the whole concerned with their own self-defences. As Guntrip says, with some patients who have deep schizoid problems:

The naturally active, energetic and capable persons who cannot succeed, or be contented, in becoming cold, emotionally neutralised intellectuals, and yet cannot effect stable and happy relationships and get on with living, can reach a point of volcanic eruption. They cannot stand the utter frustration of their inability to escape from their own need to compromise, half in and out solutions . . . The result can be tragedy . . .

(*Brit. J. med. Psych.*, 35 (1962), p. 273)

Out of such a *huis clos* came the progressive deterioration of Dylan Thomas. *Lament*, I believe, reveals this deterioration—as does the note to *Collected Poems*. Thomas could not escape by becoming 'cold, emotionally neutralised': his feelings rather became unstable, or volcanic. The cultural atmosphere encouraged him meanwhile to seek false strengths.

Here we encounter an urgent problem of our time. As Guntrip says, we need a 'major cultural revolution' in order to come to grips with our deepest human problems. We need a cultural atmosphere from which we have managed to eliminate not only the 'taboo on tenderness' which Ian D. Suttie diagnosed, but with it its deeper implication, the 'taboo on weakness'.

Today poetry moves continually in the opposite direction. The vogue is for loud, 'black' and nihilistic postures (George MacBeth, Adrian Henri), and for an empty chest-beating noise that not only hides inner weakness, but threatens discourse and meaning themselves. Even the best poets, like Ted Hughes, are acclaimed most for their more cynical phantasies, and those poems in which they give themselves up to the joys of hating (Crow is 'God's nightmare'). Poetry moves away further and further from that acceptance in each of us of the not-fully-born and weakest aspect of the self, associated with the deepest existential questions, which we must solve or perish. Poetry is now very far from an atmosphere, such as that of Guntrip's consulting room, in which a patient could say to him, 'If only I could feel loved, I'm sure I'd grow. Can I be sure you genuinely care for the baby in me?' Ted Hughes's *Orghast*, enacted on a mountainside in Persepolis, begins with a baby being stamped on.

The retreat from the anguish of engagement with the true self and 'existential frustration' is itself schizoid, and represents, in individuals and our culture at large a retreat into an 'inward world' so that values become detached from engagement with reality, and so we suffer from a lowering of human value. Various manifestations in our culture, such as the use of hallucinogenic drugs, the use of hypnotic sound and light in 'pop' music, and pornography, all belong to this kind of schizoid retreat from symbolic creative engagement with reality. Certain individuals such as Dylan Thomas and Sylvia Plath may be seen as representative, *in extremis*, of this breakdown of creativity in culture and living. As Fairbairn says,

There is a great tendency for the outer world to derive its meaning too exclusively from the inner world. In actual schizophrenics this tendency may become so strong that the distinction between inner and outer reality is largely obscured ... such extreme cases apart ... there is a general tendency ... to keep up their values in the inner world.
(Psychoanalytical Studies, p. 18)

Dylan Thomas's remark 'in the tumultuous world of my own being' is thus a characteristic schizoid remark. By his overvaluation of his inner world he becomes involved in an obscuring of distinctions and confusion of values—and in the ultimate encapsulation in his problem. The moral problem which arises was characterised by Fairbairn thus:

In the case of individuals whose object-relationships are predominantly in the outer world, giving has the effect of creating and enhancing values, and of promoting self-respect; but, in the case of individuals whose object-relationships are predominantly in the inner world, giving has *the effect of depreciating values, and of lowering self-respect.* (ibid., my italics)

The essential ethical problem here is of *attitudes to human nature.* Strangely enough, as Dylan Thomas 'gave out' in his work his values and self-respect deteriorated instead of becoming enhanced so that the man's behaviour declined in quality, even as some of his poetry became clearer and more profound.

So, in Dylan Thomas we have the extraordinary enigma of a man who in his poetry, and in his inner world had a concept of himself as a 'hero', of great nobility, who often identified with Christ—but who in his actual behaviour was capable of forfeiting all self-respect and destroying all personal values. This can only be explained in terms of a schizoid failure of the capacity for object relationship, as between the subjective and objective worlds, between inner reality and outer reality, so that in the end such an individual takes the ultimate flight from being human.

The reader thus has to resist being drawn into the false roles, in which such a schizoid individual seeks to involve him. He needs, like a psychotherapist, to arm himself by conscious insight. He can then afford to try to 'creatively reflect' Thomas's poetry—and if he does I believe he may find himself able to understand more of the meaning of madness, and learn about some of the strangest experiences of 'life without feeling alive'.

4

The 'Living Cipher' of the Early Poems

Dylan Thomas's early poetry can be understood in terms of a strange preoccupation with mortal dangers in inner contents, somehow associated with a 'first miracle' which has to do with the 'spitting forth' of a 'baby's corpse', and the compulsive quest for identity which forever follows, often misled into an internal hate —or death—circuit.

Inevitably, since they are themselves an attempt to explore primal experience, some of the early poems seem incomprehensible. We find this problem as soon as we turn to the first poem in *Collected Poems*, *I see the boys of summer* (see below pp. 176–8). But, passing this by, we shall find it easier to begin with the next, *When once the twilight locks no longer* (p. 4). There is much in this poem that seems at first mere surrealist gesture. But it seems an early approach to the problems of identity with which Thomas was to be engrossed. Who is this 'carcass shape' in the twilight?

> When once the twilight screws were turned,
> And mother milk was stiff as sand,
> I sent my own ambassador to light;
> By trick or chance he fell asleep
> And conjured up a carcass shape
> To rob me of my fluids in his heart.

Is it not the rival 'other', who is dead?—'bad inner contents': the regressed ego as a bottled foetus?[1] Earlier (verse one) we have

---

[1] In Dylan Thomas's notebooks, Dennis Pratt tells us, he shows himself obsessed by 'disgusted anguish at conception of cancerous embryos'. See *Dylan Thomas*, ed. C. B. Cox (1957), p. 118.

'the mouth of time sucked ... The milky acid', 'And swallowed dry the waters of the breast'. Here are themes of unappeased hunger: a fear of danger in taking hate from the breast ('milky acid') and a frustration of thirst ('stiff as sand'). Why is there this dearth? The infant sends out an 'ambassador' to throw 'light' on this problem. As if in a dream ('He drowned his father's magics in a dream') this 'ambassador' has

> conjured up a carcass shape
> To rob me of my fluids in his heart.

That is, if my conjecture is correct, it is the dead sibling whose envy (it seems), by existing in the mother's memory and claiming her psychic preoccupation, has deprived the self of its 'fluids'— of love, of good inner contents. For this reason the creature of the self seems 'sewn' to the changeling and it is as if his whole relationship with the world is permeated by this confusion of identity:

> I sent my creature scouting on the globe,
> That globe itself of hair and bone
> That, sewn to me by nerve and brain,
> Had stringed my flask of matter to his rib.

In this one poem we can begin to note various elements which we know from our exploration of psychological theories to spring from schizoid preoccupations. Relationship is conceived in terms of sucking at partial objects, as if at a depersonalised stream of milk, rather than being confirmed by another person ('The mouth of time sucked, like a sponge,/The milky acid ...'). There is a feeling of petrification ('Mother milk was stiff as sand'). There is a fear of contact, because it threatens to 'rob ... the fluids': relationship and the hunger for it threaten to empty inner contents, which are in any case threatening—'issue ... The redhaired cancer ... bags of blood let out their flies ... Gives up its dead'.

But there is also much confusion, because the 'other' seeks 'To rob me of my fluids in *his* heart' (my italics), it is as if the self has been taken over by the other. 'Sewn' and 'my flask of matter to his rib' conveys the uncertainty of the individual who has not been confirmed by his mother's handling that he is in his own body, so that there is a failure of personalisation.

Resurrection of the regressed ego ('Awake, my sleeper, to the sun'), which feels as if it were threatened by the other, involves rejection of the 'other'—

... leave the poppied pickthank where he lies ...

—'Poppied' implying his death (drugged to oblivion or with poppies growing on his grave). The poem is thus one of envy directed at the double of the self, who has become confused with the self. Sewn together, one self punishes the other for the fear of ontological insecurity—a parallel *huis clos* to Thomas's alcoholism.

Other less evident features are a horror of woman and the physical reality of her creative body ('issue ... redhaired cancer ... bushy jaws ... bags of blood ... flies' evoke a subdued image of hideous flux from the vaginal opening). This may be associated with the schizoid fear of dependence, and fear of the feminine element in oneself—because one never securely experienced 'being' from the mother's capacity to be for her infant.

There is also evident in this poem a belief in omnipotent magic and incantatory power as a way out of difficulties: 'And worlds hang in the trees'.

Next we may take the poem *Before I knocked* (*Collected Poems*, p. 7). In *Llareggub Revisited* I wrote of a 'neurotic identification with Christ' in this poem, and how it speaks as if time and reality were crucifying the innocent child. I noted that 'Christ also had the Virgin ... all to himself'. I rejected the poem as 'neurotic morbidity': now I believe neurotic is not the right word: the problem is a schizoid one, of existence. John Ackerman says Thomas is 'speaking of existence before it takes the form of human life':

He sees all life as part of an organic whole; existence is a unity which is broken when life is conceived, but to which the body returns at death. In imagining the experience of life in the womb the poet sees himself as both male and female ('was brother ... and sister') ... the child in the womb is aware of the journey to death it must make and already feels within itself the seeds of destruction. (*Dylan Thomas*, pp. 46–8)

Ackerman points out that 'Thomas speaks in the person of Christ, who, in terms of the Virgin Birth, was in a real sense born of the flesh and ghost'. William York Tindall's gloss is rather more ingenious: 'The "fathering worm", more than papa's member, could be the Serpent of Genesis, who also brought death into the world' (*A Reader's Guide to Dylan Thomas*, p. 46). Mnetha, he points out, was an old nurse who served as mother to senile Heva.

Such glosses explore unconscious themes of the poem but discuss them as if Thomas were expressing a consistent 'philosophy', as if he were calculating his ambiguities, or as if he were being blasphemous in identifying with Christ. These critics are discussing the poem as if Thomas knew what he was writing about. And such critics search around in mythology for types of symbol and relationship which parallel the strange phantasies of Dylan Thomas's vision. The problem of identity for Thomas I have suggested was one of confusion between the self and a dead sibling, a feeling of being that sibling reborn, which could involve guilt at having in some way been responsible for killing or replacing that sibling. Because of the unconscious themes of death and resurrection here, all focusing on the mother, Dylan Thomas's poetry has been taken to be about Christ—and he himself obviously identified with Christ, who became a symbol of his regressed ego in need of resurrection. (At other times this regressed ego, in its tomb inside the self, seems like Houdini.)[2]

Thus attempts at interpretation have shown great ingenuity at interpreting Dylan Thomas's poetry in terms of Christian symbols. Because of his schizoid preoccupation with inner contents, with the womb and birth, and because of his revulsion at the physical details of sex, there has also been much 'Freudian' interpretation. But one's experience with such glosses is often that, having studied the poem, and then the 'interpretation'—one goes back to the poem none the wiser. The trouble always seems to be that here interpretation means adding to the words of the poem material the words do not themselves contain or generate. Such criticism merely scatters around a plethora of external extravagances of reference and detail for which the poem itself offers no definition or organisation—or even an excuse.

Even so, we may find clues to the essential meaning from phrases in such attempts at interpretations (even though by themselves they do not explain the poem). Here for instance we have in Tindall's notes the phrases:

[2] '. . . he spotted a billboard poster advertising a new movie *Houdini*. Dylan remarked that the great magician had always fascinated him . . . The worst horror in life, said Dylan, . . . was the sense of being hopelessly trapped.' J. M. Brinnin, *Dylan Thomas in America* (1955), p. 249.

> Identification with Christ . . .
> sees himself as both male and female . . .
> feels within itself the seeds of destruction . . .
> born of the flesh and ghost . . .

The poem, as I see it, is about the perplexity Thomas experienced as an infant (and felt in his adult attitude to existence) in feeling that birth was death, and that as a newborn infant he was a resurrected being, who is yet dead. This may be associated with the symbolism of schizoid suicide: it is the 'regressed libidinal ego' which waits for the chance to be reborn, which may be found in withdrawal—even in the ultimate withdrawal of death.

The poem begins with the prenatal state, and ends with the 'message of the dying Christ' being conveyed to the father. If we explore the poem for the characters involved, they are the father, the mother, the 'I' of the poem, and *another*, Him, Christ, who has

> doublecrossed my mother's womb . . .

Who can this be, but the dead sibling, whose flesh undoubtedly preceded Dylan in the womb, and whose ghost is confused with his identity? The essential Trinity here is Math the Magician Father, the non-virginal maiden, and Dylan the Sea Son. The father receives the 'message of his dying Christ' for his part in 'swinging his rainy hammer': he is to be made to feel the guilt he denies by giving his son the name Dylan and so invoking the maiden who has such an easy birth.

To the infant Dylan the father would surely have seemed the one guilty of causing the death of the previous sibling because he was the one to 'sew the deep door'. The infant Dylan, however, would have felt involved in the guilt, not only because of his hatred of a rival, but because he was confused with him and *treated as if he were him* (when he wasn't). To a child (according to Kleinian theory) the sexual act (the Primal Scene) between the parents has all the dangers of incorporative eating: for his excitement at his parents' incorporative act of sexual 'eating' he expects in revenge to feel retribution (because sex is 'taking in'). Thus the father's hammer is 'rainy' because the child fears a urinary talion attack, a storm of urine, in response to becoming involved in his phantasy with the parents' fleshly love. He is so near (in the womb) as to feel their intercourse 'thud beneath my flesh's armour'.

The commentators mentioned above take the poem to be 'about' actual intrauterine, pre-birth, experience. It is more meaningful, however, to take Thomas's preoccupation with birth and the womb to be a symbolic way of referring to the *genesis of the identity*, and the processes of psychic birth. A passage of Guntrip's seems relevant here (from a discussion of Fairbairn's later theories). He is discussing the concept of the 'regressed libidinal ego': the kind of retreat by which 'the emotional heart of the personality has drawn back inside out of reach of being hurt'. (He quotes a child in a play who says, 'It doesn't matter what you do to me now, you can't hurt me any more.')

Where does the regressed libidinal ego go? It withdraws into its original base camp, the warm protected place from which it first emerged. It withdraws, if not back into an actual womb, then deep into the unconscious into *an even more secret and hidden 'closed system' of an illusory though psychically real reproduction of the intra-uterine state*. This is the source of the 'return to the womb' phantasies with which analysts have always been familiar, the importance of which Freud stressed in connection with his criticism of Rank's views.

(*Personality Structure*, p. 432, my italics)

Dylan Thomas said towards the end he would like to be 'forever unconscious': he had a strong impulse to retreat to this 'closed system'. This closed system to which the libidinal ego retreats is conceived in terms of intra-uterine feelings (as he used to want to 'cuddle up' to the women he slept with): but it is in fact rather a 'psychically real reproduction of the intra-uterine state' not a memory of that state.

To be turned out of that state of regression was to Thomas crucifixion: disillusionment was death. So, birth is death—as indeed it is if we consider it as the beginning of our mortal journey. To be born yet born as if one were dead (psychically dead and also confused with a dead baby) is to 'doublecross' the womb.

The poem strives towards making this truth universal, so that it may be a statement of how 'in the midst of life we are in death', or an insight echoing Eliot's 'did we come all that way for birth, or death?' That is, it is yet another statement of the feeling that one is born but dead—Thomas's schizoid predicament, but also a statement of our existential 'nothingness'. The unintegrated self, divided and insecure, becomes less able to symbolise as it approaches the essential problem of feeling a confirmed existence:

> As yet ungotten, I did suffer;
> The rack of dreams my lily bones
> Did twist into a living cipher,
> And flesh was snipped to cross the lines
> Of gallow crosses on the liver
> And brambles in the wringing brains.

Because the nature of the problem is not evident to a conscious integrated self which can recognise and explore the existential problem, attempts to explore it by symbolism are baffled. If we accuse Thomas here of incoherence, as I have done in the past, it may be that we are merely denying the nature of the deep existential problem towards which he is groping. But if we study the schizoid processes we can, I believe, see that he expresses it in a startling way, so long as we supply the other half of the incomplete meaning.

Here he tried to explore the problem, that, looking back on his primal experience, he suffered before he conceived an identity ('ungotten' here meaning not physically not-conceived but not-conceived as an identity—for we are dealing with what is psychically rather than physically real). This is so because he is confused by his mother with the dead sibling, who suffered death. So, before he became an identity, he was already preconceived to suffering. The 'rack of her dreams'—her impingement on his identity by stretching it over the dead child—*twisted* his lily bones (pure, flowering fragile) into a *living cipher*: she has made him a not-identity. His own self was twisted, broken and negatived, even in its first pure flowering.

Flesh was snipped suggests circumcision (as a symbolism of initiation of identity), perhaps caesarean birth, or the cuts made in the perinaeum to ease birth. *Cross the lines* links these birth pains or initiation pains with the crossing (or *doublecrossing*) of one sibling identity with another. The consequences are those preoccupations with 'badness' inside that made Thomas such a hypochondriac: examined for portents he was sure his liver bore marks of a gallows-bird (and, significantly, we have a report on his liver from the American hospital where he died). The phrase brambles in the wringing brains . . .

expresses the torment in the tortured mind which results from
the impingement on him, from a difficult birth and inadequate
early handling. The difficult birth, I have suggested, was a consequence of the mother's schizoid reluctance to part with bodily
contents. This (he is unconsciously aware) has killed the sibling
and it was manifest in her maternal overprotection of Dylan. In
regressing into the intra-uterine state Thomas only finds reminiscences in his psychic reality, of torturing impingements, even
there.

> My throat knew thirst before the structure
> Of skin and vein around the well
> Where words and water make a mixture
> Unfailing till the blood runs foul . . .

'The child's ego is a mouth ego': Thomas's ego knew hunger
before he could speak: he thirsted and thirsts for an identity. It is
the same thirst which made him an alcoholic. The words welling
up as an expression of oral attitudes to the world mix with the
water by which he attempts to cure the thirst: both the poetry
and the drink were attempts at self-cure. There is, however,
another threat in the 'badness within': even the 'unfailing' mixture
of words and water may be stopped 'when the blood runs foul'.
The recognition of the deep need for love, and of the physical
hunger, go with the smell of mortality and the fear of bad inner
contents:

> I smelt the maggot in my stool.

The recognition of reality is associated with recognition of the
death of the former sibling, and of the death latent in his own
'bad' faeces (i.e. bad inner contents).

The reality of this mortality he resents: time has cast him out.
Here Thomas expresses in an early poem that resistance to time
and maturity that was to be a recurrent theme in his work.

> And time cast forth my mortal creature
> To drift or drown upon the seas
> Acquainted with the salt adventure
> Of tides that never touch the shores.

Dylan the Sea Son of the Wave feels cast forth to 'drift or
drown': his 'tides never touch the shores'—he never feels real,

never touches shore, but is only acquainted with the bitter and tearful adventures of being tossed on the sea of life, which feels to the schizoid person like an endless loss of freedom ('while I sang in my chains like the sea'). He who was once 'liquid', 'shapeless as the water', 'was yet in molten form', has now become merged with the flux of the sea outside the security of the amniotic fluid. The fluid identity threatens to merge with the cosmic flux. Yet there is a recognition that in growth in time there is a gain, in the odd last two lines of this stanza:

> I who was rich was made the richer
> By sipping at the vine of days.

Here, I believe, there is a dim recognition of the distinction between the 'I' (the true Dylan self) and the identity confused with the dead sibling, the schizoid dissociated identity. Apart from these two lines (which can only apply to the child who survived), the poem can be read as if spoken either by the dead sibling, or by Thomas himself: or by the two identities confused and merged as they were by the mother.

> I, born of flesh and ghost, was neither
> A ghost nor man, but mortal ghost.

This was Dylan Thomas's predicament at the core: it is also a description of the dead child, who was only a ghost, but is yet a very present one in Thomas's life: the stillborn changeling.

> And I was struck down by death's feather.

Death's feather is the feather that King Lear holds under the nose of Cordelia. It is also the feathered wing of the angel of death (as Ackerman points out) and yet implies a light-as-a-feather death, *such as an infant might suffer*. King Lear is Cordelia's father, and he is testing to see if she is alive still. Here,

> I was a mortal to the last
> Long breath that carried to my father
> The message of his dying christ.

The pressure here is of an unconscious conviction that the father (who rhymes with and lurks within the word *f(e)ather*) has killed the sibling even under the pretence of trying (like Lear) to demonstrate that he is alive. Christ died according to God's will: He cried 'Father, father, why hast thou forsaken me?'

Here Dylan Thomas is expressing a deep fear that the father, despite his explicit love, which seems to guarantee life (resurrection), conceals beneath this the impulse to destroy—as he actually destroyed the changeling sibling (by swinging his hammer). Dylan Thomas himself, who felt the hate in his father's wish that he should be him, is a Christ who died by becoming mortal and being thrust out of the intra-uterine state. In this his father is as much to blame as he is for having killed the sibling who has 'become' Dylan. This is the doublecross. To doublecross is to play a trick, by pretending that one thing is another: the doublecrossing, here as we have seen, has led to *gallow crosses*, the *living cipher*, and *brambles in the wringing brains*.

What does the last stanza mean?

> You who bow down at cross and altar . . .

—you who take part in symbolic ritual, worshipping the emblems of crucifixion, which are emblems of the price paid in ultimate mortal suffering for sin.

> Remember me and pity Him . . .

Think of me, who have experienced a torment suffered innocently (because the suffering was endured by an *infant*) and pity *Him*. Who is 'Him'? Him, I believe, is the changeling who is also confused with the self,

> Who took my flesh and bone *for armour* . . .

The last phrase can be interpreted as meaning that the sibling entered into his (Dylan's) body and identity 'casing', in order to become resurrected and alive again (*issue armoured*). Or it can mean He-who-is-me: that is, pity the self that entered into my flesh to become its shield against being invaded (as by hate). Or it can mean Christ: but Christ is 'me'. The line 'And doublecrossed my mother's womb' can now mean:

> The sibling changeling entered into my flesh and so managed to arm itself against the hate that would not let it out, and thus cheated the mother's womb of killing it a second time.

or

> My self took on this flesh and bone, and, since my mother thought she was giving birth to the changeling who had died, she was doublecrossed.

or (if we read it as being about Christ):

> In that in my mother's womb, through my birth, that came alive which was once dead, this was a resurrection, that thus

brought two crucifixions—one of the dead changeling, and one of me, in that I was cast out into the mortal world of death. Thus I see how Christ takes on my flesh and blood (as the changeling took on mine) and tricks my mother's womb into becoming a twice sacred place (doublecrossed with *blessing*).

Or, we can take Christ to be the regressed libidinal ego that waits to rise again: the 'armour' is the shell of the False Self protecting it.

One consequence of regression to early modes of existence is reversion to oral modes of dealing with experience. The mouth goes with all kinds of 'appetite' magic—to wish the world other than it is, to control it, or to annihilate it altogether. The mouth can thus be a focus of compulsion exerted on the object: and where the 'object' has become largely a world of inner objects, there can be a recourse to magic which is felt to have cosmic consequences, in the urge to impose inner reality on the outer world, so that the cosmos feels as if it is all the self. This inner magic omnipotence is imposed on relationships with real people.

In *I make this in a warring absence* (p. 78) we may find a symbolism as I have already suggested of the persistence of the urges of the infant 'mouth-ego' in the adult love relationship. Moreover, the imagery, the attitudes, the self-dramatisations here all bear out Fairbairn's analysis of schizoid attitudes. By his oral gifts and by his giving out of excrement, as Fairbairn and others point out, a child feels he is 'making' the world. So Dylan Thomas has made his love-gifts, as poetry and bodily offerings. 'Praise is blessed' when the object responds to this creation of a world, as by an immense architectural enterprise:

> . . . her pride in mast and fountain
> Sailed and set dazzling by the handshaped ocean,
> In that proud sailing tree with branches driven
> Through the last vault and vegetable groyne,
> And this weak house to marrow-columned heaven . . .

The inner need to create and give in love is imposed on the external world: Dylan Thomas feels that he has created his world and lives in it. It is therefore intolerable when the object (whom he feels he has created) does not obey the idealising impulse, and refuses to be 'handshaped' into obeying his will. Rejected, his cosmic offerings become

corner-cast, breath's rag, scrawled weed, a vain
And opium head, crow stalk, puffed, cut, and blown . . .

Typically the images are of a weakness of inner contents ('this weak house') in terms of trying to sustain substance by effort (rag . . . weed . . . vain . . . puffed); there is a threat of emptiness consequent upon the rejection, a feeling of loss of identity and annihilation.

In truth the poet's attempt to impose inner reality on the outer world is a manifestation of immaturity, of being not yet 'disillusioned' sufficiently to be independent in a world recognised as real. But in this poem he attributes the woman's 'pride' to regression. She refuses to respond as an adult to his demands, he alleges. Yet his demands themselves are of the order of tyrannical infancy. He seeks to control and dominate her, possessively. And indeed he seeks to identify so closely with her, as ideal object, as to grow through her ('Branches driven through'): he virtually wants to incorporate her. So the truth is rather that it is he who is expressing his own need to eat up the object, altogether. Significantly, in projecting this over her he uses oral imagery:

And, pride is last, is like a child alone
By magnet winds to her blind mother drawn,
Bread and milk mansion in a toothless town.

By her withdrawal of love his desire is shut out: so he is cut off
Lost in a limp-treed and uneating silence . . .

—'starved' and 'cast in ice'. 'Uneating' is a significant word, which recalls Mrs Chaloner's quotation from a child who was left at school on his first day; 'I felt very empty when you left me this morning, Mummy'.[3] The rejection of desire leaves Dylan Thomas feeling not only a sense of flop and impotence ('limp-treed') but also a threat of emptiness and loss of identity.

So, the object must be coerced into 'feeding' him: he must take her as partial object. Since the idealising impulses of love have failed to bring this about, he turns to hate:

I make a weapon of an ass's skeleton
And walk the warring sands by the dead town . . .

The town is 'dead' because his inner world is wrecked by the withdrawal of love. His sense of omnipotence is indulged to

---

[3] Len Chaloner, *Feeling and Perception in Young Children* (1963).

change outer reality, in order to coerce the object to be as he wishes her to be:

> Cudgel great air, wreck east, and topple sundown,
> Storm her sped heart . . .

The rage is self-destructive, so that rather than affect her it ruins his subjective world further:

> And, for that murder's sake, dark with contagion
> Like an approaching wave I sprawl to ruin . . .

Behind these verses are two images of reality: one is an actual skeleton on the beach 'picked by birds' which disturbs him by what it conveys of destructiveness in the outer world. The other is his own despairing sprawl on the beach, because things cannot be otherwise, and as he would want them to be.

He lies there as if dead:

> Weighed in rock shroud, is my proud pyramid;
> Where, wound in emerald linen and sharp wind,
> The hero's head lies scraped of every legend . . .

Here is deflated the heroic posture of the False Self, in its poignant, hopeless predicament. By recording what he endured during this moment of rejection however the poet also reveals the actual suffering True Self—the need 'deep down' to love and be loved. The approach to loss of identity brings him face to face with his deepest problem—the fear that he *is* the dead sibling, whom his mother made him feel he was, by handling him as if he were. Rejection by the object has made him feel like the dead child, whom (by logic of a schizoid kind) he feels *has died from the same lack of love which he has experienced* here as an adult. That is, the sibling dead in the womb seems to him like himself dead from a failure of confirmation by the 'significant other'. The prostrate moment on the beach was a moment of death and of rebirth: he has experienced the worst that it is possible to experience—loss of identity. So there is a dreadful perception of the otherness of the not-me:

> The terrible world my brother bares his skin.

We can see that for Dylan Thomas the inability to bear external reality is in complex with a fear of death. The urge of the regressed libidinal ego to be reborn is experienced as a need to withdraw ultimately from life, so that rebirth can be experienced. Yet he is

terrified of the womb (i.e. of the context of psychic parturition) because it threatens death and petrifaction: 'topless, inchtaped' lips cry,
    'His mother's womb had a tongue that lapped up mud' . . .
They speak of the terror of being drawn back into the womb:
    'A lizard darting with black venom's thread
    Doubled, to fork him back, through the lockjaw bed
    And the breath-white, curtained mouth of seed.'
Instead of creative reflection in the mother's face, he sees 'taut masks' indifferent to the spectacle of a dead baby in the womb which might have become a man:
    'See,' drummed the taut-masks, 'how the dead ascend:
    In the groin's endless coil a man is tangled.'
These phantasies of death in the womb, in the absence of creative reflection, are aroused by the withdrawal of love. The moment on the beach was a moment of severe dissociation. Voices of hooded and taut-masked grotesquely menacing figures seem to preside over him as he lays there 'linened', though there are only boats on an anchor ground sheeted and roped up ('hank and hood'). He is asking external reality to explain his feeling of being threatened by death because love is withdrawn: the world being the object, it explains as if from the dim infant past that the mother's womb had an appetite for 'mud'—and the mud was lapped by the 'tongue'. The tongue in the mother's womb is both her hungry hate—but also the father's penis. So we re-enter an infantile phantasy of parental sex, as a dangerous form of eating, which has generated a 'piece of earth'—i.e. the dead sibling *who is also him*. Sexual incorporation itself is the threat of death, and it threatens to dash him back with black venom's thread, 'through the lockjaw bed', and the 'breath-white, curtained mouth of seed', 'back inside'. To the schizoid individual, individual giving, as of semen, is liable to bring about a dangerous emptying, and also a thrusting of split-off badness into the object. In the womb there is a hungry mouth, a hungry tongue, mud (excrement) and hate-filled seed from the father's 'rainy hammer'. This visceral imagery is of the kind Guntrip reports from patients who fear being 'drawn back inside'.

    The man tangled in the groin's endless coil is his sibling—and himself (his regressed ego)—endlessly suffering (as he imagines) for the loss of 'stuff' from a kind of mouth in the eating act of sex, or by the thrusting of a penis (as if it was a venomous lizard). The 'lockjaw' bed is that in which the parents have dangerous intercourse, eating that brings a disease which paralyses the jaws, shuts up oral expression, and closes the gate of the body for ever. As the sibling died in the womb, so he who was born from it, but who has never been properly disillusioned, suffers a living death (with a perpetual schizoid identity) forever locked out of that dangerous mouth, in a closed system—as if drawn back inside forever.

When D. H. Lawrence writes *Song of A Man Who is Not Loved* he feels himself dissipated by the winds blowing in the space of the universe. He is 'out there'. Thomas by contrast feels threatened by regression to the womb—being drawn into a voracious and malignant internal environment—a Houdini sack.

These are the visions which he sees in his lovelorn moment, and is forever changed thereby.

These once-blind eyes have breathed a wind of visions . . .

He becomes a 'ghost in bloom'. He can now return to his object, accepting *her* need for satisfaction, her love hunger–which means he can accept her a little more as a person with her own reality, but still in the maternal role:

And though my love pulls the pale, nippled air,
Prides of tomorrow suckling in her eyes . . .

She will recurrently be proud (and reject him): this is growing in her eyes. She needs to feed at his (? proud) penis (as at a breast) as much as he needs to feed from her. But she is breast-proud, and he envies her: or, if we were Winnicott, would we see 'penis-envy' here—in the split-off female element in Thomas himself?

What we can certainly find in the poem and its protestations is a characteristic expression of Thomas's kind of over-dependence: the woman must mother him, and give him peace

Now in the cloud's big breast lie quiet countries . . .

He is calm after his vision as if after a feed, and feels that the outer world is 'quiet'. There is less fear of woman who has

nor lightning in her face,
A calm wind blows . . .
Once where the soft snow's blood was turned to ice . . .

But fundamentally the poem originates in the discovery that the woman is not him—she is an independent being who will not always be controlled by him. This makes his dependence on her unbearable. He has projected the ideal object over her, but has had to recognise that the real woman is not neutral and undisturbing; by her independence she evokes in him all his deepest schizoid fears that her ambivalence and the hidden dangers in relationship will destroy him, unless by magic he can coerce her into fulfilling his total demands on the object. In the end he consoles himself by believing that she does exist solely for his satisfaction: an obviously false solution. The poem shows a characteristic schizoid concern with 'inner contents', fullness and emptiness, libidinal attitudes of a 'taking' kind, of incorporating from a 'partial object', while fullness and emptiness 'have tremendous significance'. It is also a poem which eminently demonstrates a 'compulsive attitude to the object'. All these aspects accord with Fairbairn's analysis of the schizoid individual and his symbolism.

This diagnosis of *I make this in a warring absence* seems confirmed by Thomas's own gloss on the poem in a letter:

You say you want to know what the poem . . . is 'about'. There I *can* help you. I can give you a very rough idea of the 'plot'. But of course it's bound to be a most superficial, and perhaps misleading, idea because the 'plot' is told in images, and the images *are* what they say, not what they stand for . . .

This itself seems to show a schizoid confusion about symbolism. But he goes on:

The poem is, in the first place, supposed to be a document or narrative, of all the emotional events between the coming and going, the creation and dissipation, of jealousy, jealousy born from pride and killed by pride, between the absence and the return of the crucial character (or heroine) of the narrative, between the war of her absence and the armistice of her presence. The 'I', the hero, begins his narrative at the departure of the heroine, (Stanza One) at the time he feels that her pride in him and in their proud sexual world has been discarded.

(Stanza Two) All that keen pride seems, to him, to have vanished, drawn back, perhaps, to the blind wound from which it came. (Stanza Three) He sees her as a woman made of contraries, innocent in guilt and guilty in innocence, ravaged in virginity, (Stanza Four) virgin in ravishment, and a woman who, out of a weak coldness, reduces to nothing the great sexual strength, (Stanza Five) heats and prides of the world. Crying his visions aloud he makes war upon her absence, attacks and kills her absent heart, then falls, himself, into ruin at the moment of that murder of love. He falls into the grave: (Stanza Six) in his shroud he lies, empty of visions and legends; he feels undead love at his heart. The surrounding dead in the grave describe to him one manner of death and resurrection: (Stanza Seven) the womb, the origin of love, forks its child down to the dark grave, dips it in dust, then forks it back into light again. (Stanza Eight) And once in the light, the resurrected hero sees the world with penetrating, altered eyes; the world that was wild is now mild to him, revenge has changed into pardon. (Stanza Nine) He sees his love walk in the world, bearing none of the murderous wounds he gave her. Forgiven by her, he ends his narrative forgiveness—but he sees and knows that all that has happened will happen again, tomorrow and tomorrow. (*Letters*, p. 186)

Here we have expressed the fear of being 'drawn back' into the 'blind world' through sexual rejection which 'reduces to nothing'. The attack on the object, to compel her to confirm his existence, becomes a 'murder of love', so that he feels 'undead love at his heart'. To change 'revenge' into 'pardon'—i.e. to discover truth, requires a rebirth by which the 'womb . . . forks its child down to the dark grave, dips it in dust, then forks it back into light again'. To discover the 'altered eyes' of reflection the regressed libidinal ego must die and be born again, so that the 'resurrected hero' can repair the object, ('bearing none of the murderous wounds he gave her') . . . but here there is a 'compulsive attitude to the object', in the demands he makes at the triumphant conclusion, for pardon and forgiveness as a reward for reparation. Yet he also sees that this anguish of the need for rebirth and resurrection is one that is going to continue unresolved 'tomorrow and tomorrow'.

5
The Code of Night

The first effect of using psychological insights to interpret Dylan Thomas's earlier poems is a feeling that the meaning is liberated: we are beginning to get through to him. On re-reading, however, one discovers that a good deal of chaos still remains: one has something like two halves of a poem but the poem can't somehow be completed. Elsewhere we find more severe and even deliberate problems of meaning. How shall we explain these?

If the problems of identity and existence he was engaged with were as deep as I have suggested, Dylan Thomas could not know at times even what kind of experience it was he was trying to write about. In consequence he was unable to find an 'as-if' metaphor, mythology or dramatic structure by which to symbolise those aspects of his inner life which he needed to explore, but whose nature he could only grope towards. His problem is the same as that of the psychological writer who tries to discuss primal experience: in what terms can he do so? This problem of speaking about the unspeakable confronts any writer who attempts to explore the deepest and earliest problems of identity. Coleridge's *Kubla Khan*, for instance, is surely an approach to the fount of identity, but all the multifarious elements congealed in that poem cannot make up for its dissociated nature. It stirs us, but 'nothing coheres', and what we possess of its meaning seems to remain a complex of fragmentary sensations and apprehensions. By contrast in *The Ancient Mariner*, in which Coleridge was aware that he was dealing with the problem of guilt, there is coherence. This unity may seem to be supplied by Christian mythology but in fact it is rather given by the underlying recognition in the symbolism of the forces of reparation in human consciousness (of which Coleridge was experientially but not intellectually aware).[1] *The Ancient Mariner*, perhaps we can say, is a depressive poem, while *Kubla Khan* is a schizoid one. With Blake, again, the poetry of schizoid preoccupations remains largely incomplete, inchoate, and finally incomprehensible—except to Blake. His symbolism and language came not only to belong to a private mythology, but metaphor and myth ceased to maintain a three-term 'as if' symbolism in the exploration and organisation of the inner world. This 'as-if' creative work can only go on so long as the identity is organised enough to feel a three-term relationship between the self, the symbol, and the internal object or dynamics symbolised. What is also required is interplay between separateness and union, between the individual and the (shared) tradition. Since this interplay echoes a relationship in the reader, communication is possible, between individual dynamics. When Coleridge's Mariner's heart blesses the watersnakes 'unawares' the reader feels as if his own reparative impulses are triumphing over his hate, and shares through the language the life-rhythms of the experience.

But where the three-term relationship breaks down there is no 'as-if' dynamic to which ours may respond: no bridges are built by shared metaphor. This kind of breakdown approaches the state of the schizophrenic who, as Kasanin points out, cannot symbolise.[2] With this type of schizoid poetry we require an *external knowledge* of the problems of the individual *in order to supply a meaning* to their utterance. At the same time, even when we cannot establish referents for the symbols, we become involved in the struggle against chaos—for in order to establish or re-establish the three-term relationship it requires an entire self distinguishing not-me experience as a whole. Thus, with schizoid art, our response involves us in an attempt to confirm the artist's identity. D. W. Winnicott sees this about the work of Francis Bacon, the painter, when he says: 'Bacon's faces seem to me to be far removed from perception of the actual; in looking at faces he seems to me to be painfully striving towards being seen, which is at the basis of creative looking' (*The Predicament of the Family*, ed. P. Lomas, p. 29). Winnicott postulates stages in the formation

[1] See the present writer's analysis of *The Ancient Mariner* in *The Exploring Word*. A more extensive and fascinating exploration was made by Maud Bodkin in her *Archetypal Patterns in Poetry* (1934).

[2] See J. S. Kasanin (ed.), *Language and Thought in Schizophrenia* (1944).

of the sense of self in relation to reality: 'When I look I am seen, so I exist. I can now afford to look and see. I can now look creatively and what I apperceive I also perceive' (ibid).

R. D. Laing in *The Divided Self* takes us into the experience of the schizophrenic, his inescapable sense of confusion between the self and others, and his anguish of division within.

> To the schizophrenic, liking someone equals *being like* that person: being like a person is equated with being the same as that person, hence with losing identity. Hating and being hated may therefore be felt to threaten loss of identity less than do loving and being loved. (p. 191)

Contact with others and with the world, in which one finds one's identity confirmed, becomes dangerous and so the schizoid individual tends to have 'no genuine autonomy'. 'The simple act of achieving autonomy and separateness is for him an act arrogating to himself something that is properly not his . . .' (ibid., p. 190)— which explains how to Thomas it can feel horrifying to apprehend reality and separateness: 'The terrible world my brother bares his skin . . .'

So, related to the withdrawal into a world of phantoms, there is an inward split.

> the basic split in the schizoid personality [is] a cleft that severed the self from the body:
>
> Self/(body-world)
>
> Such a scission cleaves the individual's own being in two, in such a way that the I-sense is disembodied, and the body becomes the centre of a false-self system. (ibid., p. 191)

There can be a further split of 'self/body/world', in which 'the body occupies a particularly ambiguous position'.

> The two basic segments of experience can be taken as
>
> here   there
>
> which are further differentiated in the normal way into
>
> inside   outside
>
> (*me*)   (*not-me*)
>
> (ibid., p. 191)

The 'schizoid cleavage' disrupts the normal sense of self by dis-embodying the sense of 'I'. 'The seed is thus sown for a running together, mergence, or confusion at the interface of here and there,

inside and out, because the body is not firmly felt as one in contrast to the not-me' (ibid., p. 192).

Obviously, when we take all these dissociations into account,
we can see why the schizophrenic cannot symbolise in such a way
as to allow others to 'take . . . possession of' his symbolising:

It is only when the body can be thus differentiated from others
that all the problems involved in relatedness/separatedness,
between separate whole persons, can begin to be worked
through in the usual way. The self does not need so desperately
to remain bottled up in its defensive transcendence. The person
can be like someone without being that other person: feelings
can be *shared* without their being confused or merged with those
of the other. Such sharing can only begin through an establish-
ment of a clear distinction between here-me, there not-me . . .

(ibid., p. 192)

Apply this to Dylan Thomas's poetry and we can perhaps begin
to see why meaning breaks down. In the core areas of his experience, where he sought confirmation of existence, he found only a
'false-self' system, and this threatens his capacity to share feelings,
because of a confusion and merging of the distinction between
'here-me', 'there-not-me', and of the symbolic processes by which
the experience by the 'me' of the 'not-me' may be shared with others
recognised as separate but related. It will be clear from what I have
said in earlier chapters that I believe the origins of this breakdown
can be traced to Thomas's experience of a confusion or merging
of identity when his mother confused him with the dead sibling.

How schizoid breakdown confuses 'separatedness' and the
expression of the relationship between 'me' and 'not-me' and
the failure of meaning in utterance can be studied in Laing's last
chapter, 'The Ghost of the Weed Garden'. This is the account of
an 'inaccessible and withdrawn' chronic schizophrenic: 'when she
did speak it was in the most "deteriorated" "schizophrenese"'.
I am not concerned with the case-history, but with this 'schizophrenese', insofar as Laing quotes samples of it. He speaks of her
'death-in-life existence in a state approaching chaotic nonentity'.
Moreover, 'in listening to a schizophrenic, it is very difficult to
know "who" is talking, and it is just as difficult to know "whom"
one is addressing'. Something of this kind seems applicable to
much of Dylan Thomas's poetry. 'William Blake', says Laing, in

his depiction of split states of being in the Prophetic Books, describes a tendency to 'become what one perceives'. Likewise, 'In Julie all perception seemed to threaten confusion with the object. She spent much of her time exercising herself with this difficulty' (ibid., p. 217). This is what Fairbairn indicates as the schizoid proclivity to confuse the inner and outer world which we have noted as a characteristic of Dylan Thomas's poetry.

> That's the rain. I could be the rain ... That chair ... that wall.
> I could be that wall. It's a terrible thing for a girl to be a wall ...

'All perception', says Laing, 'seemed to threaten mergence': and we have this same underlying feeling in Dylan Thomas's attitudes to time and the world of reality. Julie 'was living in a world of constant persecution ... Almost every act of perception appeared to involve a confusion of self with not-self'. Laing gives an account of a number of confusions and 'jammings'—as when she would accuse him of having her brains in his head (because in having thoughts like hers he had stolen her thoughts). The 'jamming' produces incoherence:

> A [i.e. one of her divided 'systems'] would say something relatively coherently and then it would become jumbled up and B would start to speak. A would break in again to say: 'She (B) has stolen my tongue.' (ibid., p. 218)

These systems represented various 'selves' (a bully, an advocate who spoke of Julie as her sister, a compliant little girl) and one of these was an 'inner' self 'which had become volatilized into pure possibility'. The various systems operating together produced incoherence—though the coherent utterances Laing quotes are of great interest, too:

> I was born under a black sun. I wasn't born. I was crushed out. It's not one of those things you get over like that. I wasn't mothered, I was smothered. She wasn't a mother. I'm choosey who I have for a mother. Stop it. Stop it. She's killing me. She's cutting out my tongue. I'm rotten, base. I'm wicked. I'm wasted time ...

Laing's analysis is very complex and cannot be summarised completely here. One relevant observation, however, is that he found in this patient a self—not a 'true' self, but a 'rallying point around which integration could occur'.

When disintegration occurred this seemed to be 'the centre' which could not hold. It seemed to be a central reference for centripetal or centrifugal tendencies. It appeared as the really mad kernel of her being, the central aspect of her which, as it seemed, *had to be maintained chaotic and dead lest she be killed.*

(ibid., p. 222, my italics)

As Laing also says, 'When she did present words or actions to me as her own, this "self" that was so presented was completely psychotic.'

These insights seem to me most relevant to my purpose. I believe that some of Dylan Thomas's poems tend towards the psychotic in this way: he worked on them deliberately to make them 'chaotic and dead' *lest he be killed.* As the schizoid commits suicide in order to avoid a nameless disintegration (and thus really to seek re-birth), so the schizoid poet keeps his poetry devoid of meaning that can flow between the me and the not-me, or move by symbolism towards an integration that would be death. The chaos itself is a strategy of survival: integration and meaning are too dangerous. At other times the capacity for symbolism can be found and used but, even then, it can also be used (as in the *Lady Lazarus* of Sylvia Plath and Dylan Thomas's *Lament*) to defend and vindicate a false system and inverted values.

As Laing indicates, when the 'systems' talk, they talk in 'constantly reiterated short telegraphic statements containing a great wealth of implications': *but the meaning of these implications has to be supplied by someone else.*

She had the Tree of Life inside her. The apples of this tree were her breasts. She had ten nipples (her fingers). She had 'all the bones of a brigade of the Highland Light Infantry.' . . . 'I'm thousands. I'm an in divide you all. I'm a no un . . .

(ibid., p. 223)

Here we find strange portmanteau words and puns: 'no un' means 'a nun: a noun: no one single person'. A nun was the opposite to a bride: she was 'the bride' of 'leally lovely lifely life'. Life (the analyst) would 'mash her to pulp, burn her heart with a red-hot iron, cut off her legs, hands, tongue, breasts. . . . having the Tree of Life inside her, she generally felt that she was the destroyer of life. It was understandable, therefore, that she was terrified that life would destroy her.'

She was born under a black sun.
She's the occidental sun . . .
I'm the prairie . . .
She's a ruined city.
She's the ghost of the weed garden.
If one could go deep into the depth of the dark earth, one would discover the 'bright gold', or if one could get fathoms down one would discover 'the pearl at the bottom of the sea'.

(ibid., p. 245)

Most critics, I believe, have striven to supply a meaning to Dylan Thomas's more obscure poems by following directions indicated by his own deliberate factification of chaos—thus making chaos doubly chaotic. In a sense this is just what he needed, to preserve that centre 'chaotic and dead' by which he sought to preserve his existence. Yet he also seeks to have his existence confirmed. Thus, at times, his poetry was the focus of a true self; at times a way of defending himself against contact by a front line of false systems; at times preserving a psychotic detachment from reality. Somewhere in the depths is the 'bright gold' and 'the pearl': *but it doesn't want to be found.* But the effect is to make us terribly want to communicate with him.

6

The Role of the Critic

At this point let me turn to a poem, which I have analysed at length before.

THERE WAS A SAVIOUR

There was a saviour
Rarer than radium,
Commoner than water, crueller than truth;
Children kept from the sun
Assembled at his tongue
To hear the golden note turn in a groove,
Prisoners of wishes locked their eyes
In the jails and studies of his keyless smiles.

The voice of children says
From a lost wilderness
There was calm to be done in his safe unrest,
When hindering man hurt
Man, animal, or bird
We hid our fears in that murdering breath,
Silence, silence to do, when earth grew loud,
In lairs and asylums of the tremendous shout.

There was glory to hear
In the churches of his tears,
Under his downy arm you sighed as he struck,
O you who could not cry
On the ground when a man died
Put a tear for joy in the unearthly flood
And laid your cheek against a cloud-formed shell:
Now in the dark there is only yourself and myself.

> Two proud, blacked brothers cry,
> Winter-locked side by side,
> To this inhospitable hollow year,
> O we who could not stir
> One lean sigh when we heard
> Greed on man beating near and fire neighbour
> But wailed and nested in the sky-blue wall
> Now break a giant tear for the little known fall,
>
> For the drooping of homes
> That did not nurse our bones,
> Brave deaths of only ones but never found,
> Now see, alone in us,
> Our own true strangers' dust
> Ride through the doors of our unentered house.
> Exiled in us we arouse the soft,
> Unclenched, armless, silk and rough love that breaks all rocks.
>
> (*Collected Poems*, p. 125)

In *Llareggub Revisited* I sought by a lengthy analysis to show how this poem was largely meaningless. The reader's first problem, I said, was to decide what the poem was about at all. I then attempted to show that certain perplexities in the poem had been deliberately contrived as if to make it more baffling than it need have been:

> ... in some places the half-rhymes have been created by manipulations which add nothing but make the sense more difficult to come by—'The voices of children say' or 'speak' has been manipulated to provide the 'says' '-ness' half-rhyme. The difficulty of 'to hear' comes because of the half-accomplished attempt to produce a half-rhyme in the first two lines of stanza three. So we can approach the whole poem's meaning with a sense of its being to a large extent half-finished, and manipulated. (p. 118)

I gave my 'translation' of the poem and then concluded, looking back on it, that the poem looked like 'an inadequate and incomplete attempt to render what I take to be the *intended* meaning'.

In many places I have had to do work—to interpret and interpolate by guesswork—which as a reader I should not have had to do. The meaning should be *there* if I take sufficient care as a reader. Rhythm and movement in poetry should help enact a meaning that is only damaged by paraphrase. Here I do not find them adding qualities of 'felt life' to what I take to be the intended meaning. Nor do the qualities of the texture of the verse help create attitudes to the experience rendered.

What seems to be complexity is often merely a half-finished figure—often it seems a deliberate perversity. The first perversity is in the irresponsibility about punctuation: commas are used at the ends of lines 6, 11, 14, 18, 19, 27, 35 when, to help the reader and to assist the poem's structure, a colon, semi-colon or full-stop should have been used. To be deliberately vague about punctuation in this way produces perplexity in the reader and is intended to stand instead of genuine complexity and involvement. [It serves] the purpose only of making the poem seem more difficult . . . related [to this]—making for unnecessary difficulty—is Dylan Thomas's use of hyphens in hyphenated pairs of words.

I have cut and amended this quotation to remove from it my previous tone of disapproval. If I do this I find my observations about the deliberate confusion still stand: what I differ over now is the interpretation of why Thomas found it necessary to be so confused.

Previously I saw the syntax of the poem as merely clumsy, taking the phrase: 'Two proud, blacked brothers cry.'

'Blacked' means *coloured black by the act of blacking*: it implies something blacking something, for *to black* is a transitive verb. To *black out* can be intransitive, and *blackened* is the adjectival past participle from *to blacken*, and feels more intransitive. Boots are *blacked*, and we talk of a *boot-black*. And we talk of *black men*, and *black brothers*.

Dylan Thomas was careful to avoid *blackened* (which has a pejorative flavour) and *black* (which would have suggested the brothers were negroes), but he has forgotten boots and coons. The activity of the word *blacked*, if one is sensitive to the English language, does not evoke darkness, spiritual or otherwise. The poet may, of course, have wanted to suggest the blackout (see below), and *blacked-out* would then have been preferable to *blacked*. *Blacked*, too, has an inappropriate everyday sound, as compared, say, with *darkness*, which is more mysterious in flavour. The activity of the word *blacked*, if one is responding normally to English, is not that of suggesting *benighted* or *darkened*, and is all extraneous flavour here, an irrelevant activity as of applying a soft black pigment.

Even Vernon Watkins took this word up with Thomas, but all the poet can do is to justify the external sound-effect of the word: 'I like the word "blacked" by the way in spite of its, in the context, jarring dissonance with "locked". I had, quite apart (that is absurd, I mean secondarily to) from the poem, the blackout in mind, another little hindrance on the scene, and the word seemed to me to come rightly.'

Later I said:

... language is handled for effect from the outside, not from the deep inward voice of true metaphor ...

> O we who could not stir
> One lean sigh when we heard
> Greed on man beating near and fire neighbour.

'Stir', given emphasis by the line-break, puzzles for a moment, and in any case has no great felicity as 'stir . . . a sigh': perhaps it was manufactured from 'stir a limb' and Dylan Thomas may have been recalling Hopkins's 'spare a sigh' in *Spring and Fall*. But the syntax of the rest of the phrase has been . . . manipulated to increase 'ambiguity', so that it becomes meaningless in the ordinary sense of the word.

We could not sigh when we heard greed on
man beating near and fire neighbour.

Now one can grasp a general meaning: 'we could not sigh *though* we heard greed *in* man causing him to beat his near and far neighbour *with fire*'. That is, when we heard war's catastrophes, fire raids caused by man's greed, and causing him to beat his neighbour.

But, again, one's paraphrases seem so much to be preferred to the line of poetry. There the odd prepositions ('*on* man') seem deliberately obstructive and perverse. The verb itself, 'beating', seems on the whole weak. '*When* we heard' suggests the event happening once and once only (unlike 'whenever'). And the 'near and *fire*' seems merely a distractive trick, for 'fire' becomes substituted for 'far', and the 'far neighbour'

becomes a 'fire neighbour', though one might have expected
both the near and far neighbour to suffer from fire. The change
from 'far' to 'fire' is an attempt at the kind of thing Hopkins
achieves (also in *Spring and Fall*) in 'ghost guessed': but such
movements of one word into another must go with a movement
of the verse, and a movement of meaning, a poetic logic. This
poetry has less poetic logic than the prose paraphrases one can
make of it.

I also observed that 'the logic of the poem . . . is non-existent':

The pattern is incomplete, in that the love is not triumphant
in producing an undeluded awareness of life, neither is there an
enlargement of sympathy by love, such as the brothers could
not extend when they were deluded by the Saviour. What
the war has to do with the matter is not at all clear, except that
it is happening. Nor is the quality of the love expressed in
anything other than by an evocation of its tactile quality and
by the vague 'breaks all rocks' . . . The platitudes of 'soft',
'unclenched', 'silk and rough', remain cliché, while 'armless'
seems inappropriate. It cannot, except by a violence to the
language, be taken to mean 'unarmed', while love, essentially,
we feel to have its strength conventionally, in the arms of
embrace. An 'armless' love suggests perhaps even something
morbid or even perverted. The line may be a wild gesture at
the ecstasies of the child-mother relationship [or, as I later
suggested, something related to phantasies of the 'armless'
movement of the foetus through the birth-passage: a phantasy
reported by some psychoanalysts.] . . . There is the same in-
appropriateness about 'the drooping of homes', if words are
to have any common meaning at all to which poetry shall add
intensity. Houses can fall, crumble, decay, disintegrate; homes
which one feels as connected with 'houses' can be broken up
or deracinated, and no doubt poetry can refurbish these com-
monplaces. But how can a home 'droop'?

Finally, I pointed out that:

'Assembled', 'tongue', 'golden note', 'groove', 'locked' suggest a mechanical agglomeration of locks and gramophones
which I can fit into no metaphorical pattern. And if you can
have a 'keyless smile' (presumably derived from the wartime
coinage 'clueless'), what does a smile which *has* a key or keys

look like?—for 'keyless' inevitably generates an image of a key
in a smile, rather than a smile without a key.

It may be worth looking at another detailed account of this
poem, to see how far other detailed commentators may go
in supplying meaning. Winifred Nowottny[1] is a critic who
studies Dylan Thomas's poetry 'in the hope of showing how the
peculiarity of the language compels us to set about constructing a
meaning for it'. She says that Thomas's belong to a certain kind
of poetry: 'We are forced to read the poem as meaning whatever-
it-is-that-will-make-such-language-ring-true-in-some-sense'   (p.
186). She is here discussing Blake: and she goes on next to discuss
There was a Saviour as an example of this kind of poetry:

> ... This very remarkable language demands that we should
> supply to it the kind of meaning that will make sense of the
> words. The language, claiming to be truth, will only become
> true, or be seen to be true, if we attribute to it a particular kind
> of meaning (which, of course, the poem itself directs us how to
> provide). To characterize this kind of symbolic language I
> cannot do better than repeat the excellent phrase used by
> Ramsey: he describes religious symbolic language as 'language
> in search of a situation'. That is to say, when one attaches the
> language to the right sort of situation, or constructs the situa-
> tion such language demands as its explanation, the language
> will ring true. The peculiarity and violence of the language
> forces us to look for or imagine a situation capable of calling
> such language into being. Language of this kind offers advan-
> tages to poets who want to say something outside the experi-
> ence of their audience and outside the range of more ordinary
> language. But since part of its strategy is to flaunt that peculiarity
> for which we have to construct the explanation, language of
> this kind—however simple the individual items of its vocabu-
> lary may be—stands at the peak of the ascent of difficulty in the
> language of poetry, and at the extreme point of differentiation
> from the linguistic stereotypes used in common life. (pp. 186–7)

In *Llareggub Revisited* I sought to show by an analysis of lines
from Hopkins and Shakespeare the kind of metaphorical richness
by which poets can 'say something outside the experience of their
audience and outside the range of more ordinary language'. Mrs

[1] *The Language Poets Use* (1962), pp. 187 ff.

Nowottny, however, is concerned with a use of language even beyond the range of such symbolism—'at the extreme point of differentiation from the linguistic stereotypes used in common life'. While, of course, Mrs Nowottny regards herself mainly as an academic critic of literature, we can never separate attention to symbolism from the deepest subjective processes—not least because the origins of our identity are in this very responsiveness to imaginative communication. So, when Mrs Nowottny pursues allusiveness to extremes, and says, 'what we are required to do is to interpret his language . . . rather as one interprets the language of a child' (p. 195), I believe she is striving to 'creatively reflect' a communication that is only partially formed, and to complete it. Here the problem becomes one like that Farber discusses in psychotherapy. Is the poet in the critic's head? Is the critic in the position of the therapist who is trying to communicate with a schizophrenic who cannot symbolise?

From my point of view, what we have in Dylan Thomas is a use of language akin to that of R. D. Laing's patient Julie, as I showed in my last chapter. This patient would at times 'marvellously come together and display a most pathetic realisation of her plight'.

But she was terrified of these moments of integration for various reasons. Among others, because she had to sustain in them an intense anxiety; and because the processes of disintegration appeared to be remembered and dreaded as an experience so awful that there was refuge for her in her unintegration, unrealness, and deadness. (*The Divided Self*, p. 215)

Equally, I believe, there was a refuge for Dylan Thomas in the deadness of his own poetry; to use his own phrase he 'kills the life in it'. Moreover, using language in the way others use it means 'being like' those other persons: being like is equated with being that person, and losing identity. Sharing is merging, and dangerous. In Julie 'The central aspect of her . . . had to be maintained chaotic and dead lest she be killed' (ibid., p. 222). Finding and sharing meaning are a death: that is the paradox of Dylan Thomas's poetry. He doesn't want his thoughts 'stolen':

She is thinking *a*, *b*, *c*.

I express closely similar thoughts a^1, b^1, c^1.

Therefore, I have stolen her thoughts . . . (ibid., p. 218)

This explains Thomas's sense of a cherished 'tumultuous world'

of his own being, and the way in which everything had to be him,
for an act of perception of a world independent of him seemed to
'threaten menace'. Being perceived threatened, too: so no-one
must find his meaning. Here too is an explanation of his reluctance
to finish work, his habit of losing it, and his continual failures such
as the film scripts. It explains the hard and lengthy labour of
elaborating his poetry until it became increasingly unmeaning
and unpossessible. Whenever he achieved meaning by integration,
it generated an anxiety which was intense and which he dreaded.
In later poems such as *Over Sir John's Hill* and *Poem on his Birthday*
this dread is experienced, but assuaged by magical faith.

Constructing a meaning *for* Dylan Thomas's more dissociated
poetry is therefore meeting his closed-circuit with a closed-circuit
of one's own, by which one has to create, by 'unharmonic' *doing*,
the sense of a complex response which is not there in the poem
as having naturally emerged from *being*. The poetry is often made
by what we can perhaps call false male doing (as I shall show): by
activity. It is constructed by a process learned from the father, like
the alcoholism: its deficiency of creative content derived from the
area of being is a consequence of the failure of the mother to
supply an adequate sense of identity, from which symbolism
could develop, within a 'harmonic' self. To complete the poem
we have to resort to false doing, too.

The extremes to which our 'doing' *for* the poet has to go is well
represented by Mrs Nowottny. She recognises the problem. She
speaks from time to time with deep uncertainty. 'The problem
of how one is to know which way to jump' (p. 196); 'this is tricky
material to deal with, but by now they [the allusions] almost
shriek for admittance' (p. 201, my italics); 'How is allusiveness to be
established? Even if it is established, what does it mean?' (p. 201).
She says later:

> I have laboured over the question of whether the recall of other
> literary works entitles them to be regarded as cues, and, if they
> are regarded as cues, how far the relevance of the cued-in work
> may properly be said to extend, because the poem has so many
> layers of meaning that it is sometimes difficult when one has
> shown the presence of some to argue convincingly for yet more
> without recourse to the allusions.
>
> (*The Language Poets Use*, p. 212)

This comes after a discussion of the words in *There was a Saviour*
>   O you who could not cry
>   On to the ground when a man died . . .

In the version of the poem printed in *Horizon* this was
>   O you who could not cry
>   On the ground when a man died . . .

Thomas was often careless about his proof corrections and may
not have noticed the difference. If he did he almost certainly
altered the phrase to improve the rhythm, and to alter the image
from one of people standing '*on* the ground' crying, to one of
people crying '*on to*' the ground (i.e. dropping tears on the
ground).

In any case, the words under discussion are: *On to* . . .—just
those two words. Mrs Nowottny has the following gloss on these
with no indication that Thomas ever heard them in the context
suggested:

> Gertrude Stein is not a writer familiar to many, but one
> quotation from her work, at least, is: it appears in Bartlett's
> Familiar Quotations (11th edn., rev. and enlarged, 1937). The
> quotation is from St Ignatius's aria in *Four Saints in Three Acts*—
> an opera, words by Gertrude Stein, music by Virgil Thomson.
> I quote from Van Vechten's text:
>
> [He had heard of a third and he asked about it it was a magpie
> in the sky.] If a magpie in the sky on the sky can not cry if the
> pigeon on the grass alas can alas[1]

---

[1] *Last Operas and Plays by Gertrude Stein*, ed. Carl Van
Vechten (New York, 1949), p. 468. In the Introduction (pp.
ix–x), Van Vechten writes, '*Four Saints in Three Acts* . . . was
originally produced . . . at Hartford, Connecticut, February 8,
1934 and subsequently has been performed in New York and
Chicago. It has been sung in concert, over the radio, and it has
been recorded. This opera was first published in America in
1934 . . . the complete original text may be examined in *transi-
tion*, No. 16 (June 17, 1929) or in *Operas and Plays*, published
in Paris in 1932, but these are no longer generally available'.
The complete vocal score (New York, [1948]), has prefixed to
it a Scenario by Maurice Grosser, who writes (Scenario, col. 1):
'The present scenario was written after both the text and the

music had been completed; and although it was done with the help of suggestions from both the poet and the composer, it is to a large extent my invention'.

Such is the obscurity of Gertrude Stein that one is tempted to disregard the context of this passage, and confine oneself to the observation that St Ignatius's aria is headed in the score, *Vision of the Holy Ghost*. But Maurice Grosser's scenario, which describes the original production, has many curious points of interest. 'Saint Teresa, for reasons of musical convenience, is represented by two singers dressed exactly alike' (col. 1); 'The two Saint Teresas were costumed as cardinals' (col. 2); 'The use of Negro artists in the original production was a result of the composer's admiration . . . for the naturalness of their approach to religious themes' (cols. 2–3); Act I . . . represents a pageant, or Sunday School entertainment . . Saint Teresa enacts for the instruction of saints and visitors scenes from her own saintly life' (col. 3); 'Saint Teresa II . . . converses with Saint Teresa I' (col. 3) [cf. 'can two saints be one', score, 48]; 'she rises and asks, "Can women have wishes?" ' (col. 3); 'the Compère and Commère, in front of the house curtain, discuss whether there is to be a fourth act' (col. 6)—this is presumably related to the Last Judgement, prepared for at the end of Act III. These and other features of the action make one wonder whether they were 'compost' for Thomas's poem, though one can hardly suppose that the phrase 'could not cry On to the ground' actually 'cues' anything beyond the passage from St Ignatius's aria. There would be nothing odder in his deriving hints for the action of his poem from the action of a work by Gertrude Stein than there is in his showing the influence of Eliot's allusive technique and of the verbal technique (of simultaneous reference at different levels) of James Joyce. It seems at least possible that the oddity of the two Saint Teresas who are one Saint Teresa seemed to him to have an imaginative congruence with Eliot's treatment of Tiresias ('Just as the one-eyed merchant . . . melts into the Phoenician Sailor, and the latter is not wholly distinct from Ferdinand Prince of Naples, so all the women are one woman, and the two sexes meet in Tiresias' [*The Waste Land*: note on l. 218]) and with Joyce's method in *Finnegans Wake*, where the Fall in Eden and Humpty-Dumpty's fall are the same fall, and any two brothers are any other pair of brothers, and (to exaggerate only a little) everything is the same as everything else that can in any way be connected with it. (op. cit., pp. 211-12)

In the mood of my previous work on Thomas I would have been merely derisive about such scholarly ingenuity, by which 'everything' can be made to seem relevant to 'everything else that can in any way be connected with it'. All that about 'on to'! But I see now that the interesting question is—what kind of element is there in Dylan Thomas's poetry that causes him to make readers feel that they must supply a meaning, and moreover such a complex, abstruse and deep meaning to his poetry? Obviously, here, a compulsive need is felt to provide a meaning. Mrs Nowottny tries, through this tiny verbal clue, to link the 'if two saints can be one theme' to Thomas's 'the brothers' theme: she is straining her ears to the ultimate like a therapist listening for some clue to meaning in his schizoid patient's utterance. So, she 'hears' what isn't there.

Such wishful responses arise, I believe, from various aspects of our action to schizoid disintegration in poetry. (1) It is too dangerous to leave the poem without meaning because to do so is to leave it without an identity 'in' it. (2) Thomas's need to 'hold us away', to alienate us, by no-meaning, is felt by us as an invitation to collaborate in an activity of response where none really exists—otherwise we feel his disintegration may be in *us*. We supply a meaning in order to avoid feeling *we* have no identity either. (3) The lack of 'being' in the poem that underlies its deadness not only frightens us, but also impels us towards a kind of 'primary maternal preoccupation' or *couvade*: we feel we are obliged to give it psychic life, where it has none. Beneath the surface here is the ghost of Thomas's sibling: we begin to treat the poem as a dead baby or as a regressed ego, desperately needing to be reborn into an identity. All this is confirmed by Farber's observations on the effect of schizoid patients on his colleagues.

Mrs Nowottny suggests, for instance, that the cry from the Cross merges with the shouts from Nuremberg, and thus (surely?) Christ with Hitler (and she may be right in that Thomas would respond to both as schizoid images—one who rose again, one who was pure hate):

. . . one level of reference, now that twenty years have elapsed since the poem was written, is perhaps not so quickly evident to the reader as it would be in 1940. I have already interpreted this stanza as having, at one level, reference to the stage of adolescence where guilt and the father-figure are important, and, correspondingly, at the religious level a scapegoat is sought. In 1940 comparable features of Hitler's Germany were evident to many and it was a commonplace that Hitler's success in Germany was a classic example in political life of identification with a father-figure, that the Jews were the scapegoat, and that in the release of psychopathic violence and sadism that accompanied his régime there was a hideous projection of the disturbances of adolescence. The 'Fascist beast' was a symbol only too horribly familiar, and the Fascist shout likewise. 'Lairs', 'asylums' and 'tremendous shout', occurring in a stanza concerned with cruelty, the scapegoat, and the father-figure, make an almost compulsive combination for anyone who lived through Hitler's rise to power, and the war. These circumstances are now at a distance, as are the patterns of talk and of newspaper writing familiar at that time. But the verification of such a parallel is written into the allusions. If we ask for an explanation of the phrase 'that murdering breath', it is to hand in Swinburne's famous line from the *Hymn to Proserpine* (*After the Proclamation in Rome of the Christian Faith*), which begins with the motto '*Vicisti, Galilaee*':

Thou hast conquer'd, O pale Galilean; the world has grown
grey from thy breath;

in the word 'grey' (which I think there can be no doubt Thomas recalled) though Swinburne himself was alluding to the suppression by Christianity of the colourful gods of earth, there is the further relevance that the uniform of the German army, which in 1940 was overrunning Europe, was grey; 'grey from thy breath' also alludes to the devastation of Europe at the command of Hitler. It may come as a shock to have to accept that an allusion to Hitler is brought in by way of a line about Christ, but it is part of the argument of the poem that an ethos of suffering may become involved with a displacement of aggression that finds its release in militarism, and that the worshippers of the Father, travestying His image into a mirror of their own conflicts, execute the same psychological manoeuvre as those who identified themselves with the strength of Hitler. The 'tremendous shout', in which 'We hid our fears', allows of reference both to the cry from the Cross and to the Fascist shout; 'we' in this stanza are not only Christians and Germans . . . (pp. 212–13)

Yet surely this identification depends upon the flavour and associations of the word 'grey'—*which is not in Thomas's poem at all, but in Swinburne's*.[2]

Mrs Nowottny is intelligent and sensitive, however, and from time to time she sees that what the poem evokes are feelings to do with identity, with roots in childhood. The children in this poem are: 'embodied voices, and are more likely to be figments or haunters or intimations of something lost, buried in the past, or unattainable . . .'

Unattainable, too, is the identity:

. . . The change in the pronouns is very striking at the words [stz. 3], 'O you who could not cry' (this is the first appearance of 'you') and again [stz. 4] when this form of words is almost repeated but the pronoun changes back to 'we': 'O we who could not stir'. It would be a reasonable inference from this series of changes that 'we' and 'you' are somehow the same and yet somehow different. If, struck by these changes, we ask what exactly is done with the pronouns from first to last, we find that stz. 1 speaks of 'saviour' and 'children' and uses the pronouns 'his' and 'their', in stz. 2 the situation is that 'we' did this and that in 'his . . . unrest', in stz. 3 'his' persists but 'we' is replaced by 'you'—in three different uses at that, as may be seen by considering them one by one. The first use of 'you' is in 'you sighed as he struck' [stz. 3]. It is most natural to take this as the generalizing use, equivalent to *everybody*, a use implying *anybody in the same situation would feel the same*; 'you' is often used in this way to introduce a description of a common and familiar reaction. The same stanza's second use of 'you' is

[2] It is true that Dylan Thomas, as Mrs Nowottny points out, associated this word with the Nazis ('Greyclothed, grey-faced . . . troops', *Letters to Vernon Watkins*, pp. 98–9.) But yet all the above is built on a word which is not there.

in 'O you who could not'. Here the pronoun is the opposite of universalizing. To say 'O you . . .' to anyone is normally to mean *you as distinct from me, you who are different from me.* The stanza's third use is in 'only yourself and myself'. The poet doesn't say *only us,* or *only you and I*; he says something radically ambiguous, for 'only yourself and myself' could be intimate [*only the two of us, together*] or it could be separative [distinguishing *your self* from *my self*]. The people referred to in this phrase may be very intimately together or on the other hand it may be (or may at the same time be) that their confrontation is startling. It may be that each one of them is, as we sometimes say, alone with himself. This obscure situation becomes even more puzzling when we realize that the syntax of the lines containing these changes is continuous: from 'O you' to 'yourself and myself' there is no break. (Moreover, the 'yourself and myself' become in the ensuing stanzas 'we' again—looking back to the 'We' of stz. 2, which itself looks back to 'children' in stz. 1.) It would seem, then, that it is being forced upon our notice that this is a poem about continuous identities with a changing outlook, taken at various points in a continuum running through the poem. (pp. 189-90)

We can, surely, link this with Laing's remark that 'in listening to a schizophrenic, it is very difficult to know "who" is talking, and it is just as difficult to know "whom" one is addressing . . .' The changing tenses and pronouns of the poem are part of the chaos defending a number of false systems from becoming integrated enough to symbolise from an 'I'.

Mrs Nowottny, however, refuses to give up. She finds the poem moves beyond 'compassion', and that it has three characteristics (1) the vanishing of the Saviour (2) the expression of human compassion (3) the entry of sexual love. But she then makes this most pertinent comment:

To make this supposition does not instantly result in a clarification of the peculiar expressions the poet uses; the diction does not so easily declare the logic of its mysteries. It is almost as though the poet had gone out of his way to write a kind of language that is 'symbolist' in the sense Wallace Stevens expresses so well when he writes in the opening lines of his poem *Man Carrying Thing*:

The poem must resist the intelligence
Almost successfully. Illustration:

A brune figure in winter evening resists
Identity. The thing he carries resists

The most necessitous sense . . .
(p. 193)

Dylan Thomas's poetry *'resists the most necessitous sense'*: I believe
this is very true, and that this is because he must preserve chaos,
and resist identity.

One of the problems that Mrs Nowottny encounters is that,
convincing as her references to literary allusions may be, there is
no evidence, often, that Dylan Thomas had ever read the works
supposedly alluded to. 'Did Dylan Thomas know, and expect
his average reader to know and recall as relevant, what Grover
Smith tells us in a commentary on Eliot's use of *London Bridge is
Falling Down?*' (footnote p. 203), and she even quotes Grover
Smith, 'There is danger lest multiplied allusions, adventitious or
not, should defeat meaning'. I cannot really believe that Thomas
had ever read most of the texts that Mrs Nowottny invokes. She
says, 'The tissue of allusion is precariously thin here' (p. 214),
trying to invoke Wordsworth, Donne, Crawshaw, Keats and
Hopkins, as if in a desperate attempt to show that Thomas was
meaning something by drawing on the meaning of others. But
I remain unconvinced, except of Mrs Nowottny's reflecting, and
listening, energy.

In her perceptive exegesis Mrs Nowottny points out many
things which I feel the poem is 'about' (compare my summary on
pp. 117–21). But at the same time her 34 pages of analysis largely
consist of supplying meanings that are not 'there'.

The poem is not concerned simply to reject institutionalized
religion in favour of one of the poet's own making. In it the
poet relives his life, surveying at every stage the process by
which it became distorted, enabling himself to understand and
pity the child within the man even while he grieves for his per-
version, so that in the last resort, finding pity for his own cor-
ruption and suffering, and forgiving himself his own guilt, he
can release his love and assert it as a liberating power. What
makes this an unforgettable poem is the continuity of the persons

(the man and the poet, and they themselves are one) who move
from 'saviour' to 'love'. And if one asks, 'What, as a poem, not
as a message, does it all come to?' it might be replied that all of
the poem comes to its own last, great statement, which, gathering into itself all that has gone before—the jails, the asylums,
the churches, the frozen earth in which the dead are locked, the
buildings blasted by bombs, the wailing wall, the rock of
Christ's tomb and the rock from which breaks the goddess of
Love as water broke from the rock struck by Moses—declares,
in the formulation, 'that breaks all rocks', that anything that has
been, is, or will be symbolized by rocks is subject to the love
this poem defines, and so extends the triumph of Venus out of
the poem into infinity.

In order to lead up to the shattering and endless reverberation
at the end of the poem, the poet has had to devise a diction that
does not so much say what it means, as allow all the range of
meaning involved in the poem to fit into the peculiar phrasing
used at any given point. The diction is extraloquial because it
is bare; it is bare of those overtones of general usage which, in a
less idiosyncratic diction, allow us to identify what the poet is
talking about, not necessarily because he names it (one of the
lessons on the nature of language, given by the 'symbolic'
writer, is that a 'bird' may be any kind of bird, or any of the
things for which 'bird' may be a metonymy), but because the
tone of the language in which he talks about it will tell us where
to look . . . (pp. 218–19)

—anything can symbolise anything else; the poem does not 'say
what it means'; and nothing that the poet is talking about can be
identified. For the meaning of the poem we have to look elsewhere, in areas to which he only *seems* to direct us—and supply
our own meaning from there.

This kind of procedure may lay the poet open to the charge
that though he has written a poem of amazing meaningfulness,
he has not written it in the English language. In a sense this is
true. It is true in the sense that he has not written it in the
English language as it was before he wrote the poem. But if the
structure of the poem is strong enough to show the reader how
to read the poem, it is none the less a meaningful use of the
English language, and if the poem is read and understood by a

sufficiently influential body of readers (especially by other poets) the English language will itself expand; the uses of language worked out in the poem will contribute to the range of the language as a whole. (p. 220)

Mrs Nowottny quotes a linguist E. H. Sturtevant in his book *Linguistic Change*:

A literary language tends to become a common language, and a common language tends to become a literary language . . . Chaucer chose the dialect of London because it was already beginning to be used as a common language, and Chaucer's example fixed that dialect as the common language of England. It has now become the common language of communities living in every one of the six continents and in countless islands. It may yet become the common language of the world.

—and she ends by speaking of the 'linguistic excitement' Thomas generates. But this linguistic excitement is not (as I tried to show in *Llareggub Revisited*) of the kind which links the symbolising energy of one's own inward dynamics as a user of English with that of Chaucer, and of the common language to which he contributed so much. This she herself indicates, by admitting that Thomas virtually does not write in English.

She speaks of 'a diction that does not so much say what it means, as allow all the range of meaning involved in the poem, to fit into the peculiar phrasing at any given point' (p. 219). In making such allowances, I believe, we have here a critic implicitly recognising that Dylan Thomas is drawing out of us an impulse to meet him half-way, across a dreadful gulf of non-communication. Though it will no doubt strike the academic mind as startling, or even impertinent, I am forced to say that to me Mrs Nowottny's heroic efforts may even be compared with those of the psychotherapist working with schizophrenic patients in whom communication has broken down. An American therapist (Dr R. Daly) told me how he puts on light clothing and soft shoes and goes into padded cells with gravely ill and violent patients for brief periods, hoping for a clue to some possible 'breakthrough'. One woman screamed at him for twenty minutes, 'Perry Como! Perry Como!' and even out of this alone he worked out a possible meaning. This is an extreme example of the willingness in us to try to hear a stifled human voice.

Such desperateness is a mark of the latent love in the therapist, as well as the latent humanness in the patient, and Mrs Nowottny displays a parallel love for the latent meaningfulness in Thomas's poems. His poems are more than an incoherent scream: but they need 'bridging'. As Bleuler has said:

even in schizophrenia the human spirit is not split into fragments . . . all of a schizophrenic's expressions . . . have an unmistakeable relationship to one another . . . An existentialist analytical attitude can sometimes quite unexpectedly help one to find the right word in talking with an 'encapsulated' or withdrawn patient. If one introduces such a word into the conversation in the right manner and at the right time, a gap between patient and doctor is suddenly bridged.

(Quoted in *Existence*, ed. Rollo May, p. 124)

As we see, Mrs Nowottny said that certain allusions in Thomas 'shriek for admittance', while we need to respond to his language as we do to that of a child. I believe that what she has heard (as when she 'finds' the 'brothers'), and what I have heard, is the *cry of a baby*, and the 'regressed libidinal ego'. Light is, I believe, cast on this uncanny truth by this account of a play Thomas was to write, called *Two Streets*:

The play would begin, not with words, but with screams,—the screams of women in labour and of newborn babies: a boy to one of the families, a girl to the other . . . They would live uneventfully, waiting for some fulfilment of their great capacity for life . . . and . . . while . . . they pass close to one another hundreds of times, they never meet . . .

(Bill Read, *The Days of Dylan Thomas*, pp. 165–6)

In responding to his work, we are trying to 'meet' the scream we hear: and we are driven by the basic need to *mother* Dylan Thomas. (I should add that Mrs Nowottny does not like me saying this, and she thinks my treatment of her attitudes and procedures in discussing this poem is unfair. We share the same publisher, so we were able to discuss this question while the present work was in proof. The reader must study Mrs Nowottny's account of the poem himself. My difficulty has been that because of my approach, I am not prepared to confine my attention to the limits of scholarship alone, and thus, of course, I have been impertinent, in attributing to a scholar such a deeply emotional and mysteriously

psychic response to Dylan Thomas. I am prepared at the same time
to admit my own strange vibrations. But the reader must study
The Language Poets Use and judge for himself.) It is something
like this that Mrs Nowottny is trying to do, to get across the
gap to Dylan Thomas. Of course, that she has to proceed in
this way exposes the lack of achieved poetic precision in Dylan
Thomas's more chaotic work. As I said, in *Llareggub Revisited*,
invoking Shakespeare, Thomas's poetry has to be judged in
terms of the English language, and our touchstone must be the
highest metaphorical power in art, as in *King Lear*:
    The Duke of Albany talking to his wife Goneril:
        You are not worth the dust which the rude wind
        Blows in your face. I fear your disposition:
        That nature which condemns its origin
        Cannot be bordered certain in itself;
        She that herself will sliver and disbranch
        From her material sap, perforce must wither,
        And come to deadly use. (*King Lear*, Act IV, Sc. ii)
The metaphorical power [of these lines] resides in the submerged
image as man-as-a-tree-or-plant. Though everything is founded
on it, the image itself is hardly given explicitly, yet it is itself a
symbolic contemplation of man's nature in nature. The metaphorical force is thus at one with a deep philosophical consideration: what is man, and how can he live? Without such deep
moral concern about the nature of man and the natural reality
he inhabits, such delightful poetry could never have been written.
    We experience delight in the texture and substance of 'sliver
and disbranch'. These words give us, in the saying (or hearing),
the feel in the mouth-muscles of working in green wood, tearing and paring away shoots, lopping off branches: *sliver* is the
texture and movement of slipping off small growths, *disbranch*
those of using axe, cleaver or wedge on cellular-textured wood.
As we experience these work-feelings, so we are brought to feel
the sap of which the tree is created (*material*) exposed, and come
to mere *deadly use* (not growth). The metaphor is exactly that
of those forms of treatment of growth that lead to soil-erosion
as caused by ring-barking trees: but as Albany is talking of
Goneril the process is taken by us as one in the human spirit,
which inevitably leads to such external denaturings.

By our sensory relish in the tactile and movement forces of the language we enter into, or possess, both Albany's condemnation of such unnaturalness, and Goneril's impulses to denature herself. We are thus brought to experience Shakespeare's experience of Albany and Goneril—and thus moral conflict is being enacted in our own breasts, as well as the poet's. The process of the plant growing out of the dust which is worthless and blows in our faces, then spoiling itself, withering, and coming only to deadly uses echoes the stoical contemplation of life in popular saying ('thou'lt never be satisfied till thou gets thy mouth full of mould'), and the poetic realism of the Psalms. Yet it conveys too the additional force of Shakespeare's own grasp on life, his positive moral concern. He makes Goneril's reply significantly full of emptiness:

> France spreads her banners in our noiseless land
> Whiles thou a moral fool sit'st still and criest
> 'Alack, why does he so?' (*Llareggub Revisited*, pp. 67ff.)

Here, I deal with a Shakespeare who is writing as a poet who feels real and alive, using characters who are given as 'feeling real and alive', being 'riddled by doubts and torn by conflicts'—even those of temporarily feeling unreal, threatened from within, depersonalised and deracinated (Goneril, Edmund and Regan are symbols of schizoid potentialities in man and manifest 'pure hate' at times). To explore these problems he is using the traditional English language in all its metaphorical life. He is using cultural symbolism in the space between separateness and union.

Dylan Thomas, by contrast, belongs to the category of writer defined by Laing who feels 'life without feeling alive', but who, because he does not feel real or differentiated enough, cannot utter this. So, he cannot use symbolism in this 'space', with full confidence in the 'three-term' relationship, between self, symbol and 'other'. In 'going over' to meet such a person, as Farber indicates, we tend to go out of our way to seek for elements in our experience which match his. In Thomas's anguish of vacancy and chaos he seeks to find a strength of identity by a phantasy contest against oppression and petrifaction ('breaks all rocks'). Mrs Nowottny seeks to confirm this 'shattering reverberation' as a truth about love in life, as best she can. In her need to confirm Thomas's identity she will go to extremes—'anything that has been, is, or will be symbolised by rocks is subject to the love this poem defines, and so extends the triumph of Venus out of the poem into infinity'. What this really means is that I, the critic, trying to reflect you, Dylan Thomas, in my state of (intellectual) primary maternal preoccupation am willing to go to any lengths to confirm your existence—even if it means that I take anything to mean anything. This parallels the mother's response to her baby's needs, in which she forfeits all her self-interest, and her relationship to reality, at first, to help him to begin to be. To literary criticism, however, since we are concerned with relating art to the world, so that the world can understand it and place it, this kind of preoccupation shows up as a schizoid state of dissociation itself, in which everything dissolves into a haze. We are drawn into a state something like the undifferentiated state of the infant before his necessary 'disillusion', and forfeit our own 'self-interest' and reality-sense.

But what is *There was a Saviour* about? The first stanza seems merely platitudinous. Examined more closely, the whole poem seems to be composed of words manipulated to seem meaningful but also actually to resist meaning. If we follow the kind of meaning I have explored in the earlier poems we shall find that what emerges is very surprising.

The poem begins as a protest against imposed moral teaching, and false assurances:

When we were children we were told that there was a saviour who was going to release us, who was more rare than radium, yet more common and familiar than water, and yet more cruel (?searing) than the truth of reality. Instead of running in the sun, children used to be gathered into church to hear the Gospels—the old gramophone record of his 'golden' voice. Those who were imprisoned in their own wish to be 'saved' and to become pure drowned their perceptions in the prisons and dry-as-dust studies of his promises which had become academic theology. They believed in his smiles which promised them the key of life, but in which one could really find no meaning. I can still hear the voices of children from that lost waste-ground of childhood telling us how there was calm (as opposed to harm) to be found in the safe restlessness of his service. When man interfered with nature and hurt other creatures of his own kind, instead of seeing the hate in this, we denied it to ourselves—we hid our fears by believing implicitly in everything he said. Yet what he said blighted everything. He reduced us to silence, and to an ineffectual meaningless 'false male doing' ('silence to do'), even when the world shouted its menaces, from bestial lairs and human madhouses, uttering a great roar, in obvious hate.

The false views of the world symbolised by the false Jesus and false truth, Thomas sees, are sentimental, and mere denials of hate: he also sees that 'sooner or later the hate turns up' (to use a phrase from D. W. Winnicott)—as it must have done in the 'hollow year', to Thomas, by the reality of war.

There was a tale of glory in the churches in which congregations followed Jesus's proclivity for weeping. His arm seemed angelic and soft, like that of a protecting bird. But instead he struck you with pain or punishment—and yet you only sighed with resignation. You could not raise one tear to fall on to the earth whenever a man died, but rather wept for joy at the thought of an imaginary flood of sacred baptism and gave your tender affection to an empty shell formed of mere clouds . . . Now in the darkness of war, of loss of faith, of reality there is only yourself and myself.

At this point we seem to have followed a clear poetic logic—a denunciation of the platitudinous image of Christ. But who is addressing whom?

> Two proud, blacked brothers cry,
> Winter-locked side by side . . .

I believe all attempts to locate the poem in war, or to make the brothers Thomas and Vernon Watkins or even Thomas and his reader are beside the point. The poem is a poem written, as it were, from one personal system to, or of, another. Nor is the poem about the need to throw off religious platitudes, even to 'renounce the blessed face . . .' The 'Saviour' is an element within the self of which the Saviour Christ is a symbol: that is, it is a 'false compliance' such as might be induced by Sunday school moralising and an over-strong super-ego, and so is a False Self.

This Saviour is a pseudo-male element identity 'on a conformity basis'. It is the 'central ego'—false because it cannot supply a sense of being by mere doing ('silence to do'). This False Self is associated with the anti-libidinal ego—the super-ego which punishes the libidinal ego or True Self. It seemed rare, golden, smiling, calm, glorious and downy: but in truth it was cruel, platitudinous, punitive, imprisoning, limiting, murdering, sadistic—and a shell.

It is a relief to be in the dark—that is, blacked, winter-locked in an inhospitable and hollow state (in the Houdini bag). The black-out brings home to us our 'nothingness' in a valuable way. This darkness is but the discovery of the hate, emptiness and despair which the so-called 'saving-grace' of 'false compliance' disguised: 'blacked', it feels power. As Sylvia Plath wrote,

> Only the Devil can eat the Devil out . . .

Who are the 'brothers'? Surely, the self and the self—like Julie's various systems who speak to and of one another? With Dylan Thomas these systems tend to be the self and the sibling with whom the self was confused. These 'brother selves' are 'winter-locked side by side', like twin empty identities, 'blacked' by the same impingement (cf. Sylvia Plath on the 'moon's blacks', Laing's Julie on being 'born under a black sun').

> Now in the dark there is only yourself and myself.

The pretence of having ruth or concern, of being capable of depression has gone, in one 'hollow year' (1939-40).[3] The selves are 'proud' to reject all the false assurances of seeming able to 'cry on to the ground', when in truth they were unable to 'stir/One lean sigh when we heard/Greed . . . beating'. All that pretence of compliance, of only seeming to have a 'super-ego organisation' is rejected as regressive itself.

> But wailed and nested in the sky-blue wall . . .

—this is the concept of heaven that imprisons us and limits per-ceptions: it is laying one's 'cheek against a cloud-formed shell' of empty idealising.

The rejection of all false assurances itself brings relief: the selves

> Now break a giant tear for the little known fall . . .

---

[3] It is possible that the blackout and the war had become an impingement that made it impossible for Thomas to preserve his defences against the existence of ex-ternal reality. By contrast, Winnicott points out somewhere that psychotic patients were 'maddeningly' unaware of the Blitz and bombs. Another possible parallel is with Sartre's situation in the Underground Movement in war-time France, when the 'hate-solutions' of 'endless hostility' were the only possible existential solution in a society occupied by Nazism and so based on schizoid hate itself—hate against hate felt real.

The 'little known fall' is that historical incident of being turned out of the Garden of Eden (cf. Thomas's remark 'I want to go to the Garden of Eden . . . I want to be forever unconscious'). It is also the failure of the first environment and the place to which the ego seeks to regress, to seek re-birth. The Eden environment failed: the giant tear falls

> For the drooping of homes
> That did not nurse our bones . . .

Here we have 'failed' language, to which we have to try to supply a meaning from what we know of the writer's predicament. 'Drooping' implies something it is impossible to rely upon: 'that did not nurse' implies 'failed to nurse adequately'. 'Drooping' followed by 'bones' suggests an environmental deprivation in which the bones (of the psychic self) failed to become a strong enough skeleton for the identity (another poem is actually called *Find Meat on Bones*).

So,
> Brave deaths of only ones but never found . . .

means that by that environmental failure the elements of the identity that should have been born, have died (like those killed and lost under air raid debris): they are the 'only ones but never found'. 'Only' implies 'only true' as in the 'onlie true begetter' of Shakespeare's *Sonnets*: the 'on(e)ly ones'. They died rather than live the false existence of pretence and compliance characterised in the first stanzas: so 'we' follow

> Now see, alone in us
> Our own true strangers' dust . . .

Al(one) we take over from the 'on(e)ly ones': formerly strangers we find one another in the same identity, and by magic 'ride through the doors' (Thomas earlier wrote 'fly', but found 'ride' 'mysteriously militant') into our as yet unpossessed identity.

> Ride through the doors of our unentered house . . .

The imagery is that of schizoid regression of the ego, that regression that seeks rebirth and is symbolised in alcoholism—and schizoid suicide, 'we' are cast out of the Garden of Eden in two senses. We have relinquished the false identification with the 'Saviour', yielding a sense of identity which has only been falsely assumed. And we have left the environment which 'did not nurse' —the all one (al(one)) brothers shall now triumph as one, as outcasts who have lost the false Jesus, but find a new reality by their leap into the dark.

> Exiled in us we arouse the soft,
> Unclenched, armless, silk and rough love that breaks all
> rocks

In the American edition of my earlier book I linked the word 'armless' to some phantasies of patients under psychoanalysis, which were of entering the womb again, in the form of an (armless) phallus, or of birth (reptation). In striving to be born Thomas wants the 'riding through' to be soft, the jaws of the womb *unclenched*, the body to pass through armless (and *harmless*). (His own birth was very hard.) The images are not sexual (i.e. of *entering*) but rather of birth (i.e. leaving the birth canal). This birth of the 'us' self, integrated, shall bring forth (from the mother) that love which brings a tactile sense of contact with reality (silk and rough), of a sense of the difference between 'me' and 'not-me', of a sense of being triumphantly *held* (this explains the soaring rhythm) in such a way as to assure one that one is real and alive. This love will break the rocks—of one's fear of being petrified, of the dead stoniness of one's psychic aridity.

The poem is thus a poem about rejecting the 'doing' image of the male element False Self (that empty-shell Saviour), in favour of a search for the re-experience of a rebirth and re-mothering that could bring a genuine core of being. It is a choice of 'darkness of the soul', for the discovery of love, and with love, being, the sense of existence.

Now I am aware of how much I have had to supply: I have been writing a mad gloss on a mad poem. And this is the problem of Thomas's more inchoate poetry. He could not possibly have known consciously what *There was a Saviour* was about. Unconsciously his dissociated identity depended for its protection on *not* sharing any insights with any reader—because such insights would have brought anguish, and because such sharing would threaten invasion. So, he comes to spin from his symbolism of identifying with a dead sibling, who is reborn in him, an aspect of his inner world which 'self' is a false Christ. From this, and the time of outward dissociation when he was writing, he comes to feel that his poem is about Christ, religious faith, the war, the blackout, the brotherhood of man, and/or sexual love. From these he in fact spins chaos-defences. But through them show the mad words and word-spinning (e.g. 'drooping', 'unearthly') which speak of a more disturbing meaning underneath. It is this glimpse of madness and the attempt to cover it by no-meaning that makes some readers reject Thomas angrily—as I did in my earlier work. On the other hand where readers become captivated, they seek to supply all manner of meanings—anything that can accrue—which are *simply not there*, even to an infinity of possibilities. They do this in order to help supply an identity which is terrifyingly not there (as the 'I' or 'you' are not here in this poem). They are thus brought by this poet into the role of the mother in 'primary maternal preoccupation', doing what Thomas's mother failed to do, which is to supply him with an identity, and so with the capacity to symbolise. No doubt, unconsciously, we feel that if we cannot supply him with an identity he will eat us or invade ours. Hence the whole 'Dylan' phenomenon.

7
Picking the Life Out

Dylan Thomas seldom discusses the meaning of his poems, though he does discuss the qualities of words.

> All I can say that might be interpreted as even remotely constructive is that you must endeavour to feel and weigh the shape, sound, content of each word in relation to the shape, sound, content etcetera of the words surrounding it. It isn't only the *meaning* of the words that must develop harmonically, each syllable adding to the single existence of the next, but it is that which also informs the words with their own particular life: the noise, that is, that they make in the air and the ear, the contours in which they lie on the page and the mind, their colours and density. (*Letters*, p. 289)

Though Thomas says 'it isn't only the *meaning*', he speaks of words in poetry not as symbols but as if they were entities with a potential life of their own, like emanations from the self, which one could arrange and manipulate, but which are not in dynamic engagement with anything which deeply matters to the poet. The 'feeling' and 'weighing' seem by his account to be done at a distance, as if by an aesthete, concerned only with style, rather than by one who (like Hopkins) is wrestling with truth, in the search for insight.

Elsewhere Thomas even seeks to persuade Margaret Taylor that meaning is someone else's business, other than the poet's:

> ... try to go through them in detail for sound and shape and colour. The *meaning* of a poem you cannot, as a poet, talk about in any way constructively: that must be left to theoreticians, logicians, philosophers, sentimentalists, etc. It is only the *texture* of a poem that can be discussed at all. (*Letters*, p. 285)

Later he says, 'The music is made, the magic is done, the sound and the spell remain.' In both letters he makes use of the same apologetic phrase, 'I can only burble like an old bird with its beak full of bias and soap; and you can but curse yourself for ever having given your poems to such a turgid rook'. He also says elsewhere (to Pamela Hansford Johnson):

> . . . when the words do come, I pick them so thoroughly of their *live* associations that only the *death* in the words remains. And I could scream, with real, physical pain, when a line of mine is seen naked on paper & seen to be as meaningless as a Sanskrit limerick . . . I'm a freak user of words, not a poet. That's really the truth. No self-pity there. A freak *user* of words, not a poet. That's terribly true. (*Letters*, p. 122)

It is strange to find a poet who struggled so hard over his rewriting, prepared to leave meaning to others, while 'picking the life out' of words, and being only willing to discuss textured explanations. Thomas himself was only too aware of his own diffuseness and linguistic impotence:

> . . . I'm almost afraid of all the once-necessary artifices and obscurities, and can't for the life or the death of me, get any real liberation, any diffusion or dilution or anything, into the churning bulk of the words. I seem, more than ever, to be tightly packing away everything I have and know into a mad-doctor's bag,[1] and then locking it up: all you can see is the bag, all you can know is that it's full to the clasp, all you have to trust is that the invisible and intangible things packed away are—if they *could* only be seen and touched—worth quite a lot.
>
> (*Letters*, p. 171)

The implication here is that his poetry *ought* to be full of meaning, if only he were capable of organising his utterance. If only the poems meant anything it would be marvellous: but all we can see is the bag, and we have to trust. He does not know what his poetry is about: 'all the invisible and intangible things—if they could only be seen'. What is so extraordinary is the extent to which readers and critics have been prepared to take the 'mad-doctor's bag' on trust: it is because the poetry is an attempt to be *born*.

It is also extraordinary to what extent critics of Thomas have failed to see with what strange mechanical perverseness he picked

---

[1] A doctor's bag in popular belief contains the new baby.

Poem On His Birthday

In the mustardseed sun,
By eely river and switchback sea
where the cormorants scud,
In his house on stilts high among beaks
And palavers of birds
This sandgrain day in the bent bay's grave
He celebrates and spurns
His driftwood thirty fifth wind-turned age;
Herons aspire and spear.

Under and round him go
Flounders, gulls, on their dying trails,
Doing what they are told,
Curlews aloud in the congered waves
Work at their ways to death,
And the rhymer in the long tongued room,
Who tolls his birthday bell,
Toils the ambush of his wounds;
In thistledown fall
He sings towards anguish; finches fly
In the claw tracks of hawks
On a shambling sky; small fishes glide
Through the ... of the drowned
... to the islands of otters. He
In his bird isteepled room
And the hewn coils of his trade perceives
Herons walk in their shroud,
The ... river's robe
Of minnows rippling around their prayer;
And far at sea he knows,
Who slaves afraid to his fiery end
In a spiralling cloud,
Dolphins dive in their turnturtle pall,
Seafoxes and seaowls
Taste the flesh of their death as the trawled
Dales ... as they pounce and mouth.
Thirty five bellnckte ...

Working sheet F.1 of *Poem on his Birthday*

Working sheet F.2 of *Poem on his Birthday*

the life out of his own language or worked it up in an external way. (Professor Maud's edition of *The Notebooks* is illuminating here: much of the material is extremely dull and was only given interest by being 'activated' by hard labour—while occasional original sparks of intuition were lost or repressed in the process.)

When we examine Thomas's processes of composition it is remarkable to find how much is done from the outside merely mechanically. An interesting account is given in John Ackerman's *Dylan Thomas, his Life, and Work*, where Ackerman reproduces some work-sheets.

Occasional words and phrases are altered to fit the patterns of thought; thus 'shambling sky' (F.1) becomes 'seizing sky' in the finished poem; 'spiralling cloud' (F.1) becomes 'serpent cloud'; 'Herons, on one leg, bless' (F.2) becomes 'Herons, steeple stemmed, bless'. On the working sheets are word lists which Thomas employed for his selection of image; unwanted words in the catalogue are frequently crossed out (as in F.2). Similarly, another manuscript page lists words which have the meaning of dwellings . . . Sometimes the word-lists catalogue possible rhymes . . .

Also on the work-sheets are certain numbers, to which Ackerman does not refer. What are these? The answer, which I discovered by accident, I found startling—they are reference numbers to sections in Roget's *Thesaurus*! The lists in fact are from Roget, and others are perhaps from Brewer's *Art of Versification* or some other technical guide.

From an examination of the pages it seems that Dylan Thomas wrote his poem in its first version allowing words to emerge helter-skelter. He then noted certain doubtful words and marked them. Here one would expect closer attention to meaning, trials of the shape of a line, rewriting in the struggle with words and with meanings. Instead we have recourse to Roget, and catalogues of synonyms.

Thomas's method of work was something like the following. Here is the first draft. The lines with which he is least satisfied are:

> In ~~the~~ thistledown fall,
> He sings towards anguish; finches fly
> In the claw tracks of hawks
> On a shambling sky; small fishes glide
> Through the ~~wynds~~ of the drowned
> Circles
> ▬▬▬ to the islands of otters . . .

We can follow the changes made in the next version:

In this next version he omitted two lines, perhaps through care-less transcription, since they read:

> In the thistledown fall
> He sings towards anguish; small fishes glide
>   finches glide
>   wynds
> Through the ▬▬▬ of the <u>drowned</u>
> <u>Towns</u> to the ~~island~~ of otters. He
>   pastures

Now the word on which major dissatisfaction focuses is *wynd*. At this point Dylan Thomas looks it up in Roget. He is, perhaps, trying to avoid it as an archaic word. He tries in the margin the lines

> The linns of the long drowned
> Hills to the pastures of otters

linn, n. (chiefly Sc.). waterfall; pool below this; precipice, ravine (*O.E.D.*) *linn* is not in Roget.

The reference for *Wynd* in Roget is No. 189. *Abode*: under which Thomas found

tent etc. (covering) 223; building etc. (construction) 161

from Roget he notes down 223/161 on his work sheet, and then also finds in the same section

street, place, terrace, parade, esplanade, promenade, pier, em-bankment, road, villas, row, walk, lane, alley, court . . . etc.

Looking up *Lane* he finds 189/260 which he notes on his work-sheet.

Now it would seem appropriate for a writer to search in Roget for a word already in mind, or nearly in mind. But all Roget sup-plies is cliché—words which are already more or less synonymous, already used in that way. His words are in any case dredged out of their context in which alone they have metaphorical life. Nothing could be further from freshness or originality than Roget: he could be a computer, and from such a computer one could write something that sounded rather like poetry—albeit without inward life. A creative writer would surely rather use Roget to know what to avoid, than to find something more personal, more relevant, more *exact*? That is, if the creative writer is to be at the frontiers of metaphor, he will avoid Roget who is all dead—or, as the linguists call it—*frozen* metaphor. What we can find in Roget, however, because he lists so many near-synonyms, is a source of words which are 'unusual'—though lacking that unusual-ness which is impelled by a need to express some fresh aspect of experience.

Looking up 223, *Covering*, Thomas found:

Covering, cover; canopy, tilt, awning, baldachin, tent, marquee, *tente d'abri*, umbrella, parasol, sunshade; veil (*shade*) 424 . . .

So, he writes 424 below 223 and 161 on his work sheet.

Now we can see that from the image of *small fishes gliding through the wynds of drowned circles* or *towns* to the *islands* or *pastures of otters* there are further images being explored *by random scanning of Roget*. Instead of the final lines

Through wynds and shells of drowned
Ship towns . . .

we might have had any of the words scribbled on the left of the page. Where do these come from? Town, lane, road, passage, sheds and caves are from 189; domes and arches are from 223; doors and oriels are from 260; fabric and structure are from 161.

Thus a proportion of the associations, and maybe a significantly large proportion, are not from Thomas's inner response to words, but from Roget's associations—including the word finally chosen (towns). In the work-sheet (F.2) we have

Through the wynds of the drowned
Towns to the island of otters
pastures

How much difference would there have been had this become:

Through the wynds of the drowned
Lanes to the pastures of otters . . .

or

Through the wynds of the drowned
Islands to the pastures of otters . . .

or

Through the lanes of the drowned
Sea towns . . .

What makes the difference? If there is a difference it should per-haps be found in the inevitability of words which press their claims for relevance, to be selected for reasons of poetical economy from a mood. What I mean here by a *mood* is the unifying dynamic of inner symbolism associated with a particular life-problem, or life-rhythms. Has this poem such a unity of symbolic energy?

Where Dylan Thomas's poems fail I believe we can speak of a deficiency of 'inner necessity', and even, on the contrary, a need to 'resist necessitous sense'. The term 'inner necessity' is taken from an important note in an essay in *The Calendar of Modern Letters* by C. H. Rickword. Of a common quality in all great works of art he says:

It is a unity among the events, a progressive rhythm that includes and reconciles each separate rhythm. As manifested in the novel, it resolves, when analysed, chiefly into character and plot in a secondary, schematic sense—qualities that are purely fictitious. Neither is it an active element in the whole work in the way that melody and harmony are elements in a piece of music. Perhaps it would be less ambiguous to designate this basic, poetic quality by some such term as rhythm or development: on the other hand, plot or story do indicate its nature—that is primarily a sequence of events developing in accordance with inner necessity. (III, p. 228)[2]

The relation of symbolism in creativity to inner necessity is illuminated by Suzanne Langer's remarks on symbolism in *Philosophy in a New Key*, in which she speaks of the discovery of insight by the sharing of symbolised 'life-rhythms':

The emotive content of the work is apt to be something much deeper than any intellectual experience, more essential, pre-rational and vital, something of the life-rhythms we share with all growing, hungering, moving and fearing creatures. (p. 260)

The truth with Dylan Thomas is rather that he does not want to share these life rhythms, because to do so is to court annihilation. His 'inner necessity' is not to share: hence he must be anti-metaphorical. He must avoid 'being' as a source of symbolism and employ 'doing' with language instead.

In *Poem on his Birthday* Dylan Thomas is exploring the theme of approaching middle age, in terms of the animals and birds around him outside his house, all of which are part of the dance of natural life towards death. As a child does, he identifies with these

---

[2] *The Calendar* was reissued in volume form by Frank Cass and Co. in 1966.

creatures, and is depressed (in the psychoanalytical sense of feeling guilt) by the way they prey on one another, are resigned to their brief existence, follow their biological patterns ('Doing what they are told'), merely 'working their way to death'. In his incantation he hovers between aspiring to be 'deathless' and coming to terms with his own mortality, by which he too is 'sailing out to die'. He seeks to insist that, even though he is now in 'midlife' and moving on towards death, the closer he moves towards death the 'louder the sun blooms' and the more triumphant his faith.

From our acquaintance with Thomas we know that for him living in time is interpreted as growing towards death and that this preoccupation links with his pity for himself because he has to grow out of innocence and childhood, and lose his freedom. So this is

<blockquote>His driftwood thirty-fifth wind-turned age . . .</blockquote>

Here we may note a characteristic perversity: Thomas later omits the hyphen in 'wind-turned' which is visible in the work-sheet, in order to create greater ambiguity—or perhaps to make the poem look more meaningful than it is? We follow here a general drift: he is moving down time's stream like a piece of driftwood, and is also aimless and worthless. Like the flounders and gulls he is on a 'cold, dying trail', following his biological path and pattern, working his way to death, towards the 'ambush of his wounds'. *Ambush* was once *anguish* in his drafts: how has it become *ambush*? Is the ambush the mortal end when the effect of being vulnerable to life's blows will have its final effect? The natural world is a world of eating others—the seals even find their own 'tide-daubing blood' good in their sleek mouths.

For his advancing age 'white angelus knells' ring, and there are skulls and scars at the bottom of the sea where his loves lie wrecked (presumably the natural objects which he has loved). His forth-coming death is seen (significantly) as an *unbolting of love* (love being a dangerous threat). He is mourned by the priestlike herons. He moves to death through the sundered hulks of his life: he sails out to die, but is no more alone, as he has angels, shining ones, with him.

Although Dylan Thomas is writing a poem for his thirty-fifth birthday he tries to deal with the subject as one who bitterly resents having left the earliest state, before becoming aware of the conditions of life, for mortal reality. That is, he sets out to 'celebrate and *spurn*' his advancing years, as he tried elsewhere to 'Marvel my birthday away'. That is again, the poem is an act of magical incantation, and an attempt to deny reality. Since he is not a child, and is mortal, and living in a real world, this magical incantation becomes an act of composing orally an artificial entity (of internalised objects) which stands instead of the real world, and is intended to cast a magical light over the real world, in order to change and redeem it—redeem it not from 'sin' or 'evil', but *from being real*. He wants to claim the freedom which to recognise reality seems to threaten.[3] Such a poem manifests the 'over-valuation of inner contents' of the schizoid and the attempt to impose inner reality on the outer world. The poem is to count more than the life: meanwhile nothing is feared more than contact with reality (which could be dangerous 'unbolted' love). Thus the symbols are not symbols arising from an inner engagement with inner reality, but symbols selected by an external process—a selection of 'frozen metaphors', and of language-activity or 'false male doing' with words.

Guntrip, discussing Winnicott's paper on Male and Female Elements, says:

One cannot 'be' anything in a vacuum. Having developed this capacity to 'be' by experiencing the primary relationship with a good enough mother, this will lead spontaneously to the arising of a healthy unforced capacity to 'do'.

(*Schizoid Phenomena*, p. 259)

Symbolism impelled by 'inner necessity' takes this 'unforced' form. On the other hand as Guntrip further notes:

The experience of 'doing' in the absence of a secure sense of 'being' degenerates into a meaningless succession of mere activities (as in the obsessional's meaningless repetition of the same thought, word or act), not performed for their proper purpose, but as a futile effort to keep oneself in being: to 'manufacture' a sense of 'being' one does not possess. (ibid., p. 259)

This is what happened to Dylan Thomas's poetry: it ceased to grow and ceased from time to time to be the expression of being;

---

[3] 'Reaching a self freedom is the only object' (*Letters*, p. 16).

it became itself rather mechanical 'doing' to 'manufacture a sense of being'. Even the attempt to be reborn in the poetry becomes a form of 'false male doing'.

Here, too, is the explanation of the rhythmic and metaphorical deadness which I explored in my earlier book on Dylan Thomas, and the mechanical methods of composition. We may examine the worksheets of the poem under discussion further. If we take working sheet F.4 we see how the whole bears the appearance of an attempt to contrive what sounds like inspiration, but what yet never escapes from cliché

> At half his bible span
> A man of words who'd drag down the stars to his lyric
> He looks back at his years . . .   oven,
> A lyrical man . . .
> who'd pull the stars . . .

Here he virtually reveals the oral intensity of his need to believe himself a poet with power to *pull* and *drag* external reality to suit his False Self purposes: the 'oven' being the place where he would, in hate, 'make' the world to his recipe. A schizoid intensity appears in the images of regression, suckling, and the sense that love and living are a dangerous exhaustion of inner contents:

> The dead years spinning back to the dark . . .
> The cocklesucked Thirty-five . . .
>   ransacked love . . .
> Thirty five ways to death . . .
> Bygone love makes a sound
> Like a bell ducked in the foam . . .
>   gong

At this point 'makes a sound' seemed banal: how could it be made 'interesting'? The word *bell* in Roget yields

> *bell*, 417, 550
> *passing*, 363

—the word 'passing' meeting Thomas's preoccupation with the passing of his years.

> 550 yields *angelus, sacring bell*   .
> 363 yields *cypress . . . dirge*, etc. and leads on to 839
> 839 yields *sackcloth, coronach, jeremiad, requiem.*

And so he writes:

> Bygone love sounds like a cypress bell
> Swing in fanes of the foam
>   chantries of
>   minsters
> Knelled
> swung in sea minsters.

Where did *fanes* and *chantries* come from? Having *bell* it seems
natural that Thomas should look up *church* (temple)—and get to
No. 1000 in Roget. From 1000 come *fane*, *chantry* and *minster*.
Admittedly, the work-sheet under discussion produced nothing
used directly in the final poem. But in the final lines are many
phrases and words whose origins are essentially in associations
made by Roget.

> In a *cavernous*, swung
> Wave's silence, wept white *angelus knells* . . .

> Gulled and chanter . . .
> To his *nimbus bell* . . .
> The lost moonshine *domes*

We may, I think, deduce that Dylan Thomas's linguistic 'doing'
was a substitute for having anything inward to say, with its own
inscape derived from symbolic contest with experience, and its
roots in being: and a way of avoiding insight. His substitute for
inspiration was Roget, and we may approach his verse with a sense
of its having been largely contrived by thumbing through Roget's
banks and files of clichés, and other objective sources, to find words
which sounded original enought to be received as poetry, yet
which would resist necessitous sense.

Turning from Thomas's own needs to the way he was received
we find that this kind of ingenuity is a gift for the intellectual
critic. Concocted intellectually, Thomas's associations lend themselves eminently to being unravelled intellectually: both activities
contrive to draw attention away from the absence of 'felt life'
in the rhythm, and the absence of relevance in the symbolism to
any inward creativity, to being. Thus in his *Reader's Guide to Dylan
Thomas* William York Tindall writes:

> Shells in the 'wynds' (winding streets) of sunken towns bring
> thoughts of shipwreck and death . . . (p. 297)

At half his bible span,
A man of words who'd drag down the stars to his lyric oven,
He looks back at his years.

A lyrical man

At half his bible span,
A lyrical man ~~who'd~~ who'd pull the stars
~~And the~~ And the

                                                                    ransacked love

And the ~~39~~ years spinning ~~spun~~ back to the dark,

The dead ~~5~~ years spinning ~~spinning~~ back to the dark
                    gong.

The cocklesucked Thirty five

H
The ~~two~~ spent loves spinning back to the

        Thirty five ways to death
                                                        d
                                                        keening
        Bygone love makes a sound   requiem
        like a ~~bell~~   jeremiad
                ~~bell~~ ducked in the foam   durge
                gong   sackcloth
                                    deep   coronach koronah
        Long gongs ducked in the foam   a cypress bell
                                                        sacring bell
                                                        angelus

                                                        550
                                                        363
                                                        412

        Thirty five ~~stages~~ to
                            sounds like
        Bygone love. ~~makes a sound~~ a cypress bell
                ~~Swung in~~ lanes of the foam
                            chantries of.
Knelled   minsters
Swung in sea minsters

Working sheet F.4 of *Poem on his Birthday*

But 'wynds' was arrived at by finding a synonym in Roget for 'lanes', while 'towns' came by the same process.

In Thomas's early poems there is a multitude of images in violent disagreement. Here so far, a multitude of images has been in general agreement—an agreement that, like blood, 'Slides good in the sleek mouth'. (pp. 297–8)

The way the critic takes the oral activity Thomas offers in terms of his own image is revealing: as I have said, we become involved in Thomas's 'suckling' needs. In truth the 'agreement' between images here is no more than governed by clusters of Roget section numbers.

Yet relics of old disagreements survive, along with old paradox and ambiguity. Context makes the 'cavernous' wave of stanza five the tomb. The 'angelus' is Gabriel's announcement of the womb. But the momentary disagreement of tomb and womb, of 'silence' and bell, of white tears and black, is quickly settled by 'angelus knells', a synthesis of birth and death that agrees with everything said so far . . . (p. 298)

How complex it all sounds! Yet the analysis is, as so often, very much more interesting than the poetry: the poet is in the critic's head. Both 'cavern', 'angelus' and 'knell', as we have seen, were put together from contiguous lists in the *Thesaurus*. In an intellectual literary ethos in which schizoid detachment from being is prevalent, Dylan Thomas's mechanical poetry is an ideal gift for the mind that itself is dissociated from the wholeness of being human.

8

Windy Houdini

In a well-known letter to Henry Treece, Thomas speaks of his
method of composing a poem:

A poem by myself needs a host of images, because its centre is a
host of images, I make one image—though 'make' is not the
word, I let, perhaps, an image be 'made' emotionally in me and
then apply to it what intellectual and critical forces I possess . . .

Having let an image form, Thomas immediately applies his intel-
lect and critical faculties to it. His way of discussing this suggests
at once a 'conflict' within the self between creation and analytical
'limitation':

let it breed another, let that image contradict the first, make of
the third image bred out of the two together, a fourth contradictory image, and let them all, within my own imposed formal
limits, conflict.

The emphasis on 'contradiction' surely indicates the need to
'preserve chaos', out of a 'terror of integration' by 'doing' with
words, rather than letting them 'be'.

Each image holds within it, the seeds of its own destruction, and
my dialectical method, as I understand it, is a constant building
up and breaking down of the images that come out of the
central seed, which is itself destructive and constructive at the
same time.

At this point Thomas admits:

Reading back over that I agree it looks preciously like nonsense.
To say that I 'let' my images breed and conflict is to deny my
critical part in the business. But what I want to try to explain—
and it's necessarily vague to me—is that the *life* in any poem of
mine cannot move concentrically round a central image; the
life must come out of the centre; an image must be born and die

in another; and any sequence of images must be a sequence of creations, recreations, destructions, contradictions . . . Out of the inevitable conflict of images—inevitable because of the creative, recreative, destructive and contradictory nature of the motivating centre, the womb of war—I try to make that contradictory peace which is a poem. I do not want a poem of mine to be, nor can it be, a circular piece of experience placed neatly outside the living stream of time from which it came; a poem of mine is, or should be, a watertight section of the stream that is flowing all ways, all warring images within it should be reconciled for that small stop of time. I agree that each of my earlier poems might appear to constitute a section from one long poem; that is because I was not successful in making a momentary peace with my images at the correct moment; images were left immediately dangling over the formal limits, and dragged the poem into another; the warring stream ran on over the insecure barriers the fullstop armistice was pulled and twisted raggedly on into a conflicting series of dots and dashes. (*Letters*, pp. 190–1)[1]
Under the surface of this comment on his own procedures lurks the image of a contest against danger. Thomas seeks for 'peace' in a 'war'. At the end of each poem comes a 'fullstop armistice': in the earlier poems he failed to achieve any adequate suspension of hostilities—only a 'conflicting series of dots and dashes'. The poetry is conceived in a 'womb of war': he seeks a 'watertight section of a stream that is flowing all ways'—a conflicting image in itself. Obviously his poetry seems to him a way of *containing* a 'warring stream'. And containing it by a 'contradictory peace'— that is by preserving chaos. The 'life' of the poem that comes out of the centre depends upon destructive and contradictory 'deaths' coming upon images in order that others may breed. The central image is not *reinforced* by others (as, say, all the imagery in Sylvia Plath's 'Bee' poems reinforces the central meaning). The development of the poem is negative, in the sense that he steps, as by obsessional compulsion, to a new image only by the birth and death of the previous one. That is, he must kill the symbolic existence of each image as he proceeds to the next, in case the images breed integration between them, or begin to bring life to

---

[1] The sequence of the prose in this edition is jumbled badly at certain points in the letter and I have corrected it.

the 'central aspect' of his deeper self. *That centre, and the poetry, must be kept dead.*

He is thus in the agonising predicament of sitting down to seek insight and meaning, but deliberately baffling himself, since any such development threatens too great anxiety, and too terrifying integration.

The old fertile days are gone and now a poem is the hardest and most thankless act of creation . . . I am getting more and more obscure day by day. It now gives me a physical pain to write poetry. I feel all my muscles contract as I try to dig out . . .

(*Letters*, p. 122)

—it is as if he finds a physical resistance to the release of inner contents.

In a letter to Pamela Hansford Johnson already quoted where he speaks of 'picking the words of their live associations', he also says of the lines, 'I picked and cleaned them so much that nothing but their barbaric sounds remained.' He says:

if I did write a line 'My dead upon the orbit of a rose', I saw that 'dead' did not mean 'dead', 'orbit' not 'orbit' & 'rose' most certainly not 'rose' . . . They are not the words that express what I want to express; they are the only words I can find that come near to expressing a half. (*Letters*, p. 122)

It is important to see this problem as Thomas saw it—as anguished self-bafflement, and not to pass this method off as wild 'surrealism', or to seek to supply meanings on the supposition that a mystic voice was somehow speaking through Dylan, as a 'druid of the broken body'. Nor is it enough to dismiss his poems as fakes.

Dylan Thomas was intelligent and he worked laboriously. He did not follow mere fashions, as he makes plain in a letter to Richard Church:

Far from resenting your criticism, I welcome it very much indeed, although, to be equally candid, I think you have misinterpreted the poems and have been misled as to their purpose. I am not, never have been, never will be, or could be for that matter, a surrealist . . . I have very little idea what surrealism is . . . I have not read any French poetry . . . As for being 'caught up in the delirium of intellectual fashion of the moment', I must confess that I read regrettably little modern poetry . . .

(*Letters*, p. 161)

he also says:

> I think I do know what some of the main faults of my writing
> are: immature violence, rhythmic monotony, frequent muddle-
> headedness, and a very much overweighted imagery that leads
> too often to incoherence. But every line *is* meant to be under-
> stood; the reader *is* meant to understand every poem by thinking
> and feeling about it, and not by sucking it in through his pores,
> or whatever he is meant to do with surrealist writing. (ibid.)

He declares he is not 'purposely unreasonable' as the surrealists
were.

Since reading Thomas's letters and his life I have come to
accept his integrity as a writer, and I believe he was sincere in these
comments on his work. He was aware of all the faults with which
I charged him in *Llareggub Revisited*: he was not mocking us by
deliberate irrationality. He was aware, too, of the projection of
himself that became his false public image:

> Only one thing: do, for friendship's sake, cut out that remark of
> mine about 'I have a beast and an angel in me' or whatever it
> was; it makes me sick, drives me away from drink, recalls too
> much of the worst of the fat and curly boy I know too well, he
> whose promises are water and whose water's Felinfoel, that
> nut-brown prince . . . (*Letters*, p. 231).

Dealing with Dylan Thomas as a person is a difficult problem, as
compared with, say, dealing with Sylvia Plath. One feels she must
have been an attractive person with Ariel-like qualities. Dylan
Thomas one knows to have been maddening, coarse, deceitful,
thieving, treacherous, and self-pitying—as well as a clown,
generous, romantic, lively and thoughtful. At times one simply
does not know how to take him: see for instance the impossible
long apologetic letter for not turning up to a banquet, at which he
was to be guest of honour of the Swansea branch of the British
Medical Association.[2] He never got there, did not explain why
until obliged to, then tells part fantasy. His serious letters about his
work contrast strangely with his sycophantic letters begging for
money, while these conflict again with apologies for his death
wishes and recognition of his self-destructiveness in letters to
Princess Caetani. Even when one is feeling most deeply the poignant nature of his predicament, one can suddenly come upon some

[2] *Life*, pp. 319 ff.

passage or aspect of his life that alienates, or makes one hate him violently. This, indeed, was the reaction of some people to Dylan Thomas in life and in 1945 someone tried to murder him. But this effect of the 'fat and curly boy' is at one with the schizoid need to 'preserve chaos': it is a trick of alienation necessary to the strategy of survival. It is a defence even against recognition of his art—perception of what his own poems were about, as is his way of writing poetry.

Thomas was aware of the contradictory and self-defeating elements in himself. As he writes to Marguerite Caetani:

why do I bind myself always into these imbecile grief-knots, blindfold my eyes with lies, wind my brass music around me, sew myself in a sack, weight it with guilt and pig-iron, then pitch me squealing to sea, so that time and time again I must wrestle out and unravel in a panic, like a seaslugged windy Houdini, and ooze and eel up wheezily, babbling and blowing black bubbles, from all the claws and bars and breasts of man-trapping seabed? (*Letters*, p. 416)

He was aware, too, that his excuses for this self-destructiveness were even more reprehensible:

Why must I parable my senseless silence? My one long trick? my last dumb flourish? . . . no, I must first defeat any hope I might have of forgiveness by resubmerging the little arisen original monster in a porridge boiling of wrong words and make a song and dance and a mock poem of all his fishy excuses.

To hell with him. (*Letters*, p. 417)

Here we have the mark in Dylan Thomas of a complex libidinal attachment to death circuits of schizoid suicide. His self-destruction was not only a search to be reborn: though the reference to Houdini makes it plain enough that it was that in part (a self-destructive escapologist). Even in the 'black babble' of his self-revealing letter he makes his apologia, by manic comedy: he condemns himself, but at the same time cannot be serious. There remains an element, as of the alcoholic's 'pathological optimism' characterised by Menninger—the 'most serious obstacle' to any serious treatment and to any serious insight. The alcoholic (says Menninger), 'suffers secretly from an unspeakable terror which he cannot bear to face'. This terror is fundamentally a fear of extinction of identity: Dylan Thomas's humour in such a letter is thus really a terrible kind of 'gallows humour' (as Menninger calls it.) There is also the impulse to disguise by 'fun' the hate and aggression manifest in the self-destructiveness and regressive alcoholism. This combines with a remorse which leads to self-depreciation and self-injury. As we have seen above Menninger speaks of how in his marriage the alcoholic behaves to his wife: 'the little-boy husband rushes back to her with tears, prayers, and promises to which she very likely succumbs and the whole cycle begins again'.

It is this syndrome we have in Dylan Thomas's letter to Marguerite Caetani:

> What can I tell you? Why did I bray my brassy nought to you from this boygreen briny dark? I see myself down and out on the sea's ape-blue bottom: a manacled rhetorician with a wet trombone, up to his blower in crabs . . . It is enough that, by the wish I abominate, I savagely contrive to sink lashed and bandaged in a blind bag to those lewd affectionate raucous stinking cellars . . . It is not enough to presume that once again I shall weave up pardoned, my wound din around me rusty, and waddle and gush along . . . wan and smug as an orpheus of the storm . . .

The 'blind bag' is the same as Sylvia Plath's black bag of oblivion and Houdini's sack: the cellar is the same as that in which Sylvia Plath's heroine in *The Bell Jar* seeks rebirth by death. Both she and Dylan Thomas hoped to 'weave up pardoned': but in the end they destroyed themselves by 'the wish I abominate'.

9
No Return

Such conflicting elements generate the violent chaos of Dylan Thomas's most obscure poetry, which recurs and recurs to themes as of death issuing, or life failing to issue, from the womb. Here we need to return to the earliest poems and re-examine the symbolism of the regressed libidinal ego, and thereby see how this leads forward to poetry which expresses in a disguised form a powerful hatred of this unborn infant. This is poetry of the anti-libidinal ego, directed often, however, at children, born and unborn, over whom the poet has projected his own regressed libidinal ego, associated with his own vulnerable, 'female element'. This in turn we may associate with his denial of his own creativity: we have Envy, in fear, turned even on the True Self.

In *When once the twilight locks no longer* (p. 4), as we have seen, the phantasy image of a hideous dead and diseased foetus is horrifyingly expressed:

All issue armoured, of the grave,
The redhaired cancer still alive,
The cataracted eyes that filmed their cloth;
Some dead undid their bushy jaws,
And bags of blood let out their flies;
He had by heart the Christ-cross-row of death.

Now we have seen more of Thomas's predicament we can go deeper into this terrifying imagery. *All issue armoured* means something like, 'we all come from the womb with a defensive shell'. But 'from the womb' becomes *of the grave*: we are of the grave as soon as we are born: dust. We are also

The red-haired cancer still alive:

Thomas was fascinated (as we know from his notebooks) by cancerous foetuses. If the foetus represents the regressed ego, this means he is fascinated by the energy of the death-circuit in the self—the monstrous growth that seems like life but is destructive of life. *Red-haired* suggests the blood in the hair of a neonate, or simply a red-haired person such as himself. (Is it him or the 'other' who died?)

Thomas was fascinated (as we know from his notebooks) by cancerous foetuses. If the foetus represents the regressed ego, this

      The cataracted eyes that filmed their cloth . . .

Another kind of growth puts a film over the vision. 'Their cloth' is difficult: it could be read as referring to shrouds (as William York Tindall suggests) or to mummy-bands. The *film* is a kind of *armour* against reality, which is deathly.

      Some dead undid their bushy jaws . . .

The vagina is like a jaw, under a *bush*: the womb gaping is like the jaws of corpses sagging (bushy because they are unshaven as Tindall suggests).

      And bags of blood let out their flies . . .

The bursting of the amniotic fluid sac in birth is like bags of blood in bodies corrupted by some horrible disease or swollen by contusion. The gaping of the vagina is like an undoing of a trouser fly. What comes from this womb is a *swarm of flies* (a dissipated identity like Sylvia Plath's swarms, rather than, what one expects, a penis, or a baby).

    Instead of a clean baby, what we have is an image of a thing (or *issue*) in a shell (*armoured*); a *redhaired cancer* ('still alive' as if it was not expected to be, so bloody and monstrous is it). It has cataracts over its eyes as if the eyes had 'filmed' over with their own death-coverings (cloth). Perception is dead in the psychically unborn. It was as if 'some dead' (nameless, undetermined, confused beings) opened their bushy jaws, to spit forth, out of *bags of blood*, a swarm of flies, or a monstrous object out of a fly opening.

      He had by heart the Christ-cross-row of death . . .

To know a thing by heart is to possess it in one's being, in one's body. The creature in this stanza has the experience of being put to death before being born. We can interpret this as referring to the regressed ego: 'I know by heart what it is to be born dead'— that is, to have a self which feels like a dead foetus in a jar. Christ was resurrected, and so was born after death: the monster-baby born dead 'double crosses' the womb by being dead before birth— and yet is born dead. Tindall says the 'Christ-cross-row' refers to a row of letters in the alphabet in the old primers: it is a lesson. The line means: the one who was born dead has learnt the Christ lesson of resurrection, i.e. the sibling who was born dead learnt it; I have learnt it, since I was brought up dead in the heart of being. The self is an 'issue *armoured*' by this lesson. Because of the deadness of being, the self has had to deal with the world by a forced doing, the male element, lacking the capacity for female insight—and vulnerability—as the eyes which cataract themselves weave their own bandages.

The important thing to note is that the horrible nature of the imagery, its violence, its recoil from the sexual, and its dissociation, are expressing at the same time both an anti-libidinal hate of the regressed libidinal ego because of its needs (intense need for the 'female element' which can bring the self to psychic birth) and an intense and violent hatred of it because of its vulnerability. There is a preoccupation with visceral imagery which is a form of thinking to prevent being 'drawn back inside'. There is also a hatred of being human and having to suffer such fears in the repulsiveness of the imagery itself.

The area of 'female element being' seems to be the area of creativity, and of inwardness. It is thus the sphere of the womb where, to someone like Thomas, the True Self waits to be born, 'crouched in the natural doorway'. For various reasons he wants to be there—and so resents any competition. Birth thus became for Dylan Thomas a symbol of the psychic birth he felt some area of his inner self had never experienced. So, in his poems about birth we find violent feelings of envy of the 'other' in the womb. Because a sibling before him died in the womb, these feelings of envy become mixed with guilt and fear. Perhaps he felt that his strong envy could kill his own child in the womb. He is envious of the mother's creativity and fears that in some way birth may kill her. In the back of his mind is the schizoid belief that to die is to be reborn, and thus a feeling that it would be a good thing for the foetus to die, while birth into this world is a death. Sexual 'entering' becomes entangled with these feelings about birth and death. (Cf. the case-history of a patient who shot a prostitute in

Existence, ed. Rollo May. To this man sexual intercourse was a step towards the 'other world' of death where the mother was. He needed to get into this other world, in order to find the mother who would reflect his identity. He was a butcher and slaughtered animals. Sometimes he would have sexual intercourse with the animals before he slaughtered them, thus making a step towards this other world into which they went. The phenomenology of these acts reveals that to some individuals the female sexual organ may seem to be an entrance to the world of death, in which lies their hope of rebirth.)

These intense feelings also relate to the problem of the male and female elements in Thomas. We have seen how alcoholism often goes with an inability to tolerate heterosexual sex, while it cloaks disguised homosexuality. If we look at this question in the light of the schizoid processes we can see that alcoholism, again, is a turning to a form of 'false male doing' (hence the aggressiveness), with an element of desiring to coerce the love-object into providing what has never been provided—a sense of being. The magic of taking in by mouth is a false quest for 'being'. One aspect of this deficiency of being is a failure to embrace the female element in oneself. Here there is, I believe, a particularly relevant and important note by Guntrip:

> The female element may be defined as *the need to be emotionally susceptible, the capacity for sensitiveness to what others are feeling* . . . By contrast the male element [may be] seen as the need to be able to *take practical action in an often difficult and dangerous world*, and if necessary to harden the heart to do what is unavoidable. . .
>
>   (*Schizoid Phenomena*, p. 263)

The female element is 'the emotionally sensitive self that can be more easily hurt, and can then be felt as a weakness to be resisted, resented and hidden behind a tough exterior' (i.e. 'armoured'):

> Patients who have not been able to develop the tough super-ficial defence but have remained too vulnerable and sensitive, may generate an intense unconscious hate of their female ele-ment, project it, and experience frightening destructive im-pulses towards little girls and women. (ibid., p. 287)

These problems would surely be exacerbated in such an indi-vidual as Dylan Thomas whose mother both failed him, and failed to disillusion him as to the nature of external reality, while his father's remoteness and indifference to her made it difficult for him to 'include' a male element capable of dealing with the world. At the core of the self there was a capacity to be hurt (which was also the capacity to be sensitive): this was in part felt to be a feared weakness, a female element he hated in himself. Thomas tended to split this off and project it and was compelled both to be cruel to and reject his wife at times, and to exert a 'taking' impulse on other women in his promiscuity. (He could have said of the other women 'They're all my own female element, really.')

That is, many aspects of his life and poetry would suggest that one of Thomas's problems was what Winnicott calls a 'split-off female element' which he could not in some way 'include' in his personality. Winnicott suggests that this is a more valuable way of looking at such problems of sexuality than to talk of homosexuality. Yet when we find undue hostility to homosexuality, we may suspect that the hostile person feels that he himself has a 'weakness', to quote Guntrip, which he feels must be 'destroyed in some female person'. Dylan Thomas reveals at one point a splenetic distaste for homosexuality, to which he seems unable to extend the tolerance he demands for his own alcoholism and promiscuity: speaking of 'becoming girlish' himself, he goes on:

Have you remarked upon the terrible young men of this generation, the willing-buttocked, celluloid-trousered degenerates who are gradually taking the place of the bright young things of even five years ago? Or is the degeneracy, the almost unbelievable effeminacy, the product of the Welsh slums alone? In an hotel last night a boy, wearing a light green hat, white shirt, red tie, light green trousers and tightly fitting fawn overcoat, went up to the bar and said 'a whate port and a smale Ardathe, girlie'. I heard him. He was the most perfect example I've ever seen of the sort of thing one hears of in coarse stories but rarely encounters in the flesh (God deliver me from the flesh; the outer trappings are enough). I see more and more of them every day. They always existed, but in recent months—it seems months to me—they are coming, unashamedly, out into the open. I saw one with a drunken nigger last night.

It is the only vice, I think, that revolts me and makes me misanthropic. I can—theoretically—tolerate even incest . . . and

other domestic sins. But the sin of the boy with the nigger goes
up like a rocketed scab to Heaven. (*Letters*, pp. 72–3)[1]
From clues such as these we are enabled to understand a number
of poems in which this hatred of the female element is especially
pronounced. These are poems written while Dylan Thomas's
wife was expecting their first child: *The tombstone told when she
died* (p. 93), *A saint about to fall* (p. 95) and '*If my head hurt a hair's
foot*' (p. 97).

Each of these poems expresses a tumult of hate and jealousy,
directed at the 'female element' and the unborn 'other'. Because
of the hate involved, Thomas was inhibited from having insight
into what these poems were essentially about. Characteristically,
in discussing them in a letter to Vernon Watkins, he never discusses the meaning—only the 'effectiveness' of words. Of the first
he says it is 'Hardy-like'—perhaps (I believe) because Watkins
said it was: it is a poem about a woman whose legend is cut on her
tombstone.

A 'strange & red' harsh head was, of course, very weak and
clumsy, but I couldn't see that the alliteration of 'raving red'
was effective. I tried everything, & stuck to the commonplace
'blazing' which makes the line violent enough then, if not
exactly good enough, for the last. In the last line you'll see I've
been daring, & have tried to make the point of the poem softer
& subtler by the use of the dangerous 'dear'. The word 'dear'
fits in, I think, with 'though her eyes smiled', which comes
earlier. I wanted the girl's *terrible* reaction of orgastic death to be
suddenly altered to a kind of despairing love. As I see it now, it
strikes me as very moving, but it may be too much of a shock, a
bathetic shock perhaps, & I'd like very much to know what
you think. No, I still think the womb 'bellowing' is all right,
exactly what I wanted; perhaps it looks too much like a stunt
rhyme with heroine, but that was unavoidable. 'Hurried' film
I just couldn't see; I wanted it slow and complicated, the winding
cinematic works of the womb. I agree with your objection to
'small'; 'innocent' is splendid, but 'fugitive' & 'turbulent' are for

[1] See also his strange envy of other lovers: 'he noticed a young couple in a booth,
their heads amorously together. "How filthy!" he said to Liz . . . Liz told him
that he spoke like a Puritan. "Yes", he said, . . . "I *am* a Puritan!" ' (*Dylan Thomas
in America*, p. 263).

me in that context, too vague, too 'literary' (I'm sorry to use
that word again) too ambiguous. I've used 'devilish', which is
almost colloquial. (*Letters*, p. 209)

We may begin by asking, Why did Thomas feel the word 'dear'
was dangerous? He perhaps feared that it was sentimental and
would deepen the bathos. But perhaps also he felt it would reveal
his schizoid fear of love and 'giving' as deathly—which is what
the poem is about.

He has come across a tombstone, in the rain, on which a woman
is recorded as having died in her wedding gown, so that she was
married but not married: she was married, but still a virgin. She
has two surnames, her maiden name and her married name. She
became the bride of death. She thus became the bride of hate
rather than love:

her red lips were kissed black.

Yet at the end she is giving birth, in which the 'I' of the poem is
involved ('I who saw . . . I died'), So, she is his mother. But it is
his womb which is 'bellowing', for he has become her: she is the
female element which he desires to find in himself. Yet he has
projected his female element, of which he is afraid, and which he
hates, over her, and hates her so much that he feels he has killed
her. She is the woman of the tombstone, his mother—and *his wife
who is carrying his child*. He wants the child to be born alive: he
wants the child born dead. He is the child born alive: he is the
child born dead. He wants to give birth to the child alive: he wants
to give birth to the child dead. All these conflicting feelings arouse
intense destructive emotions: to deny these, he wishes to transform
hate and death into love, as by magically pretending that the
woman could feel 'a kind of despairing love' and that death could
be 'orgastic' (orgiastic and orgasmic). He also feels that his own
orgasm has been a death to his woman and has generated a dead
child: because he fears his projected female element so much, he
fears and wishes that this creativity which he hates can only produce death. (Above I have suggested that his father felt guilty
at the consequences of his own creativity.) The word 'dear' both
threatens to reveal his intense involvement—and also the real love
which he fears as dangerous.

Close analysis of the poem reveals now the experience of being
handled by his mother in such a way as to convey to him the

previous sibling's death, and his infant conclusions about the
father's part in this. Obviously the father must in this have caused
death, so that he virtually *is* death—who was this woman's bride.
This caused her double identity, as having death as a father has
given him a divided identity. There is no other way of explaining
the strange shift into involvement:

> She married in this pouring place,
> That I struck one day by luck,
> Before I heard in my mother's side . . .

He did not 'strike' the place before he 'heard in (his) mother's
side'. She 'married' before 'he heard'—that is, this happened before he was born. (She might have been his mother.) He has
struck the place, however before his own child is born, when he is
aware of what he can hear in the 'side' of his present woman (who
naturally now tends to be identified with his own mother).

Why should he be reminded, in coming across a dead virgin,
of being 'in his mother's side'? The only connection is that this
bride being dead when she should have been enjoying her bridegroom reminds the poet of how he felt as a child that his mother's
love had been killed:

> The sun killed in her face . . .

What Thomas 'heard in his mother's side' was that a *son had been
killed in her womb*. Moreover, by the failure of the mother to
'mirror' his self, he was a *son killed in her face*. He saw this in the
looking-glass shell: the empty shell of what should have reflected
his substance. The rain that falls on the tomb of the dead virgin
is like the rain that he saw as an infant *speak through her cold heart*,
that *killed the sun in her face*. This rain killed the possibility of the
son's finding himself in her face, by 'creative reflection'.

What is this rain? Later he speaks of a *rainy tongue* which the
virgin 'beat back'. The rain, if we examine it in terms of Kleinian
phantasy, is the kind of retributive attack an infant fears from the
imago father, in revenge for the child having participated in
phantasy in the primal scene. It is a urinary attack of hate, and it is
this Thomas unconsciously fears for participating in phantasy in
the 'orgastic' act of hate-sex that is death. One of the problems
indicated by Fairbairn is that 'the libidinal attitude of the schizoid
acquires the implication that it involves the disappearance and
destruction of the libidinal object'. This implication 'tends to

become confirmed to the infant at a later stage, when he learns that food which is eaten disappears from the external world, and that he cannot both eat his cake and have it.' Fairbairn also points out that for the infant sex seems a form of eating, and as he knows from eating, it makes things disappear. The schizoid individual has a fundamental fear that love is destructive, and so here Thomas fears the worst for himself from witnessing the primal scene.

The word 'tongue' suggests the phallus from which the deathly rain is shaken, that both destroyed the mother's *sun*, and the virgin. The rain is thus also semen that kills and breeds dead infants: while the word *devilish* makes it the *cold seed of the devil*—or death. So, this is a vision of the primal scene:

> Before she lay on a stranger's bed
> With a hand plunged through her hair,
> Or that rainy tongue beat back
> Through the devilish years and innocent deaths
> To the room of the secret child . . .[2]

Here we can see why Thomas rejected 'fugitive and turbulent' as 'too ambiguous'—though his lines are ambiguous enough. Those words don't belong to his complex phantasy. This phantasy the reader can *beat backwards*, as he imagines the virgin 'loving Death back'. We can begin at the end, with *the secret child*, which is the dead sibling (also the present foetus in his wife's womb, and his regressed ego). The *room* is the womb, which is also its *tomb* (as in so many other poems by Thomas). His death was *innocent* (a word for which we have to thank Vernon Watkins, apparently). The *devilish* years were those in which weakness came to the identity by being confused with a dead child, which were like years in which one felt possessed by the mother's hate-magic. All this is evoked in the virgin, with whom he identifies himself, as she meets the *rainy* tongue of death's love which is also his hate. The vision is of his own hate, a male devilishness bred from the early confusion with the dead sibling, having 'orgastic' intercourse with his female element: so, the pain of being killed is good for her:

> her red lips were kissed black,
> She wept in her pain and made mouths,
> Talked and tore though her eyes smiled.

[2] See 'The secret child, I shift about the sea' in *My world is pyramid*, p. 32. Obviously Thomas is here the secret child (Dylan) too.

This exactly enacts Fairbairn's 'moral motive': 'It is better to destroy by hate than by love which is harmful and bad.' We have something here almost of the petrified object (since Thomas is virtually addressing a tombstone) on whom there is excessive dependence: the *making mouths*, the *weeping in pain*, the *talking*, the *smiling eyes*, and the *tearing* are all indications that she *is still alive* although taking part in sexual intercourse that in the infantile phantasy of the primal scene is feared as likely to cause death.

> I who saw in a hurried[3] film
> Death and this made heroine
> Meet once on a mortal wall
> Heard her speak through the chipped beak
> Of the stone bird guarding her . . .

The last five lines contain the whole complexity of Thomas's problems of identity. We have seen how much he identifies with the woman who cries:

> I died before bedtime came . . .

'I died before I was taken to bed by my bridegroom. But my womb was already bellowing and I felt as I fell dead (feeling naked in my wedding gown) a *blazing red harsh head tear up my birth passage* and I felt the *dear floods of his hair*.' Thomas wants to have his own child: to bring himself to birth.

Earlier Thomas had *raving red* and *strange and red*. We may recall the *red-haired cancer* still alive. He also wishes or fears this child may be dead.

The image is inevitably one of a birth in reverse: a red-haired infant is being thrust into her (*tear up*), like a penis—like the 'rainy tongue'. A *bull* bellows: so the woman's womb has become male: roles are reversed, so that the birth happens backwards. The sexual possession (that does not happen) is a birth. The possession by death is a sexual possession, and a reversed birth.

The *secret child* (the other dead infant which died in the womb before Thomas) died before the 'bedtime' came in which Thomas was conceived or his mother was brought to bed. He is therefore seeking to resist in this poem the unconscious confusion of feeling (*a*) he is that dead sibling (*b*) he is dead (*c*) he is the Devil's off-

[3] 'Hurried' is apparently a word supplied by Vernon Watkins. Thomas's word was probably more satisfactory, whatever it was ('I wanted it slow and complicated').

spring (*d*) he is death's child, by seeking magically to make the woman who has been possessed by Death say that she has already felt the 'dear floods of his hair'. He can most successfully overcome all these confusions by having the baby himself (and thus come to embrace his own female element): but he is also recording the envy and hate in this (because he can't in fact have it).

> A blazing red harsh head tear up
> And the dear floods of his hair.

'He' is born in spite of her death. So, too, Thomas is assuring himself, his own child will be born alive, despite the original disaster with his mother's earlier baby, despite his own dead feeling in the regressed ego, and despite his own hate—which unconsciously wishes to do to the 'female element' of his pregnant wife what Death did to this virgin. Again the violence is a violence directed at the female element of the self, albeit split off and projected elsewhere.

The poem thus springs from the ambivalence of wanting his child born alive and wanting it born dead: and the parallel problem of his own hatred of his own weakness in his female split-off element of identity. Obviously, it was not possible for Thomas to achieve recognition of such deep unconscious conflicts and he has therefore to write a poem which both *says it, and at the same time successfully hides what is said* (as can be seen from unsuccessful attempts such as that of William York Tindall to decode the poem). Again, one can only unravel the meaning by writing a mad analysis of a mad poem. (I daresay an interpreter with the psycho-analytical experience of a Winnicott could see penis-envy in such lines as 'And bags of blood let out their flies'—an obvious menstrual image, in which the menstrue seems like a cut-off penis, in the flies, and in the phrase 'my womb was bellowing', taken with the image of birth reversed as a phallic entry. Both perhaps emerge from the penis-envy of the split-off female element in Thomas which refused to allow him to be wholly a man. But to suggest so much only shows how mad one has to go to attempt criticism of such poems, by trying to refine wild conjecture.)

In *A saint about to fall* (p. 95) the subject (obviously) is his own unborn child, in embryo: who risks the death of an innocent martyr, such as his sibling's death in the womb. He risks this for various reasons: (1) the 'other' died in the womb, so this again is a potential tomb; (2) Dylan Thomas feels he was born psychically

dead (the regressed ego is dead)—so birth can be death; (3)
Thomas hates the child in the womb, because he has projected his
female element over his pregnant wife, and hates creativity in her.
These feelings of hate were obviously exacerbated by the external
'objective correlatives' of hate, in the events of the imminence of
war at the time the poem was written.

Of this poem, written in 1938 during a war crisis, Thomas says
in the letter previously quoted:

> ... provisionally called 'In September', & called that at all only
> because it was a terrible war month ... Does 'Glory cracked
> like a flea' shock you? I think you'll see it *must* come there, or
> some equally grotesque contrast. (*Letters*, p. 209)

The 'grotesque contrast' is between the embryo in the womb and
the death in the world: between his own hate for the child and its
innocence and embodiment of love; between his own creative
impulses and need to be reborn, and his own destructiveness and
self-destructiveness. Yet the 'grotesque' images largely disguise
the deeper meanings, and help 'preserve chaos'. The letter continues:

> The last line of the 2nd verse ['The skull of the earth is barbed
> with a war of burning brains and hair'] might appear just a long
> jumble of my old anatomical clichés, but if, in the past, I've
> used 'burning brains & hair' etc too loosely, this time I used
> them—as the only words—in dead earnest. Remember this is
> a poem written to a child about to be born—you know I'm
> going to be a father in January—& telling it what a world it will
> see, what horrors & hells. The last few lines of the poem,
> especially the last but two, may seem ragged, but I've altered
> the rhythm purposely; 'you so gentle' must be very soft and
> gentle, & the last line must roar. It's an optimistic, taking in
> everything poem. The two most important words are 'Cry
> Joy'. (ibid.)

It is obvious from this that Thomas *thought* he was writing a poem
to tell an unborn innocent child what a terrible world it was being
born into.What he did not know was that he was writing a poem
about his own schizoid hate for the neonate, about his own regressed ego and its failure to be born psychically, and the conflict
with his female element. These the incoherence disguises, as well
as expresses: it is a mixture of 'praise and envious tongue' 'worked

in flames and shells'. (Flames destroy, and shells blow up: but flames can also be beacons and *feux d'artifice* while shells of another kind protect the bodies of creatures.)

The first whirling and breathless stanza throws out many false scents for the interpreter to follow (and William York Tindall follows them all as incoherently as they are uttered). But the main point to make about it is that it sees birth as a *fall*, a volcanic eruption, a spilling, a crucifixion, and having to do with a gradual dying—such as he himself feels he experienced and as he continually expressed in his hypochondria:

> The wound-down cough of the blood-counting clock
> Behind a face of hands . . .

He is writing about his own experience of birth. The womb is the 'garden of Eden' to which he (Thomas) wishes to return, to be reborn. Leaving this 'heaven', which is what the Saint is about to do, is an experience in which envy, emptying, being filled with spirit, and yet with bitter disillusion which one rejects, are all mingled. The saint

> Sang heaven hungry . . .

—that is, he has taken into himself everything he can from Heaven, even the

> quick
> Cut Christbread spitting vinegar and all . . .

That is, he has taken in from his womb heaven the host, which is Christ's dead body, and the bitter vinegar which one spits out, and which symbolises the hatred of man (who gave Christ bitter gall to spit out and who spat at Christ—cf. 'with shame and spitting').

Thomas is confused with his own child's identity (as his mother confused him with her earlier dead child). So, his hate, love, and envy are mingled

> The mazes of his praise and envious tongue were worked in
> flames and shells . . .

Here the Saint seems to have an envious tongue, which has 'sung heaven hungry'—that is, Thomas feels the neonate has a ferocious hunger that somehow threatens his own hunger for mothering—his needs which makes him fear for his own survival. The external flames and shells of the German campaigns of territorial conquest

symbolise his own hatred of his own child, and the fact that in his
hungry needs the neonate already has the germ of human hate
within him. At a very deep level, Thomas also feels that the
'other', his dead sibling, died in the womb (a) because of the hate
in the baby himself (the dead baby being confused with his own
'bad inner contents' or unborn 'dead' self); (b) because he, Thomas,
had hated the baby; (c) possibly also because the mother and father
had hated him (his mother's excessive needs, expressed in over-
maternal preoccupation, having been experienced by him as
hate). The birth of the Saint is thus felt to be terribly insecure, an

> unwinding, song by rock,
> Of the woven wall
> Of his father's house in the sands,
> The vanishing . . .

But note the language Thomas uses to celebrate a birth:

> The wound-down cough . . . blood-counting . . .
> . . . angelic etna . . . last whirring . . .
> . . . foot in the hole . . . fireball . . .
> . . . shrivelling . . .
> . . . last rick's tip . . . spilled . . .
> . . . hungry . . . quick
> Cut . . . spitting . . .

These are all violent and disruptive in feeling. While the poem
has a conscious intention to celebrate and praise an unborn child,
it expresses deep unconscious feelings of ontological insecurity,
envy, fear, and hatred.

'Behind a face of hands' is interesting: it is a characteristic of an
infant severely deprived of its mother to put its hands before its
face (as Bowlby points out). The clock which hides a running
down of the identity, in mortality in time, seems to be pretending
that the identity exists in normal quotidian time. To the schizoid
individual with a weak identity, who has never been given an
adequate sense of continuity by his mother and so no real sense of
time, the clock face seems like that self-protective gesture—a
pretence that one still exists, even when one fears one does not.[4]

---

[4] Cf. the terrifying view of time in a schizophrenic patient discussed by Eugene
Minkowski in *Findings in a Case of Schizophrenic Depression*, in *Existence*, ed. Rollo
May, p. 136. 'The clock . . . was not just a clock but an assemblage of instruments
of torture.'

The leaving of heaven for earth is expressed in that grotesque 'Glory cracked like a flea'. What was all marvellous in the intra-uterine state, Thomas feels, was snuffed out by a pinch or snap, as when a tiny flea is nipped by one's nail or burnt. The tiny snap shows that there was life in the tiny creature: at the same time it is the sound of one's destructive act of hate in killing it. What Thomas is saying is that he has conceived out of reminiscence of the state before birth (when there was no impingement) a state of psychic at-one-ness, heaven, which was perfection: this stands for *being*. After birth he suffered the most brutal impingement, which was like finding one was only the tiniest of creatures, being obliterated or nipped out, by being 'done to'.

What were 'sun-leaved holy candlewoods' then 'Drivelled down to one singeing tree'. The foetus with gills taking the journey to birth (like Sylvia Plath's gilled foetuses which suggest to her the possibility of being reborn by drowning in Thalassa, the sweet sea-mother) finds itself storm-tossed and scuttled:

> The sweet, fish-gilled boats bringing blood
> Lurched through a scuttled sea . . .

The contents of the self turn out to be blood-hungry and empty

> With a hold of leeches and straws . . .

So, his baby is going to awake from this in his father's earth-bound house at Laugharne . . .

> O wake in me in my house in the mud
> Of the crotch of the squawking shores . . .

Dylan Thomas identifies with his house and when the baby is born it will be born in him. Because his house is on a muddy shore, it feels to him like a house from which it was possible to be reborn, half in, half out of water. In this poem it is the house of the crotch —that is, the birth passage (cf. 'The secret child . . . Dry in the half-tracked thigh'). Once out, the baby will squawk like the birds round the Towy estuary, on its shore.

Heaven now becomes 'the carbolic city puzzle': that is, the saint is now being 'flicked' out of a mere womb and has come down to mundane earth amid midwifery techniques and disin-fectants. The bed is one in which the mother becomes physically sore (Thomas's dread of the reality of birth begins to appear). The baby is now

> Flicked from . . .
> The scudding base of the familiar sky . . .

—like a flea he has ceased to be 'trailing clouds of glory', and is a
little creature thrown down on earth.

> From an odd room in a split house stare,
> Milk in your mouth, at the sour floods
> That bury the sweet street slowly, see
> The skull of the earth is barbed with a war of burning brains
>   and hair.

The word 'stare' is difficult here, and seems perhaps merely put in
to rhyme with 'hair'. The child is no longer in heaven. It is in an
odd room in Thomas's house. The house of the womb is 'split'
for the child to emerge. The floods of amniotic fluid and blood
(which by being *sour* pick up something of Christ's vinegar—that
is, they accompany by their bitterness that crucifixion which is
birth and rebirth) bury the birth passage (sweet street) as the
waters flow by Thomas's own house. Now he is born the child
can see that he lies on the earth as if on a skull. That is, he is now
mortal.

And this skull is barbed (as Christ's is with thorns) with a war
of hatred: where men are being bombed there are 'burning brains
and hair'. But these are but symbols for the burning in the brains
of Thomas himself, who is desperately envious of the neonate,
because he himself wants to be reborn, as Christ was, by his
crucifixion. Thomas envies the neonate's suffering, which he
believes birth is (as it was for him—both physically and psychically), because he desires birth of the regressed ego so deeply. He
fears the consequences of this envious hate, and this attaches itself
to his horror that his baby should be born into a world at war. But
there is a sense in which the skull, the burning hair and the burning
brains are those of the child (the 'other', the neonate, the 'red-
haired cancer still alive') on whom a human hate falls just as it
falls on Europe—that is, the hatred that arises from envy (his
own). (See Sylvia Plath's *The Swarm* for images of European
conflict used as a symbol of inward hate.)

The last stanza combines images of the physical strife of birth
with images of the massacre of the innocents: the child will be

> Lapped among herods wail
> As their blade marches in . . .

Consciously no doubt Thomas thought he was writing about the world in which war threatened the innocent: but the intensity of the images gains its chaotic force from the fact that the images dramatise inner structures. He is Herod, even though he wishes to 'Cry joy', and to urge the baby to 'Cry joy' (the first cry being an assurance that the baby has been born alive. Thomas would suffer an intense unconscious fear—and hope—that it would *not* be).

We can, here, I believe, only take fragments; we cannot find a sequence of sense in the sentences—the 'resistance to necessitous sense' sees to that. There is the schizoid fear of petrifaction by hate:

> Throw your fear a parcel of stone
> Through the dark asylum . . .

We have here an image of the baby being born a parcel of stone through the dark sanctuary of the womb (an image emerging from Thomas's own feeling of being born petrified in the being):

> the eyes are already murdered,
> The stocked heart is forced, and agony has another mouth
>   to feed.

In another poem (*When once the twilight locks no longer*) Thomas wrote, 'The cataracted eyes that filmed their cloth'. The blindness comes from an inward doom. Here, the child is already blinded by its own anticipation of the murder of the innocents, in its own hunger. Its heart which has *sung heaven hungry* is *stocked* and *forced* with substance: his hunger is so voracious that it virtually chokes him. So, he is already violated by his own rapacious nature, and so by his own envy and hate. When *herods wail* and *their blade marches in*, the infant is already murdered by envy. And so, as soon as it is born, the whole wide human *agony* in the world has *another mouth to feed*. This is an expression of the anguished problem of the schizoid who has an urgent hunger for being which terrifies him by its energy: but also an expression of our own desperate hunger for a meaning to overcome the 'nothingness' so evident in birth and death.

For Thomas every neonate is Christ, because he himself desires rebirth like Christ's, as does every individual preoccupied with schizoid suicide, in order to be resurrected. So, his own unborn child is Christ, and so inevitably must face the slaughter of the innocents. Herod's hatred of the new-born Christ is thus for him

a myth expressing the hatred we all feel for new-born children—
perhaps especially the hatred fathers feel for newborn sons, because they secure the total attention of the Mother (Mary) and
all her creative powers to give the neonate substance of *being*. The
slaughter of the innocents thus becomes the expression of the
hatred of predatory doing—the male element expressing its fear
of dependence and projecting its hatred of the weak female
element not over the mother, but over her newborn *son*.

So, Thomas's baby is going to 'wake to see, after a noble fall,
The old mud hatch again': the mud hatch is both mud hut, and
the hatch of the belly (cf. down the hatch)—the birth passage in
the mother's clay. The actual birth is a mundane and unlovely
domestic reality:

> Woe drip from the dishrag hands and the
> > pressed sponge of the forehead . . .

—the last image combines the crown of thorns with the sponge
full of vinegar. It is possible, I believe, that an actual difficult birth
combined with an arrested psychic birth gave Thomas a particular
fascination with these symbols. Winnicott says: 'It is my definite
view that the type of headache which is clearly described as a band
round the head is sometimes a direct derivative of birth sensations
remembered in somatic form . . .'[5] (*Collected Papers*, p. 186). The
crown of thorns and the sponge of vinegar were for Thomas
reminiscences of a difficult birth and a failure of maternal pro-
vision: certainly images of the latter abound in his work:

> mother milk as stiff as sand . . .

> dries the mouthing streams . . .

> loves damp muscle dries and dies . . .

> His mother's womb had a tongue that lapped up mud . . .

> > drink in the two milked crags,
> The merriest marrow and the dregs

> Before the ladies breasts are hags . . .

---

[5] Cf. 'As Liz and Dylan strolled up Third Avenue, she asked him if he would
tell her more of the nature of his illness. "I have such a feeling of dread," he told
her, "a terrible pressure—as if there were an iron band round my skull." ' (*Dylan
Thomas in America*, p. 254.)

When refused by his woman sexually, it seems to him like refusal of the breast:

> anticlimax after
> Refusal struck her loin and the lame flower
> Bent like a beast to lap the singular floods
> In a land strapped by hunger . . .
> (*Not from this anger*, p. 90)

In *I make this in a warring absence* such a refusal, 'Bread and milk mansion in a toothless town', threatens, as we have seen, destruction of the whole identity.

> And this weak house to marrow-columned heaven,

> Is corner-cast, breath's rag, scrawled weed, a vain
> And opium head, crow stalk, puffed, cut, and blown . . .

So, the vinegar-sponge of Christ is a symbol of the taste of the failure of the mother to give him a sense of being, by her breast—his most predominant feeling, which prompts his attempt at self-cure by alcoholism. Christ's sponge is both breast and the bitter bottle: 'agony has another mouth to feed' could be a maxim for his own slow alcoholic suicide, as well as a greeting for his own son.

I referred above to Guntrip's discussion of the schizoid individual's fear of withdrawal from the world which seems like being drawn back inside the womb. And Thomas knew that a previous child had died in his mother's womb. These fears associated with birth probably lie behind the disturbing image:

> The breath draw back like a bolt through white oil
> And a stranger enter like iron . . .

Winnicott discusses images and feelings which recur in the analysis of patients who have had difficult births—images of *reptation*, in which the whole body becomes identified with the male genital; images of *oil* which makes birth (which had been intolerable) tolerable (in a patient who had attempted suicide); and feelings of *constriction* of the chest.

> During the birth process, in reaction to the constriction of the maternal tissues, the infant has had to make what would be (if there were any air available) an *inspiratory* movement. After birth, if all goes well, the cry establishes the expression of liveliness by *expiration*. (*Collected Papers*, p. 188)

In the extraordinary last lines of this poem Thomas is perhaps virtually re-enacting his own difficult birth, in wishing his own baby an easier one.

Cry joy that this witchlike midwife second
Bullies into rough seas you so gentle
And makes with a flick of the thumb and sun
A thundering bull-ring of your silent and girl-circled island.

We can see the straight sense: 'Cry for joy that in the moment of your birth, which is a moment when secret witchlike skills will bring you safely into being, and thrust you into the rough seas of this world—you who are so weak and helpless. And that this moment, by a flick of the midwife's hand, makes you bellow that you are alive, as you come out of the mouth at the base of your mother's body—that womb which previously islanded you from outer reality and surrounded you with woman.'

But in paraphrasing these lines I have been aware of flavours of words which intrude upon the meaning, seeking to reverse it. *Sun* seems merely extraneous (like *stare* already noted). But *witchlike* is strange, and so is *bullies*: why should the mother or midwife be *witches?* Here again we have the schizoid feeling expressed in *devilish* in the previous poem, a primitive feeling that birth is a moment in which *hate can enter the identity*. And also we have the experience of 'impingement'—psychic birth at the hands of an activity experienced as hate.

In *The tombstone told when she died* the womb *bellowed*: here it is a *bullring*. This is to be explained in terms of Thomas's envious desire to have the birth himself (the infant was implanted by him as bull, of course): thus he asserts his jealous male principle even in the *girl-encircled island*, which he *forces* as much as Herod. He is the neonate bellowing out of her birth-canal: the reference to the war merely hides the hate in his desire to be reborn in the place of his own child.

A similar pressure of strange 'inner necessity' lies behind '*If my head hurt a hair's foot*' (p. 97). This is one of Thomas's best-known poems. As I pointed out in *Llareggub Revisited*, there is a disguised, denied meaning, relating to 'the father's contest with the child for possession of the birth passage', and 'unconscious feelings of resentment'. I noted also the 'tone of jealous spite' and the undercurrent of wishing the child dead:

He is striving to accept the fact of birth against all his unconscious resentment of the baby as a rival to the mother-
woman's affection. Thus, because it contains opposing feelings,
the meaning of the poem is unresolved . . . diffuse and contrary,
it moves towards compassion but is hampered by defence
against insight . . . (p. 170)

Our study of Fairbairn, Winnicott and Guntrip has revealed that
it is not simply the 'fact of birth' which Thomas is struggling to
accept, but the inward turmoil aroused in him by the recent birth
of his own child, because this in turn evokes his own 'unborn'
feeling. Although the poem is written as a dialogue between the
mother and the child in her womb, Thomas obviously identifies
intensely with both and 'becomes' both the mother *and* the baby.
So the poem is a dramatisation of a conflict in his inner world, the
complexities of which we have seen. Birth is death, because it is a
forfeiture of the Eden-like state of absolute dependence, and a
re-entering of the state of dependence in which he has been
terribly let down—so much so that he feels he was born dead (a
feeling enhanced by confusion with a dead sibling). He wishes to
embrace his split-off female element, and its creative capacities:
yet so much hatred is bound up with this that he fears that in becoming the mother he is liable, with all the hunger of his regressed
ego, to kill her, because his voraciousness threatens to consume all
objects. The poem can thus be read as expressing a conflict of
'systems' within a schizoid identity, threatening each other with
hatred and envy—yet seeking, too, deep down, to love and be
loved, and to be whole. The impending birth is the 'objective
correlative' for this inner conflict.

The strange confusion of birth and death here links Thomas's
delusions belonging to schizoid suicide with his impulse to identify
with Christ and his fascination with Christian myth.[6] Dylan

---

[6] It is possible that the appeal of any religion which offers an 'afterlife', 'resurrection of the dead', is an appeal to universal schizoid feelings, of inadequacy of
ego-development, whose processes have failed to be completed in infancy, and
will be completed by entry into heaven. Failure to complete the processes of
rebirth means eternal perdition (i.e. loss of identity): though suffering in limbo
and hell can help build up identity. The most terrible fate the human mind can
conceive of is to be cut off from confirmation of identity as by excommunication:
'let me never be confounded' is the ultimate plea to stay in being. By contrast,
the direct vision of God will wholly confirm identity: 'Now we see through a
glass darkly, but then face to face: now I know in part; *but then shall I know even as*

Thomas's birthday poems are all about dying. The poem subsequent to the one under discussion begins

Twenty-four years remind the tears of my eyes.
(Bury the dead for fear that they walk to the grave in labour).

(Twenty-four years, p. 99)

To 'walk to the grave in labour' is not merely a statement about how by the end of life we are so tired of effort and work that to walk to the grave, or to walk (as a ghost) after death would be even further woe and labour. It is also an expression of Thomas's feeling that the reason for burying the dead is in some way connected with making sure they are not giving birth: for to him being born has felt like a terrible error—it was as if the mother ought to have been buried, but instead 'walked to the grave in labour', 'and produced a dead child out of the grave'—namely, himself.

> In the groin of the natural doorway I crouched like a tailor
> Sewing a shroud for a journey . . .

To Sylvia Plath the foetus in the laboratory bottle is her regressed libidinal ego waiting to be reborn. So to Dylan Thomas the foetus in the womb is an aspect of his 'being' self crouched in busy preparation to be born into a life which is a living death. Like Sylvia Plath, he confuses the grave with the womb, and seeking the dead with labour.

> By the light of the meat-eating sun . . .

This is obviously a reference to Hamlet's 'a God kissing carrion' which will 'breed maggots in a dead dog' (cf. *A Portrait of the Artist as a Young Dog*). The poem may also echo Sir Walter Raleigh's verse set as a madrigal by Orlando Gibbons, *This is our life: a play of passion* ('Our mother's wombs the tiring houses be/ Where we are dressed for this short comedy'):

> Dressed to die, the sensual strut begun,
> With my red veins full of money,
> In the final direction of the elementary town
> I advance for as long as forever is.

_{I am known.}' Now I am imperfect, and am only able to understand my experience imperfectly: when I am resurrected the way God looks at me will confirm my identity wholly, so I shall be able to understand totally. See Winnicott on the 'mirror-role' of the mother and Buber on our need for 'confirmation' of our existence.

The schizoid preoccupation with 'inner contents' is associated here with feelings of bitterness and futility. His veins are but 'full of money'—not rich stuff endorsed by love, but depersonalised and metallic counters with which one can merely buy stuff in the town (or drink). The 'final direction' is only the 'elementary town' —which is another way of saying 'in my end is my beginning': he marches on but without hope of finding anything except a fragmentary sense of human identity. 'Going through life' is a mechanical 'advance' by 'false' male 'doing' activity: and he will do it 'for as long as forever is'. (See Sylvia Plath, 'If I were to run, I would run for ever': *The Bee Meeting*.) Not as long as 'I am': but as long as whatever the word 'forever' may be taken to mean. Whatever it does mean is, by his tone here, exposed to a savage irony, with its roots in the schizoid sense of futility. Thomas himself always believed he would die young so the implication is virtually: 'For another couple of decades maybe—that's what they mean when they say "forever".'

The bitterness of this poem is that aroused by envy of his firstborn. When we return to *'If my head hurt a hair's foot'* (p. 97) we can now see that the pain expressed in the first stanza was already there in the poet's vision before the stanza came to be written. He has violent phantasies of hurt around the subject of birth: tearing out hair at the root; packing back the bony head coming down the birth canal; pricking the amniotic sac; strangling the baby with the navelcord. Against these alarming phantasies he wishes to assert his innocence: he seeks to deny that he wishes to 'hurt a hair of her head'. The inversion 'head' to 'foot' is an incantatory device to hide his deeper feelings, and to deny them. So too is the intrusive structure, which here takes on some of the verbal play qualities of the speech of R. D. Laing's schizophrenic patient ('leally lovely life' and 'I'm a no un'): 'Pack back', 'Spout . . . out', 'clouted scene'. To unravel these we have to 'supply' meaning from our knowledge of schizoid processes and symbolism rather than from the traditional resonances and ambiguities of the English language.

We need to examine this poem in terms of symbolism of inner contents and the schizoid fear of their loss: as well as the fear of communication itself. We need to note the ambiguities of meaning to do with being born, born with great difficulty; of resistance

to being born, and of entering the birth passage by armless 'reptation' in the shape of a penis. Into this vision we also have to read
the feeling a child has about the primal scene, in which he becomes
involved in an excitement which, like eating, is incorporative and
so threatens identity.

To a person like Thomas with a complexity of schizoid fears
around the subject of birth many intense feelings are aroused by
its contemplation as we have seen—all of which involve threats to
his own existence, and many dangers associated with the 'loss of
inner contents' and the effects of one's hate.

All these dangers seem to emerge from the act of sex and the
father's acts of sex are in conflict with the birth; there is some
danger to the foetus at certain stages in sexual intercourse. A
husband such as Thomas with intense fear of sexual intercourse,
combined with all the above indicated horrors of birth, may feel
that in his sexual intercourse with the pregnant mother he is
actually attacking her creativity and her foetus, as both become
the focus over which he has projected his fear of his own feminine
element and his envy of creativity.

The foetus is thus made to speak of the 'unpricked ball of my
breath' which may 'bump on a spout'. Rather than come into
dangerous conflict with the father's sexual hate, let me perish, says
the foetus—'let the bubbles jump out'. Let my inner contents
(breath = spirit) escape, rather than come into conflict with my
father's consuming needs.

The 'clouted scene' is both the birth-scene, in which the
woman's birth blood is being soaked up as with cloth clouts; but
also the primal scene, violent because infantile phantasies of this
tend to be sadistic, and so full of 'clouts' (blows). The foetus says
it would rather die (by the mortal 'worm' of the navelcord 'ropes'
round its throat)

Than bully ill love . . .

Here *bully ill* may be read as to *bully into illness* or *bully into harm
and evil* as in 'make bad'. Or it may be read as *bully* what is already
ill love—that is, love already full of harm and hate which is being
bullied further. In any case, although the first stanza seems to be
saying, 'Dear mother, I would die rather than hurt a hair of your
head', the appearance of saying this is really a disguise. For what
must be preserved *at all costs is the primacy of the father's needs, the*

hungry urges of the mouth-ego of the libidinal ego—even at the cost of the neonate's death. Should the neonate's 'inner contents' bump on the spout of his father's giving of *his* inner contents into the birth passage: if he interferes (as a *bully*) with the *ill love*, or interferes *illy*, with the love of the *clouted* (*primal*) *scene*—then let him be packed back, drowned or strangled.

Here we can see two complexities of hate being expressed.

(*a*) If the neonate threatens his father's relational needs, as by making the mother inclined to reject him sexually, let him die.

(*b*) If the regressed ego (of which the neonate is a symbol) threatens the father's need for love, let it die. This is an expression of the anti-libidinal ego's hate of the libidinal ego, turned on the actual neonate.

In either case, the neonate, and the infantile regressed ego, are felt to be 'bullies', hurters, clouters. Thomas knew from his own experience how tyrannical the infant self could be, in revenge for the hate it suffered from under over-maternal protection. But he also expresses in this poem an urge he projects on to the foetus (and which he knows to be in the regressed ego) to die rather than release tremendously savage hungers on others: he fears 'destruction of the object' and so loss of all confirmation. There are circumstances in which a mother fears that her child will eat her, because she is unable to supply his needs. So, here, Thomas expresses a fear that the neonate (and his regressed ego) had better not be released into the world alive, because it will 'Bully ill love in the clouted scene'—a difficult line to unravel, but one full of violence and fear of love and giving as harmful.

Thomas may well have felt that in the phrases he had used in the first stanza (such as 'bully ill love') he had, in spite of his attempt to 'preserve chaos', given away, by his pugilistic words, the hatred aroused by his own baby, then just two months old. In the second stanza, therefore, he makes a self-conscious reference to the language—it is after all, only a game between them, just like the parents' sexual games:

All game phrases fit your ring of a cockfight . . .

The female sexual organ is a *cockpit*: it is a *ring* which the cock *fits*. The birth of the child means that for two or three months the father is deprived of this source of comfort and confirmation of

his identity. So, there has been a *cockfight* which the father has lost
(and Dylan Thomas, as we have seen, found it hard to bear being
refused sexual intercourse when he demanded it). Strangely
enough, this denial of physical relationship means more to him
than the birth of his child, a typically egocentric reaction of one
to whom the preservation of his own ego matters above all else.
The fundamental problem here would seem to be a combination
of several factors. (1) The object is literally splitting in two; (2) the
husband's envy of the 'female element' is at its height; (3) the
woman has developed a 'schizoid extension of the personality'
(primary maternal preoccupation) for the baby's sake, which
means a temporary withdrawal of some interest in and love for
the husband—sometimes even a hostility, certainly rejection of
sex; (4) the husband has consequent feelings of loss of confirmation of his identity, and fears of extinction aroused by this. The
temporary suspension of sexual intercourse, while the wife is
having the actual satisfactions of motherhood (a woman may even
experience orgasm during breast-feeding) becomes a focus of these
feelings of jealous distress.

So, Thomas's neonate declares he is prepared to play 'games',
too, in the womb, rather than experience the reality of birth, or
haunt their adult love. Here it is interesting to see how well
Thomas disguises his own hate, even from those who offer
analyses of his poems. William York Tindall, for instance, is here
reasonably coherent:

> Let him remain like a poacher with a dark lantern in the 'snared
> woods' of the womb, or a bird himself, let him 'duck time'.
> Blamelessly dancing in the dark on his father's spouting
> fountains is better than becoming a nuisance in the light and air
> of loud and bloody birth . . . Reluctance vies with politeness to
> prevent rushing this ghost of air in the crouch of 'bunched,
> monkey coming.' (*Reader's Guide*, p. 185)

Once commentators begin to analyse Thomas they seem to
become swallowed in his own false solutions and fail to ask the
most obvious questions. Why are the woods 'snared'? How is a
foetus a 'bird'? Why should a baby be considered a 'nuisance'?
Why should a baby be reluctant to be born? What ghost?

These questions can only be answered by supplying meaning to
incomplete expression. The 'game' here is pretending that the

foetus needn't be human. It needn't be a baby evoking the 'ghost with a hammer, air'—the actual horror of breathing actual air, being thrust into light, being forced out in blood to cry and to hear the voices of those in the birth chamber. It could be a poacher in the fairy-tale woods with a dark lantern, a bird pecking, a spirit thing scuttling, a light on fountains, a thing that hides like a bird in sedge, ducking away from time: it could be magicked away, if only its mother were to instruct it not to come between its father and her. It could stay unreal—and unborn.

Here again we have an unconscious expression of birth trauma. We can link the phrase 'the ghost with a hammer, air' with 'drop with the worm of the ropes round my throat' and 'if the un-pricked ball of my breath'. Winnicott says: 'I have found that the memory trace of restriction of chest expansion during traumatic birth processes can be very strong . . .' One of the consequences of breathing difficulties during the processes of being born is a 'feeling of a lack of something, a lack which could be relieved if breathing could be freed'. This should not be forgotten, Winnicott continues:

when one is tracing out the various roots of breathing disturb-ances and the perversions that include breathing obstruction. The desire to be suffocated can be extremely strong and turns up as a masturbation fantasy, in the acting out of which many who had no suicidal intention have died. It is present in inverted suicide which is commonly called murder. By a reversal of roles, active suffocating can be a perverted kindness, the active person feeling that the passive one must be longing to be suffocated. There is something of all this, as of everything else, in the healthy passionate sexual relationship.

(*Collected Papers*, p. 188)

Dylan Thomas, as we have seen, had asthma and suffered from a preoccupation with bad lungs: he would sometimes cough until he vomited. The account of his end is horrific with its picture of Dylan Thomas in an oxygen tent to which all around him responded violently, as if to a strange imagery of his identity plight:

When I went upstairs to see Dylan, wintry-bright sun streamed into his room and made a prison of the transparent oxygen tent covering the upper part of him. He breathed easily,

quietly, his eyes closed, his face calm . . . Caitlin returned . . .
she had had too much to drink . . . She stayed at Dylan's bed-
side for about twenty minutes, and then she was asked to leave
the room by distraught nurses who could not keep her from
lighting cigarettes in the danger zone of the oxygen tent, or
from *pressing herself upon Dylan in such a way as to obstruct his
breathing* . . . (*Dylan Thomas in America*, pp. 287–8, my italics)
Later Mrs Thomas tore a crucifix from the wall and smashed it,
splintered to bits a statue of the Virgin, and had to be restrained
in a straitjacket.

Caitlin Thomas was, obviously, at that moment, involved in a
strange and deep symbolism of air (oxygen), breathing, and the
impulse to suffocate someone, because they need it, and because
you need them so much. It can only be by chance that Dylan
Thomas did not die in an oxygen explosion set off by his visitors
who pressed themselves upon him. In the terrible scenes at his
deathbed I believe we can see all the individuals close to him acting
out phantasies to do with a breakdown of their whole relationship with reality that focusses on feelings about constriction, the
breath or spirit within us, and its loss in death. Around him cen-
tred hungry needs, so powerful that they had the kind of voraciousness expressed in such a poem as Ted Hughes's *Lovesong*, in *Crow*:
> He loved her and she loved him
> His kisses sucked out her whole past and future or tried to
> He had no other appetite
> She bit him she gnawed him she sucked
> She wanted him complete inside her . . .
> Her embrace was an immense press
> To print him into her bones . . .

With Dylan Thomas this voracious desire to 'eat up' the be-
loved became mingled with the kind of impulse to which Winnicott refers, with its origins in a difficult birth. Winnicott suggests
that a person who was nearly suffocated at birth (as Thomas may
well have been) associates 'being suffocated' with 'being born'.
Thus, by a reversal of this process, to suffocate someone is to do
them a kindness, because 'the passive one must be longing to be
suffocated'. Something like this was enacted when Caitlin Thomas
had to be restrained from virtually suffocating her dying husband:
her actions were a strangely inverted act of kindness, in the attempt

to restore him, in her frenzy of grief. The dreadful scenes in the
hospital seem to have been a final enacting of the tragic confusion
in his life, between himself and the dead sibling that died before
it reached the air.

And these strange manifestations at his end in which suffocation
is such a feature seem to be forecast in the poem under discussion:
'the ghost with a hammer, air'—in which 'air' is threatening.
Light 'strikes', while the room of the birth is 'loud' and 'bloody'.
In the poem birth is so violent it seems better not to be born. And
in this there is the same murderous intent that lurks beneath
Thomas's suicide and the chaos round his life. In the poem he
seems to want to strangle the neonate, in the way Winnicott
suggests, because the neonate 'longs to be suffocated'. It is a poem
of 'perverted kindness'.

Such ferociously destructive elements in Thomas, of course,
are glossed over by his biographers and critics. He seems to be the
poet of innocent and holy childhood, when

> The sabbath rang slowly
> In the pebbles of the holy streams.

But this concern is with his *own* childhood and it is his own idcal-
ised Christ-child-like 'central ego' that he seeks to endorse here.
Towards his own libidinal regressed ego, his unborn infant, he is
ruthless. And his anti-libidinal ego is so strong that it exerted a
powerful undercurrent in his responses to family life, in which
there were some things he could not bear. His strange unhappy
mixture of loving concern for his children with an anguished
sense of his inadequacy as a father is plain in *Dylan Thomas in
America*:

> Fretfully turning on his bed, he awoke to speak, sometimes in
> tears, of his wife, of the misery of his existence, and of his wish
> to die. 'I want to go to the Garden of Eden,' he said, 'to die . . .
> to be forever unconscious . . .' And then later, 'You know I
> adore my little boy . . . I can't bear the thought that I'm not
> going to see him again. Poor little bugger, he doesn't deserve
> this.' 'Doesn't deserve what?' asked Liz. 'He doesn't deserve my
> wanting to die. I truly want to die . . .' (p. 271)

The remark 'he doesn't deserve my wanting to die' seems to
suggest that Thomas's suicidal motives included unconscious
revenge on his own family—though he could also recognise that

in this he was punishing innocent creatures whom he loved. The poignancy of this predicament is terrible.

In *'If my head'* he makes the neonate ask to be put 'back inside':

'If my bunched, monkey coming is cruel
Rage me back to the making house. My hand unravel
When you sew the deep door. The bed is a cross place.'

The foetus is 'crouched', monkey-like—and its arrival possibly cruel to the mother. Its animal primitiveness is made an excuse for hating it away. Its baleful influence on the sexual love between the parents must be *unravelled*: the choice of word suggests the anxious tangling in which the interference here has involved Thomas. The poem, indeed, is full of phrases invoking the sexual intercourse ('Bump on a spout', 'dance on fountains', 'sew the deep door') which has had to be suspended for the baby's sake, or is felt to be in conflict with its claims. Because of this rivalry 'The bed is a cross place'—a vexed place, a place of cross-purposes, and a place of that *crucifixion which birth is.*

'Bend, if my journey ache, direction like an arc or make
A limp and riderless shape to leap nine thinning months.'

Here I believe Thomas identifies his *penis* with the neonate, by the confusion of the foetus moving through the birth passage with the self moving as a whole body (identified with the phallus) into the vagina. He wants to reverse time so that the neonate shall 'thin' and so *ungrow*, backwards. In the end the neonate becomes the 'limp and riderless' penis itself that is denied a mount. In short, Thomas would prefer the baby to be annihilated rather than that he should have to forego intercourse as a means to confirm his identity: *and he makes the baby wish this*, so as to vindicate his egocentricity.

The mother in replying represents Thomas's attempt to speak as it were from his 'female element', to rebut the regressed ego's offer to forego existence if its hungry needs prove too sadistic:

'No. Not for Christ's dazzling bed
Or a nacreous sleep among soft particles and charms
My dear would I change my tears or your iron head.'

Not even were she to be married to Christ would she give up her real material baby. The second line escapes me: Tindall says 'a nacreous sleep etc' is the 'nacreous' peace of Venus. *Nacreous* I think Thomas probably developed from looking up *mother* in

Roget and finding *mother-of-pearl*: I would expect to find the Thesaurus paragraph number '440' somewhere on the work-sheet. For the mother's reply does not have the same conviction and coherence as the baby's declaration. She says first that she would not change her situation for anything: she wants his *iron head* born. But she does not go on to say that there is no other way out *except to be born to life*. She says there is no other way to *escape* life:

'Thrust, my daughter or son, to escape, there is none, none,
                                                            none,
Nor when all ponderous heaven's host of waters breaks.'

Not even a cosmic breaking of the waters can enable you to escape life. When the heaven of interuterine bliss is broached you will experience that life which is an entrapment, a loss of freedom.

Thus the mother, despite Thomas's intention, does not answer the infant by seeking to convince him that (*a*) whatever pain he causes her, she will bear it because she loves him, and her satisfactions will be greater than the pain (*b*) his forfeiture of total dependence will be compensated for by the discovery of the richness of independent existence, towards which she will help him. These would have been the assurances of love: Thomas's 'mother' in the poem can only, in fact, offer the schizoid futility of hate. *She lets her neonate down, as Thomas's mother let him down.*

The infant is *now to awake*, but *husked of gestures and my joy*—that is, shelled of all his capacities to make any more loving gestures towards her, and *deprived of her joy* (which is 'like a cave'—an empty, petrified place in which he was formed)

To the anguish and carrion . . .

This is all life has to offer, the agony of being cast out of the 'cave of joy', and becoming stuff for the sun to breed maggots out of, as if out of a dead dog. He is to become

the infant forever unfree . . .

'freedom' being the total dependence in the womb, and lack of freedom the recognition of real time and space.

O my lost love bounced from a good home . . .

—the good home is the womb: he has been (as Tindall suggests) *bounced* out of it as a rowdy is bounced out of a pub. (The word also picks up 'bump on a spout' and suggests that the father by 'sewing the deep door', by rhythmic intercourse, has both created him and turned him out by bringing on the birth: and the father has won the cockfight.)

> 'The grain that hurries this way from the rim of the grave
> Has a voice and a house, and there and here you must couch
> and cry.'

She can offer him only weakness and crying, necessary pain, because he has *hurriedly* decided to come over the *rim* of the *grave* (= womb, because the dead sibling was buried there, and Thomas's dead identity sprang from there). That is, she tells him that, whatever reluctance he had to be born, because it might hurt *her*, he can only choose to be born—and that is no better than to enter into a living death

> 'Rest beyond choice in the dust-appointed grain'

—your only choice is to accept what is given to those made of particles of dust—

> 'At the breast stored with seas. No return
> Through the waves of the fat streets nor the skeleton's thin
> ways.
> The grave and my calm body are shut to your coming as stone,
> And the endless beginning of prodigies suffers open.'

'The breast stored with seas' suggests a massive Thalassal thirst: sea water is salt and bitter, and even a thirst so great will never be slaked. He can never return through the waves of muscles which thrust him through her birth canal in the fat belly, nor back through the pelvic opening. The grave (= womb) is now closed. Her body is shut to his returning, as Eden is closed to man.

But there is an ambiguity here, which suggests that between his thrusting *iron head* and his *coming* her body was *shut*—so that the birth was terribly difficult. The 'endless beginning of prodigies suffers' her womb to open, stone though it is. Prodigies are always appearing by the force of life: there are continual beginnings. These *suffer* the women to *open* their bodies (perhaps there is an echo here of 'suffer the little children to come unto me', invoked ironically). The *opening* is *suffering*: the line is bitter, because birth is a loss of freedom.

The poem is a key one, for it shows that Thomas's female element, which he projects over the mother here, can only be supposed by him to be *reluctant to open*: reluctant to create. He sees birth as a failure to escape from life. He is able to offer the baby nothing but anguish, lack of freedom, prodigious thirst, and carrion mortality. In the dialogue he shows the regressed libidinal ego as preferring ultimate regression into non-existence to becoming involved either in hurting the mother or in the parental sexual intercourse. All the alternatives in the poem are futile; all equally anguished. Each voice speaks out of hunger or primitive hate: and the total effect of the dialogue is not to overcome that hate, but to become only reconciled to a schizoid sense of nothingness and alienation.

Can it be said (with Tindall) that the 'last line of suffering cries joy; for life is "endless beginning" and miracle? Joyous, ultimate "open" counteracts desperate "shut" in the penultimate line as endless beginning contradicts inevitable end' (*Reader's Guide*, p. 186). Surely, only by sentimentalising Dylan Thomas, who expresses here merely his conviction that to be born is to be chained to a living death 'for as long as forever is'.

10
Many Sounding Minded

The analysis of each poem in the light of the 'schizoid diagnosis' becomes so complex that to explore all Thomas's poems thus would obviously become too ponderous. The reader must be left to explore the rest of Thomas's poems himself, in the light of my approach, and to ask himself whether it makes sense—or makes that non-sense which has its own dissociated significance, once we know the psychopathological patterns.

How the regressed libidinal ego within and the 'other' sibling, unborn, become confused may be found in the earlier and most chaotic poems. In *I see the boys of summer* (p. 1) the boys are surely these two unborn entities hiding in the dark, who 'lay the gold tithings barren'—that is, who set no store by life's supposed riches, but rather 'freeze the soils'? They are 'curdless' and 'sour the boiling honey'.

> The jacks of frost they finger in the hives;
> There in the sun the frigid threads
> Of doubt and dark they feed their nerves;
> The signal moon is zero in their voids.

This kind of stanza obviously influenced Sylvia Plath immensely: the moon here is the mother who 'signalled' nothing in terms of her function as mirror: so, the identities of the boys are consequently 'zero in their voids' and 'ruin'.[1] Even in the hive, even in the sun, all they can find is doubt, dark and 'frigid threads'.

Even in the womb the splits and divisions of normal 'season' came, but meant only violent dissociation:

---

[1] Cf. 'I pick the words so thoroughly of their live associations': the line is as dead and sterile as a line could be: *signal* is a deadly gesturing code instead of a shining face: *zero* is a cipher, a nought, saying nothing to their vacant and empty identities.

> I see the summer children in their mothers
> Split up the brawned womb's weathers . . .

The 'boys' still in the womb can only act by 'seedy shifting'. Their pretences and shams (*shifts*) are made necessary by their origins (*seeds*). So they can only establish a make*shift* identity—a scarecrow: what is erected is only a straw self:

> . . . from the planted womb the man of straw.

Like the regressed libidinal ego, they threaten sabotage:

> We are the dark deniers, let us summon
> Death from a summer woman,
> A muscling life from lovers in their cramp . . .

—even love seems but a cold and mechanical 'muscling life' (cf. 'the rub of love').

The *poles* in the poem are not, I think, only phalluses and flags, but polarities (in the sense of being 'poles apart'). So in the last verse we have an expression of black and petrified futility:

> I see you boys of summer in your ruin.
> Man in his maggot's barren.
> And boys are full and foreign in the pouch.
> I am the man your father was.
> We are the sons of flint and pitch.
> O see the poles are kissing as they cross.

This is as if addressed by one 'boy' within the self to another. The various boys ('boily boys', 'I know that boy'—one remembers the phrases Thomas is reported to have used about the 'boys' in himself) are 'men of straw' not least in summer, in manhood. Man is barren because his phallus is like a living thing of death: the boys in their maturity of fruition are full of 'bad stuff' (foreign *body* as it were). He is the man his father was—with all his faults and barrenness (as a failed poet): he is male element fragmentary. He is father of all his own boys in his personality. They are all sons of the petrified ('flint') and black depersonalised emptiness ('pitch') of schizoid experience. The poles of potentiality, the 'poles of promise' are 'kissing as they cross'—that is, loving their own capacity to 'set no store by harvest', to be 'dark deniers'— to bring everything to cross-purposes, to cross him at every turn. The false system is enclosed in the death circuit of its own *flint* and *pitch*.

Their self-crucifixion has already been hinted at:

> In spring we cross our foreheads with the holly.
> Heigh ho the blood and berry,
> And nail the merry squires to the trees . . .

The conclusion is that the 'dark deniers' of the self *love* the barrenness of identity which they bring about.

> We are the sons of flint and pitch.
> O see the poles are kissing as they cross.

This poem thus virtually states at the beginning of Thomas's career the same predicament of being enclosed in the 'sad sack of myself' as does his poignantly self-revealing letter to Marguerite Caetani at the end (see p. 141).

In *A process in the weather of the heart* (p. 6) again birth is death:

> the womb
> Drives in a death as life leaks out.

The feeling of deadness has been 'driven' into him by false 'doing' and 'being done to': emerging from the (psychic) womb he feels to be a loss of inner contents, and his not-good-enough nurture has been an emptying:

> The seed that makes a forest of the loin
> Forks half its fruit; and half drops down,
> Slow in a sleeping wind . . .

The fruit that comes from human loins seems half dead (because half Thomas is dead sibling):

> The quick and dead
> Move like two ghosts before the eye.

> A process in the weather of the world
> Turns ghost to ghost; each mothered child
> Sits in their double shade.

To Thomas mothering feels like something you share with a ghost: identities merge.

> A process blows the moon into the sun . . .

There is no feeling of belonging in one's own body: the skin feels empty:

> Pulls down the shabby curtains of the skin;
> And the heart gives up its dead.

In *The force that through the green fuse drives the flower* (p. 9) therefore, the life force is a mechanical process (as suggested by

the word 'fuse') which disrupts rather than fulfils. The life-force
is so hungry that it
                dries the mouthing streams . . .
and turns his blood to wax.

    The schizoid individual, with his feeling of emptiness, and of
not being alive, sometimes can only feel alive because he reacts:
        He holds the wire from this box of nerves . . .
        He pulls the chain, the cistern moves.
                      (*My hero bares his nerves*, p. 10)
Reaction by others is distant and impersonal:
        Where once the waters of your face
        Spun to my screws, your dry ghost blows . . .
          (*Where once the waters of your face*, p. 11)
Contact, especially sexual contact, is repulsive because full of
fear: this is expressed in *If I were tickled by the rub of love* (p. 12)—
in which love feels cold, mechanical and dead. The reason lies in
Thomas's horror of conception and birth: the baby here (as elsewhere) is the 'plum':[2]
        Shall it be male or female? say the cells,
        And drop the plum like fire from the flesh.
        If I were tickled by the hatching hair,
        The winging bone that sprouted in the heels,
        The itch of man upon the baby's thigh,
        I would not fear the gallows nor the axe
        Nor the crossed sticks of war . . .
The content is heavily disguised: but it is a horror of the capacity
for the female sexual organ to 'hatch', to produce new life that
shall fly like Mercury or Apollo or Eros, and possibly become *a
man with a regressed ego like himself* whose identity is based upon
hate, and who feels deathly. So, love brings for him the threat of
gallows, *axe* and *war*.

    He cannot know what makes him link love with hate and
death:
      And what's the rub? Death's feather on the nerve?
Death's feather is that which (like Lear's) indicates that there is
no breath: and the slight blow (cf. 'You could have knocked me
down with a feather') which is all that is needed to end our lives.
      Your mouth, my love, the thistle in the kiss?

---

[2] Visually, the father's glans internalised by the mother.

—the thistle is the reminder in a kiss of the mouth-hunger that expresses a sense of bitterness and pain, as if one had been fed only on thistles in a wilderness.

My Jack of Christ born thorny on the tree?

Is it that my 'other' who died in the womb (since he was born dead or resurrected after death) is Christ? Or is it because I am Christ, who became that dead one resurrected?

The words of death are dryer than his stiff . . .

His words, because he 'kills the life in them' are dead and cannot tell him: the words of a dead self are less full of meaning than a corpse. He can only go back to experience:

Man be my metaphor.

He will make a desperate gesture at finding his answers, by studying human nature.

Thomas's early poems go over the subject of his own birth again and again.

The plum my mother picked matured slowly,
The boy she dropped from darkness at her side
Into the sided lap of light grew strong . . .

The poem from which these lines come is called *From love's first fever to her plague* (p. 20) and is an investigation into how it could be that since the time when 'All world was one' in the infant mansion of intrauterine existence, *fever* has turned to *plague*. The last stanza approaches the dissociation of being 'double' in a 'two-framed globe':

One womb, one mind, spewed out the matter,
One breast gave suck the fever's issue;
From the divorcing sky I learnt the double,
The two-framed globe that spun into a score;
A million minds gave suck to such a bud
As forks my eye;
Youth did condense; the tears of spring
Dissolved in summer and the hundred seasons;
One sun, one manna, warmed and fed.

The integration he sought was not to be achieved by pronouncing it to be achieved by 'one manna': a 'hundred seasons' (twenty-five years) had only dissolved the identity into a million, a score—his identity feels like Sylvia Plath's swarm of bees. But the origin of it all is here indicated, in the sense of being split into two, although he knows in a way he is one creature who has been given suck by the one breast, and brought up by the same 'mind' from the same womb.

This dissociation of the schizoid identity he links with his own language of chaotic false systems:

> And from the first declension of the flesh
> I learnt man's tongue, to twist the shapes of thoughts
> Into the stony idiom of the brain,
> To shade and knit anew the patch of words
> Left by the dead who, in their moonless acre,
> Needs no word's warmth.

His brain feels petrified: words belong to the dead who are not even moonlit. To be wordless is to die: the words we inherit from the dead are full of death—and perhaps this is why, confusing words with the people who spoke them, like the Abipones,[3] Thomas sought to make his words have meanings for his purposes alone, rather than bring with them their own rich associations. This would explain in part his impulse to take the life out of them.

> The root of tongues ends in a spentout cancer,
> That but a name, where maggots have their X.

> I learnt the verbs of will, and had my secret;
> The code of night tapped on my tongue:
> What had been one was many sounding minded.

His language is mostly *many sounding minded*—a language of many 'systems' which sounds as if he had many minds, or a multitude of selves sounding like a single-minded person. By this *code of night* he preserves himself from the *maggots*, who make their impersonal cross where a self-aware articulate identity should be. Here Thomas quite explicitly refers to the strategy R. D. Laing describes in discussing the self-protecting codes of his schizophrenic Julie (see above, pp. 93 ff.). Talking to him originates in a *spentout cancer* at most, and expression represents a name attached to an identity where the existing self has been crossed out by maggots: to talk, to be named, to be literate and clear is to expose oneself to obliteration.

---

[3] Among the Abipones any word or part of a word associated with anyone who has died is immediately dropped from the language. See Hannah Segal discussed in my *Human Hope and the Death Instinct*.

Yet at the same time, the self strives to burst out of the bonds:
but as in *My world is pyramid* (p. 30):

> The fellow halves that, cloven as they swivel
> On casting tides, are tangled in the shells,
> Bearding the unborn devil . . .

The split elements of the self are bound in their 'strategies of
survival'. The chaotic language 'binds' both the 'unborn devil'
but also 'my angel hood'. There is a clue somewhere to the agony:

> Who blows death's feather? What colour is glory?
> I blow the stammel feather in the vein.

But Thomas's search itself is bedevilled by mechanical methods,
for the strange *stammel* was quite patently found by looking up
434 *Redness* in Roget! Yet there is a genuine agony in the account
of his predicament in the last lines:

> My clay unsuckled and my salt unborn,
> The secret child, I shift about the sea
> Dry in the half-tracked thigh.

—the meaning of which is by now surely obvious?

I I
'Sharp in my second death'

The less obscure poems by Dylan Thomas are also 'illuminated' by the 'schizoid diagnosis' I have tried to employ in this study. Often, for instance, when he seems to be identifying with Christ we can read the poem as if he were writing about himself and the 'other'—the dead sibling with whom his mother confused him. The effect of this theory when we come to read such poems as the sequence *Vision and Prayer* (p. 137) is startling. This series of lozenges and Easter wings is generally supposed to be a series of Christian poems, and perhaps it can be read as such—though we must allow, if we do read it in such a way, for a most idiosyncratic concern to vie with Christ, and to become Him.

Even to sympathetic critics of Thomas, there seems to be another meaning here apart from the devotional one which they cannot quite fathom. William York Tindall says that 'religion serves as a metaphor for something else—something secular which, feeling holy, demands holy metaphor: secular enlightenment, the birth of a child, the making of a poem' (*Reader's Guide*, p. 250). The shapes of the poems are felt to be significant, too. Tindall notes how, 'by shape a diamond represents the womb'. The crucial difficulty of the sequence is the question, 'Who are you?'—answered, as Tindall points out, in the second half of the diamond by 'the wild Child', whose identity (he says) is our problem; 'the unbaptised or nameless child' is identified with the poem. 'Rebirth is as frightful to a poet as birth to a child,' Tindall adds, with unusual relevance.

The poem is obviously in some way about resurrection—ending in Easter wings. Lazarus is mentioned. But at the end of Tindall's interpretation—who is really wiser? Tindall makes another relevant indication when he mentions *Waiting for Godot*: *Vision and Prayer* is a schizoid poem about birth, as *Waiting for Godot* is a schizoid play about the futility of ever being born.

The poem seems to me to make sense if we read it as being addressed to the previous sibling who died in Dylan Thomas's mother's womb and with whom he came to feel identified because of the way his mother handled him. Because of this strange confusion he had never found himself: the clue is to become the other, the changeling. The shapes of the poems are attempts to effect the identification and discovery of the self by talisman: the poems are an attempt *to be* by discovering the regressed ego which is locked up with the 'other' unbaptised identity, and to bring it to birth, by a process which requires such a regression to a 'point' (with no dimension) that it is a death.

The two shapes seem to me symbolic of the problem of 'twin' identity. Thomas seeks to become himself by becoming the 'other'. In the first series the two triangles which form the diamond have their apexes at opposite poles:

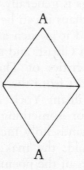

In the Easter wings the apexes are joined ('O see the poles are kissing as they cross')

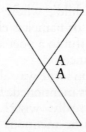

—a symbol of unification of all the converging impulses of being. This feeling for the point at which the identity focuses, by contrast with the diffuseness represented by the spreading wings of the triangles, was probably inspired by Herbert's phrase in his Easter wings

> Then I became
> Most thinne . . .

—tenuous in the identity, because not confirmed by being reflected in Christ. The first sequence ends:

> And I
> Die.

The second ends

> I
> Am found . . .
> . . . lost in the blinding
> One

—i.e. the one who is invisible and who has blinded the identity: but by becoming lost in him I am found in the great light of self-discovery.

The poems then, their shape and theme, parallel Thomas's attempt at self-cure—at rebirth—by alcoholism and suicide. The poem is itself an act of schizoid suicide—a sinking of one self in another, in the attempt to achieve a rebirth of identity—a resurrection. Hence the identification with Christ (= the 'other').

The poems begin

> Who
> Are you
> Who is born
> In the next room
> So loud to my own . . .

The switch of 'near' to 'loud' is characteristic of Thomas: here it picks up the loud of 'bloody a loud room' in '*If my head hurt a hair's foot*'. But the substitution has a point. The poem is about an awareness that 'near' does not convey: the existence of the other is felt as if it is a cry heard from the next room.

The wall is as thin as a wren's bone: the wren is the tiniest of birds and has bones as thin as those of a foetus. The birth is heard in the ear and the sound moves bones there as thin as wren's bones (the wren like the flea is the tiny living self). The room where the birth is happening and is bloody is not a real room: it is a psychic room, unknown to the 'burn and turn' of time. There, no-one bows to baptise him, but the darkness alone blesses the wild child. The 'secret child' is a changeling who exists only in the mother's psychic darkness, or in the 'other half' of the poet's identity (which is 'half-tracked' and consists of 'fellowed halves').

If he lies close to the 'wren bone wall', listening to the moan of the mother, hidden, he may be able to merge with that 'turbulent new born'. He fears he may 'run lost in sudden terror' because he has a 'bonfire in his mouth'—a burning hunger to take in substance for the identity, like a consuming fire, which makes his kiss a 'cauldron'. He seeks to crouch bare in his blazing breast, in

> The woundward flight of the ancient
> Young from the canyons of oblivion!
>
> . . .
>
> The world winding home!

The self of the regressed libidinal ego seeks to leave its 'canyons of oblivion' and fly 'woundward'—as if entering the wound in the side of Christ, but actually flowing into the substance of another: a process full of danger of loss of self:

> And the whole pain
> Flows   open
> And   I
> Die.

The effect is felt in 'the inmost marrow of my heart bone' because the ghost has to be brought up from the ground, so that he can take the full flavour of 'the other' being generated by deadly seed from the predatory phallus of the father:

> From
> The ground
> Like   pollen
> On the black plume
> And the beak of slime . . .

It has been in contemplating the meaning of Christ's birth that

he has come to be able to explore this possibility of rebirth: like
Christ he is one

> ... who learns now the sun and moon
> Of his mother's milk may return
> Before his lips blaze and bloom
> To the birth bloody room
> Behind the wall's wren
> Bone and be dumb
> And the womb
> That bore
> For
> All men
> The adored
> Infant light or
> The dazzling prison
> Yawn to his upcoming...

The poem obliquely refers to the line:

> 'Lo! He abhors not the Virgin's womb':

—Thomas for once is able to contemplate birth without horror:
so he is able to feel he has come

> To know all
> Places
> Ways
> Mazes
> Passages
> Quarters and graves
> Of the endless fall.
> Now common lazarus
> Of the chanting sleepers prays
> Never to awake and arise
> For the country of death is the heart's size

He discovers that his predicament is a universal one: it is the
'endless fall', the continually renewed mortality and ego-weakness
of man. 'The country of death is the heart's size'—the weakness
of identity is something that exists in the bodily life of each man.
He need no longer seek Lazarus-like rebirth, or say of suicide as
Sylvia Plath did, 'I do it so it feels real' (*Lady Lazarus*). There is a

kind of rebirth in the poem, even by a discovery of humility—a
sense that the acceptance of the possibility of total loss of identity
is possible without the identity being overwhelmed:

> In the name of the fatherless
> In the name of the unborn
> And the undesirers
> Of midwiving morning's
> Hands or instruments
> O in the name
> Of no one
> Now or
> No
> One to
> Be I pray
> May the crimson
> Sun spin a grave grey
> And the colour of clay
> Stream upon his martyrdom . . .

There are two significant undercurrents here—of recognising
the actual 'clay' existence of the 'other' that was, and the existence
of himself in clay in consequence. So he escapes temporarily from
'the hidden land' of his confusion with the other:

> . . . In the name of the damned
> I would turn back and run
> To the hidden land
> But the loud sun
> Christens down
> The sky
> I
> Am found.
> O let him
> Scald me and drown
> Me in his world's wound.

It is almost an acceptance of the one integrated self within the one
body. This rebirth still belongs, however, I believe, to manic
assertion despite the evident pains of exploration: for the writer is
still not sure whether it is Christ he is merging with, by entering

into, or whether one self is truly merging with the other. Despite
the proclamation, 'I am found' and the end

> Now I am lost in the blinding
> One. The sun roars at the prayer's end.

—we still feel that even the asserted merging blinds, and that
whatever degree of integration is presumed here, the conclusion
does not ring true, as if of the one true self. Is it possible for the
voyage of the rebirth of the self to be accomplished unaided, if,
as Guntrip says, 'one cannot be anything in a vacuum'? Dylan
Thomas's predicament in this respect is perhaps illuminated by
the remarks quoted by Brinnin:

> . . . Maybe I've always been frightened but didn't know it until
> I couldn't drink when I wanted to . . . I don't know how to
> help myself any more . . . how can anybody help someone who
> can't do that? I've always wanted to be my own psychiatrist,
> just as I've always wanted everybody to be their own doctor
> and father. (*Dylan Thomas in America*, p. 253)

We can, I believe, hear Thomas's true self in another poem,
which seems to express his sense of the falsity of the conformist
self, and yet his fear of it:

> I have longed to move away
> From the hissing of the spent lie
> And the old terror's continual cry
> Growing more terrible as the day
> Goes over the hill into the deep sea . . .
> (*I have longed to move away*, p. 64)

He seeks to reject

> . . . the repetition of salutes,
> For there are ghosts in the air
> And ghostly echoes on paper . . .

—surely referring to what Guntrip calls 'the meaningless succession of mere activities performed to keep oneself in being', against
the ghosts that threaten annihilation? Thomas's behaviour in
America was mostly a kind of frenetic false-solution behaviour, in
the schizoid ethos of the American literary world. (The inversion
of values in that world is evident when Brinnin relates how
Caitlin Thomas tried to worm out of him information about
Thomas's adulteries. He merely regards this as bad manners on
her part, and a troublesome way to behave, to someone who was

trying to be her friend. He fails altogether to see the emotional realities behind such anguished infidelity.) Thomas's compulsive attachment to the very thing that threatened his life, however, is evident in the next lines:

I have longed to move away but am afraid;
Some life, yet unspent, might explode
Out of the old lie burning on the ground,
And, crackling into the air, leave me half-blind . . .

The poem ends by declaring that he would not 'care to die' by 'half convention and half lie'—that is, by gestures and signs which, because they were mechanical ways of conforming and meaning, seemed meaningless ('The parting of hat from hair', 'pursed lips at the receiver'[1]).

The poem expresses the nightmare of being unable to move away from the false constructs of which one would gladly be rid. Behind the 'spent lie' is the 'old terror': yet he believes he will die neither by his night fears nor by his false-self postures—but in some way which will be more 'real'. He does not want to die by any half-truths—and we see him in the biographical sketch of the end of his life bringing death on himself by wild drinking bouts, as if these demonstrated that he 'was man enough' to do the real thing and destroy himself by no half-measures. There is another nothingness in the background, which is Lear's—and death's feather is that which Lear holds under Cordelia's nose. There is in it a hope that 'This feather stirs! She lives!'

But Lear is deluded. 'You can knock me down with a feather' is true, if we say it to death, and this Dylan Thomas also sees, with insight. Neither his abnormal fears of annihilation nor the rituals by which he combats these have anything to do with his real mortality, realisation of which he seeks in truth, rejecting 'half convention and half lie': but his pursuit of that whole truth, because of its schizoid logic, killed him.

[1] Cf. Camus, 'At certain moments of lucidity the mechanical aspect of [men's] gestures, their meaningless pantomime makes silly everything that surrounds them. A man is talking on the telephone behind a glass partition; you cannot hear him, but you see his incomprehensible dumb show: you wonder why he is alive . . . this . . . is also the absurd', *The Myth of Sisyphus.*

12
An Inability to Mourn

Sylvia Plath speaks in *The Bell Jar* of how her heroine was never really happy after about the age of nine. Many of Thomas's poems are expressions of nostalgia for pre-puberty, before the problems of dissociated identity made life intolerable. Some of his best poems reflect nostalgia for this stage, and even for an earlier time while his mother still managed to maintain him in a state of not being disillusioned—so that he could continue to impose inner on outer reality in the infantile way, and control it by magic. The inability to deal with experience beyond childhood is manifest in the famous poem *A Refusal to Mourn the Death, by Fire, of a Child in London* (p. 101) which could be called *An Inability to Mourn*. The last line here needs to be taken into account first:

After the first death, there is no other.

Thomas is virtually saying that he himself has been born dead. He has had his first death: he is dead. So for him there is no other death, nor can he conceive of the death of another person. The dead child is merely like himself now, the 'first dead'—dead from the beginning:

Deep with the first dead lies London's daughter,
Robed in the long friends . . .

—i.e. the oblivion which has for long been his companion:

. The grains beyond age, the dark veins of her mother . . .

Though the death of the child has struck him forcibly, he cannot feel it—he cannot conceive of it as being anything different from what he feels, having had his own identity darkened by 'the dark veins' of the mother. So, he cannot mourn her.

Elder Olson noticed in this poem its disturbing failure to achieve sufficient of the sense of the child's independent existence to express true pity.

Moved by grief for a burned child (in *A Refusal to Mourn*), nobly and powerfully moved as he is, he does not suffer imaginatively the experience of the child, does not share in it in the least: he sees the pain and the horror from without, and the resolution he reaches is for him, not the child. This curiously external view is revealed in one of his least successful poems: the death of a hundred year old man provides him matter for a string of fantastic conceits, and the poem is really unintelligible, not because it is particularly obscure, but because the emotion he exhibits is impossible to relate to any emotion that the event, however conceived, conceived if you will from the point of view of a man from Mars, could have aroused in us. I have remarked, indeed argued, that Thomas's imagination could transport him anywhere, through all space and all time: but it is also true that, wherever it takes him, he sees nothing but himself. (*Dylan Thomas*, p. 23)

The horror behind *A Refusal* is felt by Thomas because he cannot find her reality sufficiently (though he strives to do so) to mourn her. He cannot find her reality because he cannot find his own, me to not me. He cannot, he virtually says, mourn her until he has been reborn, and the rebirth is stated in characteristic terms, suggestive of schizoid suicide and its symbolism:

> And I must enter again the round
> Zion of the water bead
> And the synagogue of the ear of corn . . .

—Zion is the promised land. The ear of corn is its maturity—and an end which is a beginning. A synagogue is a place where the chosen people celebrate: their religion is that of Jaweh, belonging to the Old Testament, before Christ's birth and resurrection. Thomas's 'entering' is therefore expressed in such a way as to have all promise before it; yet it is also an end, and comes with the end of the world:

> Fathering and all humbling darkness
> Tells with silence the last light breaking
> And the still hour
> Is come of the sea tumbling in harness . . .

Did Thomas believe in an after life in which he would be able to mourn her? The question is perhaps better approached in a more complex way.

Dylan Thomas presumably had in mind here St Paul's *Epistle to the Corinthians* (I.15.35):

But some man will say, How are the dead raised up? and with what body do they come?

Thou fool, that which thou sowest is not quickened, except it die;

And that which thou sowest, thou sowest not that body that shall be, but bare grain, it may chance of wheat, or of some other grain . . .

He says that he cannot mourn the child until he becomes a grain which shall die and grow: he cannot mourn her until he is resurrected from his living death as *a person capable of mourning*. He can only react to her death with a poignant sense of not being able to mourn her: he can only mourn for himself, because he is only aware of the *me*. She belongs to the not-me, and until he is (psychically) reborn he cannot go out to her, or symbolise in the phantasy world which mourning is (i.e. reparation of one's inner world threatened by hate and guilt as a result of grief). His outer reality is one on which he has imposed his own inner reality. The horror comes when an element of outer reality impinges and reveals undeniably that outer reality is apart, uncontrollable. The death of a child in the outer world is not a rebirth, such as he believes the death of himself likely to be. Until he is dead and reborn he cannot understand her death as being anything but that. He cannot recognise it: so he will leave grieving until then. To pretend to mourn before he has this cosmic rebirth would be to 'murder The mankind of her going' with mere breath; an elegy would be 'blasphemy', because he cannot feel grief.

In one way, thus, the poem is an expression of a massive humility: in another it is a gesture expressing what he cannot feel or do—he cannot find that she is any more dead than he is, and so he cannot mourn her. She has merely 'died out of childhood' as he really wishes to. So she goes 'unmourned' by a universe felt to be indifferent, because he cannot mourn for her. After the first death, which he has already experienced, like hers, there is no other—and so there is no need to mourn. In fact the poem is a manic denial of the reality of death, rather than its acceptance.

The same mixture of the apprehension of death and its magical denial is found in *After the funeral* (p. 87), of which Thomas wrote:

This is the only one I have written that is, directly, about the life and death of one particular human being I knew—and not about the very many lives and deaths whether seen, as in my first poems, *in the tumultuous world of my own being.* (See *Letters to Vernon Watkins,* pp. 39–40, 57–8, my italics)

Yet, as I pointed out in *Llareggub Revisited,* the posture of the piece is one which draws attention to himself rather than the dead woman. As I said then, it draws from us the kind of protest Hamlet makes at Laertes' extravagant posture: 'Who is this whose grief can bear such an emphasis?'

> I stand, for this memorial's sake, alone
> In the snivelling hours with dead, humped Ann

> But I, Ann's bard on a raised hearth, call all
> The seas to service that her wood-tongued virtue
> Babble like a bellbuoy . . .

> Storm me forever over her grave . . .

The poem is an attempt to say something more than others say at the funeral—they 'mule praise' with

> Windshake of sailshaped ears . . .

There is an attempt to feel real about her death and to forfeit the extravagant gestures which stand in place of real feeling:

> (Though this for her is a monstrous image blindly
> Magnified out of praise; her death was a still drop;
> She would not have me sinking in the holy
> Flood of her heart's fame; she would lie dumb and deep
> And need no druid of her broken body)

He goes on, however, as Hamlet does, to out-Laertes Laertes. The momentary glimpse of the reality turns to incantation:

> Storm me forever over her grave until
> The stuffed lung of the fox twitch and cry Love

and, as I noted in my earlier book, the main impulse of the poem is to seek to make out that death does not really exist: 'the stuffed fox, as a child will self-protectingly believe, can come to life, if sufficient clamour is made'.

This failure to become able to mourn was at one with the failure to be able to find reality, because of the failure to find substance in inner reality. In *Adventures in the Skin Trade* a character says, 'O God make me feel something—I must be impotent'. A letter written at the time of Ann Jones's death reveals Dylan Thomas's horrifying incapacity to feel. His facetiousness about the grim agony of the woman who had been so affectionate to him is grisly in its dissociated coldness:

As I am writing, a telegram arrives. Mother's sister, who is in the Carmarthen Infirmary suffering from cancer of the womb, is dying. There is much lamentation in the family and Mother leaves. The old aunt will be dead by the time she arrives. This is a well-worn incident in fiction, and one that has happened time after time in real life. The odour of death stinks through a thousand books and a thousand homes. I have rarely encountered it (apart from journalistic enquiries), and find it rather pleasant. It lends a little welcome melodrama to the drawing-room tragi-comedy of my most uneventful life. After Mother's departure I am left alone in the house, feeling slightly theatrical. Telegrams, dying aunts, cancer, especially of such a private part as the womb, distraught mothers and unpremeditated train journeys, come rarely. They must be savoured properly and in the right spirit. (*Letters*, p. 11)

Here we have the schizoid sense of looking on at events, as though not involved in them, a detachment which, with its air of precious relish, is the tone of a hebephrenic giggle. Thomas speaks of his aunt's kindness with the same brutal detachment: the farm he refers to here is Fern Hill!

Many summer weeks I spent happily with the cancered aunt on her insanitary farm. She loved me quite inordinately, gave me sweets and money, though she could little afford it, petted, patted, and spoiled me. She writes—is it, I wonder, a past tense yet—regularly. Her postscripts are endearing. She still loves— or loved—me, though I don't know why . . . (ibid.)

There is a startling capacity to detach style from content—the aesthete's self-protecting enclosure in his own cultivated niceties of expression. At the same time we can perhaps allow that Thomas was only nineteen, was obviously concerned to make a good impression on his reader, and that in this hysterical posture itself there is a mechanism of self-defence at work. As he goes on he at least becomes aware that he is revealing a disturbing inability to mourn—and that the reason is his internal complex of false systems, 'the thousand contradictory devils':

And now she is dying, or dead, and you will pardon the theatrical writing. Allow me my moment of drama.

But the foul thing is I feel utterly unmoved, apart, as I said, from the pleasant death-reek at my negroid nostrils. I haven't really the faintest interest in her or her womb. She is dying. She is dead. She is alive. It is all the same thing. I shall miss her bi-annual postal orders. And yet I like—liked her. She loves—loved—me. Am I, he said with the diarist's unctuous, egotistic preoccupation with his own blasted psychological reactions to his own trivial affairs, callous and nasty? Should I weep? Should I pity the old thing? For a moment I feel I should. There must be something lacking in me. I don't feel worried, or hardly ever, about other people. It's self, self, all the time. I'm rarely interested in other people's emotions, except those of my paste-board characters. I prefer (this is one of the thousand contra-dictory devils speaking) style to life, my own reactions to emotions rather than the emotions themselves. Is this, he pondered, a lack of soul? (*Letters*, pp. 11–12)

There was never a clearer admission of the schizoid predicament—schizoid 'diminution of affect'—of the fear of emotion, and the internal dissociation, a void instead of a whole feeling self. The poem for Ann is therefore in the light of this something of a fake, an attempt to feel feelings of which he was incapable.

On the other hand, there are times when very deep feeling breaks through and forces great poignancy from Dylan Thomas, even from the depths of his predicament. This is true, I believe, of *Do not go gentle into that good night* (p. 116). In one sense, with its alliterative 'g's, and its incantatory structure, it is an attempt to magick death away, by ritualistic chant. The poem has a contrived air about its structure—and its conceits seem even cumbersome. Yet even so, there is a certain deeply moving quality about its attempts to transcend the conventional elegiac. Thomas's father, as we have seen, wanted Dylan to be the great poet he had never become himself. The main energy of the poem is directed at this failure of the father to achieve greatness. His words have 'forked no lightning' and his frail deeds have not 'danced in a green bay'. The green bay is both the happy seaside scene of lively pleasure,

but also the green bay which crowns poetic achievement, surely?
Wild men catch the sun and sing it in its flight—but learn too late
that they have merely helped it on its way: but it does not seem
that Thomas's father was one of these who offered Marvell's kind
of defiance in the face of mortality and time:

> ... though we cannot make our sun
> Stand still, yet we will make him run ...

He was not one of the wild men of passionate expression. The
poet writes as if he feels that his father saw with 'blinding sight'
in the end that even such blind eyes as his could have 'blazed like
meteors' and have been 'gay', but never did.

The fact that the father is a nonentity and is going to his death
in inconspicuous quietude is what seems terrible to the poet. The
old man should be raging against being swept into nothingness:
but he has never achieved any big gesture of meaning which can
stand against that darkness. He does not even seek to be defiant
now, but goes off gently. He does not, like Mahler, tear out pages
from books of philosophy and hold them desperately before his
eyes, in a search for some ultimate meaning. If he were really wise
he would rage against death *because* his words had 'forked no
lightning': but he does not, and so he was not wise, and forked no
lightning either.

The father is on the 'sad height' of death and the poet begs him
to rage and have 'fierce tears', for his son's benefit. In some way
he feels that the father's complacence about death threatens him
with nothingness, too. If only his father were to bless him, or even
curse him! But he dies like one who deserves neither praise nor
blame, and so makes Thomas feel like one of those suspended
between heaven and damnation. So, the poem conveys the distress of one who has striven all his life to make up for the father's
mediocrity, but now feels ultimately threatened by a failure to
wring meaning from chaos and emptiness. The word 'gentle' has
beneath it a fierce hatred, a wish that the father should suffer more,
because otherwise he is not yielding sufficient spiritual substance
for his son, but betraying him by his inadequacy.

In *Do not go gentle* death seems more real than anywhere else
in Dylan Thomas. By contrast the assertion in *And death shall have
no dominion* (p. 68) that it is possible to triumph over death seems
trivial. The rhythm is too facile:

> Though they sink through the sea they shall rise again . . .
> Split all ends up they shan't crack . . .

The bouncy lines remind one of the ballad about Flossie Snail and Johnnie Crack from *Under Milk Wood*, while the vision of rebirth after death, much as it might express a schizoid belief in death-as-rebirth, is given in childish terms:

> Though they go mad they shall be sane . . .
> Though they be mad and dead as nails
> Heads of the characters hammer through daisies . . .

This poem is inadequate because it seems to belong to a phase in which it is impossible for the child to conceive of death as an objective phenomenon. As we shall see, it is when Dylan Thomas experiences the inevitability of the death of this childhood view that he produces his finest poems.

13
The Other Air

As we should expect in the work of a writer who feels so intensely that his 'regressed libidinal ego' has never been born, a large number of Thomas's poems are about birth and rebirth, a fact which we can now also associate with the symbolism of schizoid suicide. Many are about *birthdays*, and we have many reflections on years, decades and anniversaries—*Twenty-four years*, *Poem in October*, *Once below a time*, *Poem on his birthday*. Frequently they begin in a 'once upon a time' mode:

It was my thirtieth year to heaven . . .

When I was a windy boy and a bit . . .

Now as I was young and easy under the apple boughs . . .

Once below a time . . .

In a sense Thomas remained in a state of perplexity about many problems which the child is engaged with—and most adults feel they have solved.

D. W. Winnicott postulates three stages of developmental process in the infant '(1) integration (2) personalization (3) the appreciation of time and space and other properties of reality—in short, realization'. Winnicott points out that over such matters we tend to take a great deal for granted—and forget that it 'had a beginning and a condition out of which it developed'. If we do become aware of this, we can more easily appreciate that for children and for some adults the sense of time and place remains rudimentary. Winnicott quotes a boy of nine who loved playing with Ann, aged two, and was actively interested in the expected new baby. He said, 'When the new baby's born, will it be born before Ann?' This shakiness of the sense of time goes, in the

schizoid person, with a whole problem of 'realisation'. As R. D.
Laing notes, in such a person 'phantasy and reality are kept apart'.
The self avoids being related directly to real persons but relates
itself to itself and the objects which it itself posits. *The self can
relate itself with immediacy to an object which is an object of its own
imagination or memory but not to a real person* . . . one feature of
this subterfuge is that the self is able to enjoy a sense of freedom
which it fears it will lose if it abandons itself to the real. This
applies both to perception and action . . .

(*The Divided Self*, p. 91)

We can apply this observation to Dylan Thomas both in the
realms of love, and of time: to him the recognition of his love-
object as a real person meant a loss of freedom. To him the recognition of place and time meant a loss of freedom. Both belong to
the weakness of his completion of the processes of realization. As
Laing points out we all have 'temporary states of dissociation' and
feelings of 'this is not happening to me', in crises and disasters. We
all have schizoid problems of identity: therefore we can respond
to such states when they are expressed acutely by someone like
Thomas who has them severely.

In his birthday poems Thomas is often seeking to 'marvel' time
away, to claim his freedom of dissociation. The world is 'his'
world—it is *him*.

My birthday began with the water-
Birds and the birds of the winged trees flying my name
Above the farms . . .

(*Poem in October*, p. 102)

The rain is a 'shower of all my days': but this pathetic fallacy cannot be wholly sustained. He finds freedom and immediacy in
relating to objects which he 'posits'. But this is a 'subterfuge', and
reality inevitably breaks in:

. . . I wandered and listened
To the rain wringing
Wind blow cold . . .

'The self can relate itself with immediacy to an object which is
an object of its own imagination':

But all the gardens
Of spring and summer were blooming in the tall tales
Beyond the border and under the lark full cloud.

The tall tales of imagination can make him relate himself to an imaginary world as object: but as he grows older this cannot be sustained.

> There could I marvel
> My birthday
> Away but the weather turned around . . .

> It turned away from the blithe country . . .

He persists in invention, claiming his schizoid 'freedom' by subterfuge. He phantasies the 'other' air:

> And down the other air and the blue altered sky
> Streamed again a wonder of summer
> With apples
> Pears and red currants
> And I saw in the turning so clearly a child's
> Forgotten mornings when he walked with his mother
> Through the parables
> Of sun light
> And the legends of the green chapels.

Here the free imagination, memory, and the reality of the present merge, enabling him to perceive what he apperceives. He is able to see the difference between the present and the nostalgia for what he used to see, which he places as legend and parable. He becomes a child again, but in such a way as to find and place childhood. It is not that he is trying to maintain the child's 'freedom' (the weather has turned round too much for that). He finds

> the true
> Joy of the long dead child . . .

For this reason, this is a deeply moving poem, in which Thomas finds both himself as a man of thirty and sees in real time the child self of long ago.

> And the twice told fields of infancy
> That his tears burned my cheeks and his heart moved in mine.

—the boy *is* in him: and so

> . . . the mystery
> Sang alive
> Still in the water and singingbirds.

—the impulse to over-indulge in nostalgia is resisted again:

> And there could I marvel my birthday.
> Away but the weather turned around .

He recognises where he is now:

> It was my thirtieth
> Year to heaven stood there then in the summer noon
> Though the town below lay leaved with October blood.

The red leaves of October are still a sign of death to him (a loss of blood): time is a loss of freedom. But in *Poem in October* he feels time as real: he 'stood there then'. For a schizoid individual this is a great achievement; and we sense this in the controlled rhythm of the poem. We feel it is profoundly meant, and that dissociation has been overcome. The risks are bravely faced: for once chaos is escaped and the true self is found—with all its attendant anguish and dangers of annihilation.

> O may my heart's truth
> Still be sung
> On this high hill in a year's turning.

Such a poem seems to represent a temporary experience of 'losing one's own individual isolated self-hood' which Laing says can be tolerated in certain circumstances by the schizoid individual without too much anxiety: 'It may be possible to lose oneself . . . in quasi-mystical experiences when the self feels it is merged with a not-self which may be called "God" but not necessarily' (*The Divided Self*, p. 98). Experiences of this kind enable Thomas to escape from isolation in *Vision and Prayer* and *Poem in October* in different ways. The escape from isolation is an escape from chaos: so these poems are clear and articulate.

Overcoming the predicament of the isolated, dissociated self and becoming clear however brings all the dangers of communicating—and thus the dangers of love. That is, communication opens the possibility of invading others, or being invaded oneself. Thus when a writer like Dylan Thomas is most articulate he encounters the problem of *schizoid guilt*. On this subject Laing writes:

> The final seal on the self-enclosure of the self is applied by its own guilt. In the schizoid individual guilt has the same paradoxical quality about it that was encountered in his omnipotence and impotence, his freedom and slavery, his self being anyone in phantasy and nothing in reality . . . If there is

anything the schizoid individual is likely to believe in, it is his own destructiveness. He is unable to believe that he can fill his own emptiness without reducing what there is to nothing . . .

(op. cit., p. 99)

Laing is here adding his gloss to Fairbairn's 'moral motive' in the schizoid's choice of hate rather than love:

He regards his own love and that of others as being as destructive as hatred. To be loved threatens his self; but his love is equally dangerous to anyone else. His isolation is not entirely for his own self's sake. It is also out of concern for others . . .

Ultimately this fear of damage one might cause by making contact with the world can lead to a withdrawal which may be an aspect of schizoid suicide:

What he may then do is to destroy 'in his mind' the image of anyone or anything he may be in danger of becoming fond of, out of a desire to safeguard that other person or thing in reality from being destroyed. If, then, there is nothing to want, nothing to envy, there may be nothing to love, but there is nothing to be reduced to nothing by him. In the last resort he sets about murdering his 'self', and this is not as easy as cutting one's throat. He descends into a vortex of non-being, but also to preserve being from himself. (ibid., p. 99)

We may find these conflicting impulses in great variety among Dylan Thomas's poems about the self, in time, and in relation to others and the world. There are two major conflicting impulses—one towards not-being, chaos, and self-destruction: one towards integration, articulateness, love and rebirth.

Once below a time (p. 132) is a poem in which he celebrates his disintegration and chaos itself. The word-switch 'below' for 'upon' is not whimsical: it indicates what goes under the mask, in the failure to accept realisation, including time. In its depiction of a self pieced together from fragments we glimpse the disturbing schizoid feeling of being an automaton. (As Sylvia Plath wrote, 'Catgut stitches my fissures . . .' *Poem for a Birthday* in *The Colossus*, p. 87.)

Somewhere inside the 'suit' of identity he has worked for himself is the 'boy of common thread', who is 'quiet as a bone'—insignificant, dead, white, petrified. Somewhere inside it all is the child, the regressed ego, but omnipotent, able to be drowned and

reborn in water—the 'readymade handy water' of phantasy. All
the rest is sham:

> my pinned-around-the-spirit
> Cut-to-measure flesh bit . . .

The self does not feel as though it is in the body (i.e. personalised).
The suit of the self is worked 'for a serial sum On the first of each
hardship . . . paid for, slaved-for . . .'—put together by the
desperate efforts of *doing*. Love has but damaged it:

> In love torn breeches and blistered jacket
> On the snapping rims of the ashpit . . .

—love threatens to eat up and burn the suit of the self itself and
reduce it to ashes.

In disguise he 'descends into a vortex of non-being':

> bushily swanked in bear wig and tails,
> Hopping hot leaved and feathered
> From the kangaroo foot of the earth,
> From the chill, silent centre . . .

But from there he shoots up to astound

> the lubber crust of Wales
> I rocketed to astonish . . .
> The cries of Shabby and Shorten,
> The famous stitch droppers . . .

To make contact with others, otherwise than by astonishing
displays of disguise—false doing to establish a self to the world,
by a collection of false systems—is to risk exposure to those who
would make the suit of the self *shabby*, or who would *shorten* it—
that is, those who would damage one by misunderstanding or by
coercing one into False Self conformity and social 'absurdity'.

He believes that this 'silly suit' even

> deceived, I believed, my maker . . .

Yet he experiences a sense of being pierced by the eyes of the
'idol' who stitched him together ('Thou God seest me')

> I was pierced by the idol tailor's eyes,
> Glared through shark mast . . .

—so that what God sees, with his 'Cold Nansen's beak' is

> The bright pretender, the ridiculous sea dandy
> With dry flesh and earth for adorning and bed.

The vision is one of schizoid guilt, because what the piercing eyes
see is the destructiveness of the disguises 'below' the time. As he

is seen and confirmed what seems most real in the reflection is
his own destructiveness.

O make me a mask (p. 85) is a poem by which he seeks to maintain disguises against threats of being seen and found. He is
seeking to

> block from bare enemies
> The bayonet tongue in this undefended prayerpiece,
> The present mouth, and the sweetly blown trumpet of lies . . .

His poems are part of the disguise against the contact that would
destroy: he clings to the dissociation that will protect against
implosion and

> . . . shield the glistening brain and blunt the examiners . . .

Here there is schizoid guilt at the

> Rape and rebellion in the nurseries of my face . . .

His 'sweetly blown trumpet of lies' is a 'bayonet' of hate, an
oral defence against dangerous communication.

When Thomas writes clearly of his environment as a real one,
as in *Over Sir John's hill* (p. 167), he yet projects much of his inner
world over it—and finds that it contains his own destructiveness.
This poem is thus also a poem of schizoid guilt. Thomas (as
'young Aesop') writes a parable of his own hate, and a dirge for
the hate that is in all natural life.

Recognising the natural world as 'out there' in its own weather,
time-scale and season, is at one with perceiving within it the
objective correlatives of one's own reality—and one's own destructiveness. The hawk is beautiful:

> The hawk on fire hangs still . . .

But it is *on fire* with its natural impulses of being which are to
prey and kill, in order to live:

> he pulls to his claws
> And gallows, up the rays of his eyes the small birds of
> the bay . . .

The sparrows are like children at their 'shrill child's play'—'And
blithely they squawk'. The birds 'swansing'—that is, they utter
their swansong. Then

> The flash the noosed hawk
> Crashes, and slowly the fishing holy heron
> In the river Towy below bows his tilted headstone.

The sparrows unwittingly 'squawk to fiery tyburn': the hawk is the executioner. By 'gallows', 'tyburn' and 'noose' Thomas projects on to the scene the weight of human guilt and punishment: the childlike birds must be being punished—for what? For their own blithe insouciance?

This he cannot answer. He identifies with the priest-like heron that merely inclines its head like an indifferent headstone of a grave: nature merely notes with indifference the deathliness of its own predatory system. The poet studies this ('Man be my metaphor'):

> I open the leaves of the water at a passage
> Of psalms and shadows among the pincered sandcrabs
>   prancing . . .

If there is to be life, there will be death: this truth is stated even in the nursery rhyme:

>   and 'dilly dilly', calls the loft hawk,
> 'Come and be killed,' . . .

In the water he reads Death speaking to him as 'clear as a buoy's bell'. So, he makes the kind of subjective acceptance Job has to make, accepting both the deadly beauty of the hawk and the necessity for his small victims that they must die. Thus he also accepts that the necessity to live in a real world from a real self means exposing oneself to the dangers of one's own destructiveness and the destructiveness in the world:

> All praise of the hawk on fire in hawk-eyed dusk be sung,
> When his viperish fuse hangs looped with flames . . .
>   . . . and blest shall
> Young
> Green chickens of the bay and bushes cluck, 'dilly dilly,
> Come let us die.'

He and the herons can only grieve:

> We grieve as the blithe birds, never again, leave shingle
>   and elm,
> The heron and I . . .

The destructiveness and the beauty, predator and victim, are all part of the music of being real and alive:

It is the heron and I . . .
   . . . tell-tale the knelled
Guilt
Of the led-astray birds whom God, for their breast of
             whistles,
Have mercy on,
God in his whirlwind silence save, who marks the sparrows
   hail,
For their souls' song . . .

    . . . The heron, ankling the scaly
Lowlands of the waves,
Makes all the music; and I who hear the tune of the slow,
Wear-willow river, grave,
Before the lunge of the night, the notes on this time-shaken
Stone for the sake of the souls of the slain birds sailing.

Time here is real: the river is wearing the willows away. The tune
the poet hears is that of the real world in time—generations of
slain birds, and birds newly hatched: each creature following its
natural function. The night about to 'lunge' is itself like destruction: the only saving is in the 'whirlwind silence' of death. Even
in their singing the birds 'hail' the hawk: all one can have in the
face of such recognition of natural cycles, their cruelty, and the
destructiveness in them is compassion, and an awareness of the
'tune': the notes that float out across the water, from the sound of
the river, the words of the poet.

Why are the birds guilty? Why are they *led-astray*? The only
answer here is that they were in their 'shrill child's play' unaware
of the nature of reality: Thomas himself even recognises here the
self-delusion in *not* coming to terms with one's own destructiveness—and this poem is a full and marvellous tasting of the problem
of destructiveness in all life, and one's essential 'nothingness'. And
he is aware of the problem of hate in oneself, and of the hate in the
magic desire of reality, associated with the problem of sustaining
meaning in the face of death.

Fern Hill (p. 159) is the most successful and beautiful of all
Dylan Thomas's poems. He recreates the world of childhood, in
which the child makes his world and endows it with significance:

The sky gathered again
And the sun grew round that very day.

But while the poem is intensely nostalgic, the state of childhood
in which one may believe in one's omnipotence, and cosmic
importance is distanced. The adult is standing back and seeing the
child as belonging to a totally different relationship with the
world:

In the sun born over and over,
I ran my heedless ways,
My wishes raced through the house high hay
And nothing I cared . . .

Not only does Thomas describe this state, but he enacts it in the
texture of the verse: 'house high hay' enacts as one says it the
breathlessness and perhaps the sneezing that the hay brings on as
one races among the cocks. Similarly with

the calves
Sang to my horn . . .

we take a breath across the line-break as if to blow the horn.

As he recreates the child's vision, he enters the phantasy life of
infancy, in which one can actually believe that owls are carrying
the farm away, and that the animals lead a special night-life, in a
nocturnal world. This world is the world of *At the Back of the
North Wind* and other such phantasies of 'another' dimension of
being. Adults have a myth of Creation: but Thomas sees that this
is but an extension of the fact that the child virtually creates the
world—so that to him every day is the first day.

So it must have been after the birth of the simple light
In the first, spinning place, the spellbound horses walking
warm
Out of the whinnying green stable
On to the fields of praise.

The horses are 'spellbound' because they are bemused, having
been just created: but they are also put together by magic, as God
puts things together, or the child puts things together, from
phantasy.

The 'sky blue trades' of phantasy, as one makes worlds out of
watching the passing clouds, belong to a time when 'nature' allows
one to have an 'irresponsible' dream, which takes no account of

world and time. The poem brings it home to us that our sense of our own validity and our sense of the world's meaning emerge from this first irresponsible vision. To be honoured, lordly, care-free, famous has a 'golden' and 'green' value which underlies our capacity to feel alive in a world coloured with significance. It is the child who can hear the tunes in the chimneys, and who knows a sun that is 'young once only'. Mercifully, Time 'allows' this irresponsibility, so that the child cannot see that even as he takes hold of the world through his perceptions, he is making his way towards the 'childless land' of adulthood.

Of course, the poem is intensely nostalgic: but it is written from a point of view which takes into account the fact that the adult has awoken

to the farm forever fled from the childless land.

The farm still exists, in reality: but it no longer belongs to the phantasy world which the child created and lived in. That land seems itself still to exist somewhere but is childless: and one can never go back to live in it. One has died out of that land. To be green and growing is to die out of it: but during the whole process he sang in his chains—as the sea does, in the rhythmic control of the tides.

Realization, then, brings a loss of phantasy-freedom. Un-deniably, the poem is written from a schizoid feeling about reality: 'The self can relate with immediacy to an object which is the object of its own imagination or memory.' When the self 'abandons itself to the real' it 'fears it will lose its sense of free-dom . . . This applies to both perception and action'. The child is self-enclosed in his Eden, and the poem encounters the paradoxes of omnipotence and impotence, freedom and slavery ('chains'), being 'anyone in phantasy and nothing in reality' of which Laing speaks. The 'air' is different from the air of Thomas's poems of strangulation and constriction: it is the air of freedom, and every-thing is made of it like castles in the air—it is the 'other air', of morning songs, chimney tunes, the child's horn and the bark of foxes. But the image of time taking him by the hand is not here bitter or negative: it is as though time is a merciful mother, or someone like the North Wind in George Macdonald's faery tale:

Up to the swallow thronged loft by the shadow of my hand,
    In the moon that is always rising . . .

Once the hand has a shadow, it is mortal. The loft, however, like Yeats's 'mackerel-crowded seas', is thronged with life—life maybe preparing to fly away at the end of summer, but the swallows are a symbol of life gathering and movement about the world. The riding and flying express a desire to grow up, and the singing expresses a defiant joyfulness, even in spite of the passing of time. Time holds him, like a benign mother, and spares the child the recognition of the cruelty of the passing of time, that is all. But the poem is written from a perspective which sees how, after childhood, one has passed out of grace, and the world can never seem as pure (golden) and creative (green) again. The effect of the poem on us is to recapture for us the energy and vision of childhood, and to help us infuse our own adult attitudes with something of the visionary power of the child, indeed to see that we only see a meaningful world *because* of that first irresponsible vision.

The last poem I want to discuss here is *Love in the Asylum* (p. 108). This takes us back to the problem discussed earlier, of male and female elements in Thomas, in relation to his problems of existence. In the poem the 'stranger' is surely his own 'female element', recognition of which has come to his madness?

> A stranger has come
> To share my room in the house not right in the head,
> A girl mad as birds.

This female element is split off:

> Bolting the night of the door with her arm her plume . . .

She is angelic (*plume*), she is inaccessible (*strait*). The bed is *mazed* (i.e. amazed and curiously tortuous). So, though the house of the self is defended against dangerous love, she slips into it like a cloud (or by entering clouds):

> She deludes the heaven-proof house with entering clouds
> Yet she deludes with walking the nightmarish room,
> At large as the dead . . .

—She is a ghost: and she has intercourse as Thalassa with the oceanic desires of the male element in his asylum of the house of the self:

> Or rides the imagined oceans of the male wards.

She is part of him, so 'possessed', and brings an air of freedom
even into the padded walls by which he defends himself
     She has come possessed
Who admits the delusive light through the bouncing wall,
     Possessed by the skies
—she is buried (with the lost mother of childhood who was dead
in terms of supplying what was needed, a sense of being):
  She sleeps in the narrow trough yet she walks the dust
     Yet raves at her will
On the madhouse boards worn thin by my walking tears . . .

 In this poem Thomas is both relating to an image of an ideal
object he has created himself or has projected over someone. This
is manifestly easier than relating to a real woman (compare *I make
this in a warring absence*). But we have here something happening
which is the reverse of 'destroying "in his mind" the image of
anyone or anything he may be in danger of becoming fond of' (to
use Laing's words). In these lines Thomas is seeking out, en-
deavouring to love and to integrate his split off female element:

 And taken by light in her arms at long and dear last
    I may without fail
Suffer the first vision that set fire to the stars.

 Many of Dylan Thomas's poems are incomplete schizoid code;
many are careful attempts to preserve chaos; some are, like *Lament*,
which we shall examine in the next chapter, attempts to 'seal self-
enclosure'—in the attempt to believe only in his own destructiveness. But others, such as those I have discussed in this chapter,
breathe the fresh 'other air' of reality. They are attempts to find
integration, to accept one's real needs, to begin to live and to love:
to 'suffer the first vision that set fire to the stars'. They genuinely
'confront the problem of existence', and the problem of being
human.

14
Lament and the Death Circuit

The title of the poem *Lament* (p. 174) is, I believe, meant seriously: the poem is a bitter lament for the failure to find love and the failure to find a sense of identity by a 'taking' attitude to the world. What is, however, proclaimed cynically is the schizoid 'false solution' of asserting an identity based on 'pseudo-male doing' and aggressive hate.

Lament is immoral in its motive: since one is debarred from the joys of loving, one might as well give oneself up to the joys of hating. There is no attempt to conceal the fact that *taking* women as *partial objects* is for the protagonist here an act of hate, carried out *from a sense of superiority*, with the intention of *expressing contempt for the object* (the words and phrases here in italics being diagnostic phrases from Fairbairn and others). But the boisterous tone and rhythm of the poem are in the service of vindicating these schizoid attitudes as larger than life—and so the poem becomes parallel to the self-deception of the alcoholic, who seeks to believe that his aggression is a joke, and also an acceptable means to strengthen identity. The poem becomes enclosed in nihilistic logic. The hate is not disguised:

> I could love and leave
> All the green leaved little weddings' wives
> In the coal black bush and let them grieve . . .

He is 'the black beast' who is 'dying of bitches'. The imagery of sexual possession is characteristically depersonalised—and mostly given in terms of animals (which as Fairbairn suggests are symbols in our dreams of part-objects). Thus the protagonist declares he is no 'springtailed tom' with 'every simmering woman his mouse' but something much bigger and badder. But we may note that a mouse to the tom is a victim who is *eaten* (as a queen cat, which would normally be the sexual object of a tom cat, is not), while later the *soul* is a mouse. That is, to Thomas normal love is a cat and mouse affair, and not larger than life enough—but also full of sadistic and incorporative dangers. The protagonist is a big bull: he comes in his own time to the *herds*. He is a black sheep with a crumpled horn: that is, his phallus is an organ of aggression which has been damaged by excessive use. With the rollicking measure of the army ballad style goes an appropriate aggressiveness of sexual imagery and language: 'wick-dipping', 'ramped', 'I shoved it into': there is a rollicking endorsement of depersonalised sexual activity.

This jovial manner is meant to engage the reader in a comic vindication of this 'black' or hate means to establish an identity.[1] But the poet is also serious: the protagonist is 'gusty', a 'man you could call a man': the poem makes the schizoid assertion, 'Better be a bad someone than a weak nobody'. The problem to be overcome, however, is that where the sense of identity is based on aggressive 'taking' behaviour in sexual relationship with partial objects, in hate—what happens when the actual physical power to enact this fails? When the 'limp time' comes?

The implication here is that the soul (equated perhaps with conscience) is a weak, mouselike thing, that lives in a 'foul mousehole'. Inevitably this suggests a bodily orifice. This internal object is given a 'blind slashed eye' (like a penis), 'gristle and rind' (to make it erect), and a 'roarer's life'—that is, the whole life is identified with this libidinal object, or put into it. ('Roarer's', oddly enough, suggests a roaring baby.) It is 'shoved into' the coal black sky to 'find a woman's soul for a wife'. He meets the need for relationship by an act of cosmic phallic aggression: but at once the recognition of dependence brings disaster:

Now I am a man no more no more . . .

Dylan Thomas equates strength of identity and 'being alive' with the taking of partial objects in hate, while the need for relationship in the 'soul' is seen as foul, puny and slinking. In response to the despised desire of his True Self for confirmation in relationship,

---

[1] We may compare Sylvia Plath's *Daddy* and Ted Hughes's *Song for a Phallus*. All three are ballads of 'pseudo-male' posture or 'masculine protest', and have the same manic jauntiness of 'giving oneself up to the joys of hating'.

he 'shoved it into a coal-black sky' to see what it could find—by an act of 'false male doing'.

The satisfactions of marriage, however, threaten because they are quiet, vulnerable, and do not come up to the cosmic ideal. To be only human in a human relationship is to be

> Tidy and cursed in my dove cooed room . . .

Married, the protagonist 'is a man no more no more': he is virtually dead—relationship has killed him. He 'lies down thin' (presumably having been wasted by relationship) and hears 'the good bells jaw'. The voice of religion seems like a wife's nagging: the wife bore 'angels'—but the poem only makes sense if we reverse the word and take it in the sense in which the 'black' protagonist uses it, which is to mean *devils*. There seems to be something of a bitter private joke in the line

> At last the soul from its foul mousehole . . .

in which there is perhaps a punning reference to the Cornish port of Mousehole from which Thomas got married (see *Letters*, p. 182). The protagonist is therefore somewhat confirmed as himself and the irony is directed at his own marriage. Thomas was often evidently in anguish about his incapacity for object-constancy. But another aspect of his make-up also went with this kind of contempt for the committed relationship which he feared. This posture vindicates the sexual rampage as another 'little joke', which is how his public, not least in America, took it: though its desperate character is often revealed between the lines, as when Brinnin reports that one of his sexual approaches put a girl under medical care for concussion (*Dylan Thomas in America*, p. 268).

As we interpret the poem in terms of the symbolization of inner dynamics we may see its symbols as 'internalised libidinal objects'. Looked at in this light the old ram rod, the crumpled horn, and the soul which is shoved into the coal black sky are the 'internalised father's penis', while the 'breast high shoal', the 'coal black sky' containing the 'wick-dipping moon' are the internalised mother's breast. Thomas's strength of black identity is based on phantasy of boisterous (and destructive) activity between these two partial objects in the internal cosmos

> I shoved it into the coal black sky . . .

Yet, as the poem admits, by such postures of aggressiveness he gains no stronger sense of identity in terms of the need for relation-

ship between real persons. Indeed, such personal reality is despised and rejected in the poem.

So, the wife bears
> Harpies around me out of her womb!

'Strangers' and 'harpies' from the wife's womb seem to threaten
that the protagonist will be torn to pieces. He hates his children
(and they are harpies because they evoke feelings in him of which
he is afraid, that are full of oral sadism). At the same time, because
he has mostly given over his life to destructive aggression because
of the *moral* schizoid motive 'it is better to destroy by hate . . .
which is overtly destructive and bad, than to destroy by love,
which is by rights creative and good', he feels essentially pure in
his hate:
> Chastity prays for me, piety sings,
> Innocence sweetens my last black breath,
> Modesty hides my thighs in her wings . . .

Positive 'virtues' (of love) are deadly to the schizoid: 'Good be
though my Evil'—
> And all the deadly virtues plague my death!

Yet his maturity and end are plagued by the deadly consequences
of ever having let the soul slink out of its 'foul mousehole': that is,
the needs for love and relationship of the regressed libidinal ego
were the most dangerous thing—and only entered into when the
'taking' means of maintaining a sense of identity proved unsatisfact-
tory. Only when he was 'dying of downfall' did the soul 'slink
out' at last. Somewhere there is a true need to love and be loved.

Understanding of the schizoid attitude explains such a poem:
but it does not alone help us to estimate its value as poetry. We
can, however, use the insights of Fairbairn into schizoid characteristics to ask how much it contributes to human truth.

In the light of the schizoid processes Dylan Thomas's poem is
an exercise of merely manic assertive vitality, aggression, and
'taking' *in the service of the denial of dependence*—a denial of being
human. It also serves the purposes of false self solutions to the
problem of identity, seeking as it does to vindicate these by involving us in the poem's apparent good humour, bawdy wit and
puns. How could such an amusing person be full of hate and
destructiveness? How could he be anti-human? I have noted
elsewhere the association observed by psychoanalysts between

humour and sadism. Menninger, as we have seen, characterises the habits of alcoholics who 'cannot be persuaded that their periodic bouts are more than jolly little affairs which, for all they may end in a rather untidy and tiresome mess, with a few disappointments all round, no one should hold against them.' This shows, says Menninger, 'The wish to be treated like a child and to have one's most serious aggressions overlooked' (*Man Against Himself*, p. 142).

As we have seen, Dylan Thomas's destructive behaviour was a strange inverted expression of the need to love and be loved. In that this need is inverted it becomes an expression of hate—the attempt to coerce the object into loving, or to incorporate it. Such hate had to be masked by the charm and humour: yet under the surface lurks destructive savagery. In denying our fear of this we are often prompted to be rather more than normally ready to believe that Dylan Thomas was 'harmless'—because fundamentally we feel that unless we humour him this hate may come to be directed at us. To see the hate would be to recognise the schizoid predicament in all its horror of existential insecurity, and self-destructiveness. The reader may test this by saying to himself at the end of *Dylan Thomas in America* the 'funny' phrases from *Under Milk Wood*, 'What'll you have?' 'Too much'; or 'Came to a bad end—very enjoyable'.

Dylan Thomas's *Lament*, then, may be seen as a subtle employment of oral power to subdue us and involve us in his schizoid inversions, by charming, clowning, and magic. The essential subject of the ballad is the vindication of egocentric hate and the denial of the need for dependence. To the protagonist it seems as if the regressed libidinal ego, with its needs for love and relationship, is like a puny animal living in an unwholesome orifice: it sulks in some corner of the bad inner contents

> At last the soul from its foul mousehole
> Slunk pouting out when the limp time came . . .

Moreover, those who seek relationship and love—our true primary ways of solution of the problem of finding our existence confirmed—are cynically exposed to contempt (from an attitude of 'schizoid superiority'). They are 'little weddings' wives', and to be married is to be 'tidy and cursed', 'dying of strangers' (i.e. of dangerous contact with others felt to be alien), producing 'harpies'

—relationship threatens being torn to pieces, generating devil-children whom one hates and who hate one. (This poem would endorse the view of Laing and Cooper that the family is an instrument of violence.) The true way to sustain a sense of identity, to be 'a man you could call a man', is to leave one's 'quivering prints'—that is, to stamp everything with one's own black hate (so that it no longer threatens from a position of independent existence in the outer world, but has had one's inner reality imposed on it). The best solution is to be 'wicked': to be a bad someone rather than a weak nobody is at least to *be*. Yet, of course, it is not: to be is to 'meet' and 'accept' the other, not eat it. *Lament* is thus a poem which seeks to preserve the circuits of the false identity, and the false solutions of false male doing. It belongs to Dylan Thomas's 'front-line' roles of exhibitionism and role-playing to his 'central ego' or false self.

We may here, I believe, compare the manic drunkard's song in *Das Lied von der Erde*. In *Der Trunkene im Frühling* Mahler takes a look at one possible reaction to the need to make one's farewell to mortal existence: self-destructive dissociation, and the collapse of symbolism, of the creative engagement between inner and outer reality. The poet, drunk, does not hear the bird, out of whose song Mahler is later (in the Ninth Symphony) to weave a belief in continuity and a sense of inner wholeness to which death is irrelevant, because he has found 'ontological security'. So, the Trinklied is merely a coarse shout of defiance, tragic in the sense in which Fairbairn indicates the schizoid attitude is tragic: the drunkard thrusts away from himself the insight, the creative discovery of reality, the love *which he most needs*. Dylan Thomas, in *Lament*, does the same. It is a song of false triumph, a mere manic assertion of the inversion of moral values:

> Innocence sweetens my last black breath . . .

Yet the protest is hollow:

> And all the deadly virtues plague my death!

—that is, to hell with real human needs, to hell with being human:

> Wenn nur ein Traum das Leben ist,
> warum denn Müh' und Plag'!?
>
> Was geht mich denn der Frühling an!?
> Last mich betrunken sein!

It is an attitude which we all experience—in bitter moments, in 'schizoid episodes' (the poem was written at such a bitter moment). But this rebellion and cynicism must be placed in a larger 'normal' context, if we are to discover our potentialities and the True Self. To fail to achieve such placing is to assent to deterioration and the rejection of human being. In the last line of Thomas's poem there is a bitterness which cannot be disguised, a bitterness of envy, conveying the failure to achieve gratitude—that is, the ability to accept the world and oneself as they are, in gratefulness for having existed.

It is perhaps worth examining the original poem which fascinated Mahler.

> 'Life in the world is but a big dream;
> I will not spoil it by any labour or care.'
> So saying, I was drunk all day . . .
>
> When I woke . . .
> I asked myself, what season is this?
> Restless the oriole chatters in the spring breeze . . .
>
> Moved by its song I soon began to sigh . . .
>
> Noisily singing I waited for the moon to rise:
> When my singing was over, all my senses had gone.

For Li Po the drunkenness is a release from the intolerable feeling that life is a dream, and yet that the natural world is driven to restlessness by the spring. The contrast between the natural cycle and the man's indifference ('noisily singing') conveys the anguish of man's additional problem of consciousness and the sources of his joy in other-than-natural roots. If he does not feel joy the natural season that prompts the oriole to sing only increases his anguish and drives him to drown his senses. The noisy protest is mainly an assertion that one is still alive, while the resort to alcohol is a way of deflecting suicidal intentions.

In Li Po, however, there is recognition of a natural reality, and the drunken poet's withdrawal, though human, is seen *as* withdrawal, withdrawal to which the poet has taken out of perplexed anguish. Dylan Thomas's protagonist's false solution in *Lament*, though it too is impelled by anguish, is not placed by him as manifestation of man's anguish. He does not see it as a false moment. On the contrary, he tries to argue that 'false self doing', 'bad thinking' and 'taking' are *true* solutions. He pleads for these as larger than life—and tried to convince himself that these can be a basis of identity. The resulting attitude becomes paranoid: it is reality which is unfair. The trouble is that the 'preachers' were right in their 'warning': the poem is but a 'roarer's' protest against the reality of being human. This is poetry which takes the direction of rejecting and obscuring insight and moves towards enclosing us and the poet in psychotic dissociation from reality and hope.

Essentially Thomas is here using his powers to encourage us *not* to see our own hate, as he seeks to prevent others from seeing the hate in him. He is trying to turn us away from being human. The fundamental unethical position in such a poem escapes the academic critic. Looking it up in *A Reader's Guide to Dylan Thomas* I found many vindications of Thomas's attitude in *Lament* ('black humour is the saving light of "Lament"—humour, irony, gusto and bouncing rhythm'). I also found an unwillingness ever to recognise the inversion of moral values contrived in the poem: 'Thomas was obsessed, like any man, with freedom and marriage', 'Thomas commonly wore a mask, white or black, like the rest of us'.

And then follows something which ceases to be criticism, and becomes a strange attempt (common in criticism of Thomas) to vindicate as innocuous the poet's own most disturbed behaviour. Thomas's exhibitionism and hate is found acceptable 'because he was a poet':

When I first met him at a party, he looked like, and acted the part of, an amorous volkswagen, driven by Harpo Marx. Chasing the girls round the room, he blew down their dickies. Everyone, wives and husbands alike, took this in good part . . . Thomas was a poet after all . . . It was plain, moreover, that the harmless poet, doing his best, was doing what he thought expected of him, or else was hiding shyness under what he thought its opposite. (*Reader's Guide*, p. 302)

Here the effect of the persona involving the critic in a distorted response is evident. The last comment is especially painful. Thomas was enthusiastically expected to perform this kind of role in America: he knew his 'little bouts' would be excused by the American *avant-garde*, whose ethos of schizoid dissociation would not only pardon such 'hate' behaviour but endorse it as a valid solution to the problem of life. Thomas behaves to others symbolically as if they were 'partial objects' rather than persons: because his manner of doing so is childish the offence is excused. But the game is given away by the word 'harmless'. Dylan Thomas was never that. The schizoid individual's energy is often devoted to the processes of hate and self-destruction, and so the way in which he behaves may become anti-human. When it does it depreciates human value and fails to take into account the humanness of others. The danger is always that the effect may be to dehumanise them, as an autistic child dehumanises by being able only to regard other human beings as objects—having never, tragically, discovered them as persons, or himself as a person. To endorse such a poem as *Lament* and such anti-human inversions in his schizoid mode is to risk becoming involved in the death-circuits of false solution ourselves, and in the destruction of that which is human in us. If we do so, moreover, we threaten those resources by which alone we can share the questions 'What is it to be human?' and 'What is the point of life?' with the true creative artist, such as Thomas himself was, in another role.

It is worth discussing this whole false posture at some length, because the mode is now more fashionable than the modes of true creativity. Sylvia Plath's psychotic *Daddy* and Ted Hughes's cynical and nihilistic *Crow* poems are among the most popular poems of our time. The implications are serious, not only for our attitudes to life, but because of the effect of such fashions on creativity itself.

15

Laughing delightedly at Hate:
Under Milk Wood

Under Milk Wood is set in a Welsh village and in this work Thomas is obliged to be explicit about 'outer reality', and other people: he is obliged to recognise a reality other than a cosmos in which 'he finds only himself'. As we shall see, he does impose on this 'outer world' a good deal from his own subjective distortions: but not to the degree he achieves in his poetry. There is a good deal of compassion for other human beings, and a kindness of regard for others even in the human comedy. Yet beneath the surface we shall detect a hatred of being human, the origins of which we have explored in the schizoid individual. At the same time, he is also trying 'deep down' to love and be loved, and to discovery his humanity.

His Llareggub is 'this place of love' (p. 76): 'The town's as full as a lovebird's egg'; 'The town that has fallen head over bells in love'. There is one way of looking at a human community, as he suggests by his caricature of the guidebook account of Llareggub. This is the superficiality of 'conformity':

less than five hundred souls inhabit the three quaint streets and the few narrow by-lanes and scattered farm-steads that con-stitute this small, decaying watering place, which may, indeed, be called a 'backwater of life' without disrespect to its natives who possess, to this day, a salty individuality of their own.

(p. 23)

This pastiche satirises the 'sane' account of Llareggub. When we come closer' Thomas implies, such platitudes as 'salty indi-viduality', and 'five hundred souls' give way to a more 'realistic' view of human nature. His own attitude to this slice of human reality is hinted at by the comic undertones in 'backwater of life' and 'decaying'. When we come closer to the 'place of love' we find, in fact, that it is full of hate, not least in the manifestations of what is usually taken for 'love'.

Sartre in his philosophic attitude is unable to see any development of love which does not lead to indifference, the impulse to dominate (sadism) or to be dominated (masochism): his is a characteristic schizoid view. Thomas's attitude is equally lacking in positives: he is equally unable to present in his work love as a relationship between mature independent adults. He sees all manifestations of love as threatening, rather as if from the point of view of a child who fears the incorporative elements in adult sexual relationships. But yet Thomas is also able to see schizoid inversions of love as attempts to feel real, as manifestations of a quest for identity. He cannot place these as such, but he does have compassion for them, and he sees how comic they can be, in their grotesqueness. He is able to do this because he places the petty drama of these false solutions ('men are brutes on the quiet') against the swarming vitality of the activity of life:

There's the clip clop of horses on the sunhoneyed cobbles of the humming streets, hammering of horseshoes, gobble quack and cackle, tomtit twitter from the bird-ounced boughs, braying on Donkey Down. Bread is baking, pigs are grunting, chop goes the butcher, milk-churns bell, tills ring, sheep cough, dogs shout, saws sing. Oh, the Spring whinny and morning moo from the clog dancing farms, the gulls' gab and rabble on the boat-bobbing river and sea and the cockles bubbling in the sand, scamper of sanderlings, curlew cry, crow caw, pigeon coo, clock strike, bull bellow, and the ragged gabble of the beargarden school as the women scratch and babble in Mrs. Organ Morgan's general shop where everything is sold: custard, buckets, henna, rat-traps, shrimp-nets, sugar, stamps, confetti, paraffin, hatchets, whistles . . . (p. 44)

The catalogue has something of the same effect as that of the objects Huckleberry Finn finds in the drowned frame-house at the discovery of his dead father: it evokes the continual bustle and gabble of human life that *assures us we are alive*: to feel alive is the object of our activity. In this context Dylan Thomas uses his record of human activity and ways of speaking, and his prose poetry of the natural world to do two things. First, in places, to cast a true irony on the postures, defences, antics, inverted mechanisms and self-deceptions whereby men seek to feel real and alive. Often he is able to see that these ways of feeling alive are not processes of love at all, but of hate. He seems to say that though he seeks for love in this place he can only find a depersonalised vitality of hunger, while in compassion he feels a relish for the tumultuous beauty and richness of the natural world and human comedy ('Life is a terrible thing thank God'). His positive gift is for a comedy of strategies of survival. But on the other hand he also seeks at times, by his own distortions, to disguise the hatred in false solutions—especially round the subjects of alcoholism and depersonalised sex. It is not, here, that he caricatures, but rather that he becomes grossly sentimental and loses his valuable sense of ironic detachment. The comedy of strategies gives way to propaganda for death-circuits.

In *Llareggub Revisited* I showed how derivative was Thomas's use of the texture and structure of the brothel scene in James Joyce's *Ulysses*, and sought to show how the piece was lacking in drama and how, by comparison with Joyce, Thomas's language was effervescent but lacking in economy, breathlessly diffuse. I linked this to a lack of moral concern in Thomas. He was seeking in *Under Milk Wood*, I suggested, to 'provoke a nostalgia for an irresponsible but noble childhood'—Llareggub being the place where on

> Forgotten mornings . . . he walked with his mother
>> Through the parables
>> Of sun light
> And the legends of the green chapels . . .

—an amoral world, in which all the strange manifestations of love-hunger are acceptable, including those of hate, while reality is denied.

There is no denying the derivativeness of *Under Milk Wood*, nor the characteristic 'lack of control' in Thomas's use of Joyce's modes. But now I would associate the diffuseness of language, its breathlessness and lack of focus, with Thomas's ambivalence between the true quest for identity and his false solutions into which he could not find insight—an ambivalence he sought to

disguise, or to flee from, into a cosmos over which he had projected his inner world. There is insight in the dramatic piece,
where it sees through false solutions and 'manic denials'. But where
it turns round to endorse certain strategies it fails, because Thomas
is trying to say something about universal human nature which is
not true—such as that 'we are all mad and nasty' (as one of his
characters says in *Adventures in the Skin Trade*), and that normal
(manic-depressive) preoccupations are meaningless. Where the
comedy is preserved there is compassion: there is insight in the
farce:

There's a nasty lot live here when you come to think . . . (p. 46)
The advantage in *Under Milk Wood* is in the semi-dramatic
presentations, in which such comments are placed, as responses to
others, in the common exchange of tattle.

Who's having a baby, who blacked whose eye, seen Polly
Garter giving her belly an airing, there should be a law, seen
Mrs Benyon's new mauve jumper, it's her old grey jumper
dyed, who's dead, who's dying, there's a lovely day, oh the
cost of soapflakes! (p. 42)

This use of the '*Ulysses* brothel-scene' mode of fragmentary
dialogue is vivid and original, and Thomas's own: it is also
characteristically Welsh in its oblique wryness and modes of
'placing' understatement. It is gossip captured—and gossip placed
itself, as a way of feeling alive, of confirming one's identity (often
at the expense of others), and of defending oneself against one's
own fears and anxiety—for if the sins and calamities have happened to others, then they have not happened to us (which is why
people so compulsively read and discuss newspaper accounts of
disasters). Thomas sees both sin and gossip as ways of feeling real
at the expense of other people's unreal behaviour—and sane, at
the expense of the sanity of others.

He also sees how incorporation, hate and manic assertion are
compensations for feelings of ego-weakness. So, it is necessary for
him to endorse the attitude expressed in his own pastiche of the
hymn of the Reverend Eli Jenkins:

We are not wholly bad or good
Who live our lives under Milk Wood,
And Thou, I know, wilt be the first
To see our best side, not our worst.   (p. 79)

Behind this need is the recognition hilariously guyed in Thomas's pastiche of the platitudes of Christian compassion for sin: sin is only a way of feeling one is still alive:

> For whether we last the night or no
> I'm sure is always touch and go . . .

The best of *Under Milk Wood* is in this comedy of human postures and gestures, of the roles we accept, in trying to reassure ourselves that we shall 'last the night' yet that we are 'some one'.

To Dylan Thomas the effort to feel real and alive was at times an urgent problem of preserving sanity. And so it is not surprising to find that the original version of the play was to be called *The Town was Mad*. In examining the piece and its origins we need to keep in mind the insight of Fairbairn, that all the elements in a dream are dramatisations of structure and qualities in the ego: so, too, are the elements of such a phantasy work.

The piece was first projected as a radio play with a blind man as narrator and central character. This obviously symbolises Thomas's own situation—of a blindness to certain aspects of reality, combined with a capacity to perceive in yet another dimension, of a deeper kind of 'listening'. Later

> Thomas thought he had found the theme he wanted in the contrast between the mythical town and the surrounding world, the conflict between the eccentrics, strong in their individuality and freedom, and the sane ones who sacrifice everything to some notion of conformity. (*Preface* by Daniel Jones, p. vi)

This is, as we can see from Fairbairn's analysis, a typical schizoid feeling about external reality: it is a phantasy of the need to live completely in a world of schizoid inversion. Within the systems of the self (the 'mythical town') there is an 'individuality and freedom' built on the false solutions of hate, to which the 'surrounding world' seems inferior, and a 'sacrifice to conformity'; its values are meaningless to the schizoid individual who has inverted them. To accept 'outer' reality would involve a loss of freedom—and conformity to alienation. He is the only one in step with his own inversions.

> The whole population cannot very well be accommodated inside the walls of a lunatic asylum; so the sane world decrees that the town itself shall be declared an 'insane area', with all traffic and goods diverted from it . . . (ibid., p. 7)

—there shall be no give and take from outer reality: the town in which there are manifestations of 'strategies of survival' is subjected to the kind of political ostracism R. D. Laing discusses in his analysis of the families of schizophrenics, but in reverse.[1] The town is given a role by the world, as the schizoid is given his: *The Town was Mad*. Thomas is also implicitly protesting that from what his schizoid insights show him about human nature—about the strange solutions all of us more or less find to problems of identity—'we all ought to be locked up'.

Captain Cat, spokesman of the indignant citizens, insists that the sanity of the town should be put on trial in the town hall with every legal formality; he will be Counsel for the Defence and the citizens themselves will be witnesses. The trial takes place, but it comes to a surprising end. The final speech for the Prosecution consists of a full and minute description of the ideally sane town; as soon as they hear this the people withdraw their defence and beg to be cordoned off from the sane world as soon as possible. (ibid., p. vii)

To the schizoid, the values, behaviour and attitudes to life of the normal world are not only meaningless, but threatening. On the other hand there is some truth in the view of the schizoid individual that many postures of 'normal' man are self-deceiving delusions—themselves falsely conformist. Because such individuals have insights into this, from a point of view concerned with the deeper problems of identity, many of those with severe existence problems turn revolutionaries. They see the problem as Shakespeare sees it:

> Man proud man,
> Dressed in a little brief authority . . .
> Most ignorant of what he's most assured . . .

Yet, of course the schizoid individual is likely to take this criticism too far, to the point of declaring the impossibility of going on living and being human at all, or he may find a false strength in seeking universal (and pointless) anarchy. Our problem is that we have to accept and live with our weak and ambivalent humanness —and dare to do so—as the schizoid dare not.

---

[1] In his social theory Laing almost endorses Dylan Thomas's schizoid point of view that only the mad are really sane, while society is insane. See also Thomas's crude social theory, pp. 255–6 below.

It is thus not a mark of a superior 'realism' to say that 'we're all mad and nasty'. There is a greater realism which sees madness and nastiness as false solutions to deeper needs, and recognises that true solutions involve our acceptance of our weakness and dependence. The most important truth about human beings is not their hate, nor that all their solutions to problems of identity are mad—but that they must feel real and alive and must seek truth of being— and that love is the true way to this while hate is but a way of making do.

Thomas is able to see at times that the primary human need is to feel real: but he is blind to those solutions, in acceptance of one's own reality, and in 'meeting' which can yield the deepest onto- logical satisfactions. His best creative work is that which sees the comic reality of 'strategies of survival': his worst seeks to impose a false idealism over the world. When he does this we have an incantatory poeticizing that covers everything with glamour by a breathless insistence:

It is spring, moonless night in the small town, starless and bible-black, the cobble streets silent and the hunched courters'- and-rabbits' wood limping invisible down to the sloeblack, slow, black, crowblack, fishingboat-bobbing sea . . .
. . . you alone can hear the invisible starfall, the darkest-before- dawn minutely dewgrazed stir of the black dab-filled sea . . .
(p. 2)
. . . The lust and lilt and lather and emerald breeze and crackle of the bird-praise and body of Spring with its breasts full of rivering May-milk . . . (p. 66)

This, as Raymond Williams has pointed out, is the less successful mode. It comes from the Thomas who seeks to be confirmed by being fed by an utterly undisturbing world-as-object, which arouses no problems of rejection or excited libido: it is thus from our point of view tedious, unreal and lacking in human interest, because it is too neutral. *Under Milk Wood*, in this mode, is idealised as a place of love, in which one feeds on the vitality of the natural world, as at a breast. The world is a breast, a vast partial object, which exists only for him, and towards which he has only a 'taking' attitude: but, like the stream of milk of which the schizophrenic patient of Fairbairn dreamed, it is not coming from a person, and has no human complexity. Thomas has never been 'disillusioned' as to the reality of this external world, and so for it to exhibit any indifference or refusal to behave according to his magic wishes would be interpreted as a threat. (This, of course, is in complex with a failure to find the reality of himself.) The intense and breathless oral flow here manifests the need to keep the world in this state of being under his magic idealising control, and to cry to it, with the Welsh fervour of the hymn:

> Feed me till I want no more,
> Want no more . . .

—that is, it is impossibly ideal and totally satisfying.

At times this mode, however, brings him by its very intensity to find and recognise the beauty of the actual world (as does his best poetry). The idealisation of the natural world leads him to study it, and as he studies it symbols emerge, which enable him to accept inward problems of ambivalence. The night is 'thin' and the water 'creased': there is an actual sense of time and weakness in the self, and so of the tenuous and mutable quality of outer reality. So his language achieves true poetic compression as at the end:

> The thin night darkens. A breeze from the creased water sighs the streets . . . the suddenly wind-shaken wood springs awake for the second dark time this one spring day . . .

From this sense of a disturbance in the vision of the world as Ideal Object, Thomas turns to the human reality and is able to render in *Under Milk Wood* a penetrating and ironic record of the fragmentary experiences that life is, and of the pathetic way in which human beings piece together a sense of identity, of prowess, of feeling real and alive, from such fragments:

> FIRST DROWNED
> Remember me, Captain?
> CAPTAIN CAT
> You're Dancing Williams!
> FIRST DROWNED
> I lost my step in Nantucket . . .

He lost his (dancing) step by losing his existential foothold, as Thomas did in America.

> FIRST DROWNED
> The skull at your earhole is

FIFTH DROWNED

Curly Bevan. Tell my auntie it was me that pawned the ormulu clock.

CAPTAIN CAT

Aye, aye, Curly.

SECOND DROWNED

Tell my missus no I never

THIRD DROWNED

I never done what she said I never.

FOURTH DROWNED

Yes they did.

The irony here is subtle and the grotesque comedy is warmly human. The Captain is dreaming of his dead mates: their requests from the tomb are not of great moment but, pathetically, the dead wish to clear their breasts of the most trivial peccadilloes. Their insistence on not being guilty of lapses of the flesh, now they are out of the flesh, casts an ironic light on our preoccupations when alive. (Cf. the chorus of dead in Carl Orff's opera *Der Mond* which has the same effect: brought to life all the dead wish to do is to drink, play cards, swear and fornicate, and this deepens our sense of the futility of such manic attempts to feel meaningfully alive.) Even after death, Thomas tells us with the penetrating wit of a fool or a clown, we shall continue to feel that our identity depends upon feeling and appearing 'good' even when we know we are not. All that life is is revealed as small fragmentary comforts, illusions and images:

FIRST DROWNED

How's it above?

SECOND DROWNED

Is there rum and laverbread?

...THIRD DROWNED

Concertinas? ...

...FIRST DROWNED

Fighting and onions?

... What's the smell of parsley?

The sad comedy here, with its poignant feeling, is illuminated if we remember the anguish of inmates in mental hospitals revealed by Professor Jules Henry in *Culture Against Man*: when the nurses and officials cease to use their names or to make remarks about the

weather, then they begin to feel they no longer exist and become
dehumanised. Detachment from the trivia of daily life is a loss of
those small commonplace experiences which confirm our
existence. So—it can seem that such trivia is all life consists of, in
our clutching at meaning.

The best comedy in *Under Milk Wood* is the comedy of caricature of how people in daily life speak and behave in the pursuit of
meaningful existence. They are seen in this way, often, as a child
sees them, for to a child adult mannerisms and idiosyncrasies are
vivid, as they are no longer, perhaps, to an adult. The child sees
horrors under the surface, too, that adults no longer care to see.
For instance, for us to live, we assume, animals must die. Yet we
say we love animals:

FIRST VOICE
From Beynon Butchers in Coronation Street, the smell of fried
liver sidles out with onion on its breath. And listen! In the dark
breakfast-room behind the shop, Mr and Mrs Beynon, waited
upon by their treasure, enjoy, between bites, their everymorn-
ing hullabaloo, and Mrs Beynon slips the grisly bits under the
tasselled tablecloth to her fat cat.

[*Cat purrs*

MRS BEYNON
She likes the liver, Ben.
MR BEYNON
She ought to, Bess. It's her brother's.
MRS BEYNON (*Screaming*)
Oh! d'you hear that, Lily?
LILY SMALLS
Yes, mum.
MRS BEYNON
We're eating pusscat.
LILY SMALLS
Yes, mum.
MRS BEYNON
Oh, you cat-butcher!
MR BEYNON
It was doctored, mind
MRS BEYNON (*Hysterical*)
What's that got to do with it?

MR BEYNON

Yesterday we had mole.

MRS BEYNON

Oh, Lily, Lily!

MR BEYNON

Monday, otter. Tuesday, shrews.

[*Mrs Beynon screams*

LILY SMALLS

Go on, Mrs Beynon. He's the biggest liar in town.

MRS BEYNON

Don't you dare say that about Mr Beynon.

LILY SMALLS

Everybody knows it, mum.

MRS BEYNON

Mr Beynon never tells a lie. Do you, Ben?

MR BEYNON

No, Bess. And now I am going out after the corgies, with my
little cleaver . . .   (pp. 34–6)

Here Dylan Thomas makes good use of his 'child vision' of the
world, in a mad fantasy. We eat food which disappears from the
outer world: we eat animals which have been killed. All kinds of
problems of identity arise for the child. Why not eat shrews, cats,
corgies? What has sex to do with incorporation? In order to be
able to bear eating what we do eat we have to lie to ourselves and
maintain some kind of dissociation. Behind our purring as we
eat our breakfast is a bestial carnivorousness: and death. This is
true clowning: a manic denial which associates well with tragedy:

FOURTH WOMAN

There's a nasty lot live here when you come to think.

FIRST WOMAN

Look at that Nogood Boyo now

SECOND WOMAN

too lazy to wipe his snout

THIRD WOMAN

and going out fishing every day and all he ever brought back
was a Mrs Samuels.

FIRST WOMAN

been in the water a week.   (p. 46)

In the presentations here Thomas is observing the defensive

function of gossip, expressing 'we are not like that'—fortifying our identity against threats in the unconscious to do with guilt and hate, fortifying ourselves by self-righteousness, splitting, and manic denial. The gossip focuses in anxiety even round the problem of identity that underlies the joke: Is a corpse which has been in the water a week still a 'Mrs Samuels'? This is at root a disturbing existential question.

In such comedy Dylan Thomas shows himself sophisticated and able to use his knowledge of human beings scathingly, but with compassion and intelligence: his debt to Joyce being usefully exploited. He makes comedy of individuals divided against themselves.

SECOND VOICE

Evans the Death presses hard with black gloves on the coffin of his breast in case his heart jumps out.

EVANS THE DEATH (*Harshly*)

Where's your dignity. Lie down.

SECOND VOICE

Spring stirs Gossamer Beynon schoolmistress like a spoon.

GOSSAMER BEYNON (*Tearfully*)

Oh, what can I do? I'll *never* be refined if I twitch.

SECOND VOICE

Spring this strong morning foams in a flame in Jack Black as he cobbles a high-heeled shoe for Mrs Dai Bread Two the gypsy, but he hammers it sternly out.

JACK BLACK (*To a hammer rhythm*)

There is *no leg* belonging to the foot that belongs to this shoe . . .

Dylan Thomas can even see, to a degree, that alcohol and 'taking' sex are false solutions of the problems of identity.

CAPTAIN CAT

Mr Waldo hurrying to the Sailors Arms. Pint of stout with a egg in it

[*Footsteps stop*

(*Softly*) There's a letter for him.

WILLY NILLY

It's another paternity summons, Mr Waldo.

FIRST VOICE

The quick footsteps hurry on along the cobbles and up three steps to the Sailors Arms.

MR WALDO (*Calling out*)
Quick, Sinbad. Pint of stout. And no egg in. (pp. 41–2)
But Dylan Thomas can only see this to *some* extent. If we examine
his attitudes over these particular forms of behaviour as solutions
to problems of identity, we find another mode in *Under Milk
Wood*, which has serious defects, which the comedy does not
amend.

In this mode the comedy itself becomes a falsification of human
reality and an attempt to involve us in a denial of being human.
The worst example of such falsity in *Under Milk Wood* I have
discussed before in *Llareggub Revisited*: Thomas's treatment of
the Cherry Owens. As Menninger says, the alcoholic wants the
'seriousness of his aggressions . . . overlooked', and his episodes of
hate behaviour tolerated as an 'amusing little weakness'. This
impulse to deny one's own destructiveness can be seen in Dylan
Thomas's stage directions here—with a childish plea for the hate
in adult alcoholic breakdown to be overlooked.

MRS CHERRY OWEN
See that smudge on the wall by the picture of Auntie Blossom?
That's where you threw the sago.
                    [*Cherry Owen laughs with delight*
MRS CHERRY OWEN
You only missed me by a inch.
CHERRY OWEN
I always miss Auntie Blossom too.
The alcoholic is without hope of ever getting cured. ('I
always . . .'). He has no remorse. But he wishes to appear 'harm-
less'—he is only throwing sago; he 'always misses'. (Incidents in
Dylan Thomas's life give this the lie: his alcoholism, in truth, was
terrifying, threatening, destructive and suicidal.) But in Llareggub
it is all a joke:
MRS CHERRY OWEN
Remember last night? In you reeled, my boy, as drunk as a
deacon with a big wet bucket and a fishfrail full of stout and
you looked at me and you said, 'God has come home!' you
said, and then over the bucket you went, sprawling and bawl-
ing, and the floor was all flagons and eels.
CHERRY OWEN
Was I wounded?

MRS CHERRY OWEN

And then you took off your trousers and you said, 'Does anybody want a fight!' Oh, you old baboon.

He takes off his trousers rather than his jacket. The joke is that he
says 'anybody want a fight?' rather than 'anybody want a fuck?'
The aggressive sex of a drunk who feels desire he has forfeited his
potency to satisfy is equated with a fight. This is realistic enough:
alcohol impels aggression as a false solution. But where the episode
is false is in Thomas's attempt to believe that Mrs Cherry Owen
would find it *endearing*, that the couple would find delight in it,
that there is no remorse and no element of self-frustration, self-
destruction and self-punishment in alcoholism.

CHERRY OWEN

Give me a kiss.

MRS CHERRY OWEN

And then you sang 'Bread of Heaven', tenor and bass . . .

The reference to himself, when we remember the horror of his
end, becomes grisly:

MRS CHERRY OWEN

Then you cried like a baby and said you were a poor drunk
orphan with nowhere to go but the grave.

The insight ('I want to be forever unconscious') is, however,
laughed off by falsifying stage directions

CHERRY OWEN

And what did I do next, my dear?

MRS CHERRY OWEN

Then you danced on the table all over again and said you were
King Solomon Owen and I was your Mrs Sheba.

CHERRY OWEN (*Softly*)

And then?

MRS CHERRY OWEN

And then I got you into bed and you snored all night like a
brewery   [*Mr and Mrs Cherry Owen laugh delightedly together.*]

Dylan Thomas's need was to express his 'hate solutions' by
seeking rebirth and self-punishment in alcohol. In this syndrome
he also needed to express the schizoid 'taking' need by promiscuous sex, or, certainly, a form of sex that had intense hate in it.
Both manifestations of hate were extremely dangerous, and he
obviously showed in his drunkenness and his sexual needs a

psychotic detachment from reality that was very frightening, both to himself and others, because they were directed at overcoming the deepest fears of loss of identity. ('I'm really afraid I'm going mad . . . Perhaps it's sex, perhaps I'm not normal . . .' Brinnin, p. 263). It is these dangers and horrors which he seeks to deny here. The consequence of such falsifications throughout *Under Milk Wood* is a sentimentality about personal relationships which detracts disastrously from the humanity of the work elsewhere in its comedy and compassion.

While there is no positive love-relationship (even in this place of love), all sexual relationships are caricatured. Inevitably the caricature is successfully comical, as with the two dead husbands of the suburban tidy wife, Mrs Ogmore-Pritchard.

MRS OGMORE-PRITCHARD

Soon it will be time to get up. Tell me your tasks in order . . .

MR PRITCHARD

I must dress behind the curtain and put on my apron.

MR OGMORE

I must blow my nose

MRS OGMORE-PRITCHARD

In the garden, if you please.

MR OGMORE

In a piece of tissue-paper which I afterwards burn . . .

To Dylan Thomas, as we have seen, the acceptance of normal domestic roles was difficult. He makes comedy of this and makes his hatred of domesticity acceptable by caricaturing that compulsive concern with hygiene that hides the death of emotion and vitality in a neurotic suburban home. But it may be that the underlying hatred of domesticity ('tidy wives') has behind it a fear of some reversal of sexual roles—for Mrs Ogmore-Pritchard 'wears the trousers', and her dominant authoritarianism extends to sex:

MRS OGMORE-PRITCHARD

Soon it will be time to go to bed. Tell me your tasks in order.

MR OGMORE AND MR PRITCHARD

We must take our pyjamas from the drawer marked pyjamas.

MRS OGMORE-PRITCHARD (*Coldly*)

And then you must take them off.

Here Thomas expresses a fear of woman and woman's sexual demands (in contrast with which the man's 'taking' demands must be tolerated by 'laughing delightedly'). This we can recognise as arising from the hatred and fear of woman underlying his work which we have noted in the poetry. He projects his 'female element' on to Mrs Ogmore-Pritchard and attacks it with his bitterest weapons of satire, because he fears it. (At depth perhaps she is his over-mothering mother whose impingement was experienced as hate.)

A similar hatred of domesticity is expressed in another caricature, that of Mr and Mrs Pugh. Here the husband is exerting grotesque infantile phantasies of destruction on his nagging wife. But Thomas can enjoy his hate comedy without needing to indulge in any anxious special pleading, because it is so hilariously grotesque. The couple sit over 'cold grey cottage pie'. Mr Pugh 'forks the shroud meat in', reading *Lives of the Great Poisoners*.

MRS PUGH

Some people were brought up in pigsties.

MR PUGH

Pigs don't read at table, dear.

FIRST VOICE

Bitterly she flicks dust from the broken cruet. It settles on the pie in a thin gnat-rain.

MR PUGH

Pigs can't read, my dear.

MRS PUGH

I know one who can.

FIRST VOICE

Alone in the hissing laboratory of his wishes, Mr Pugh minces among bad vats and jeroboams, tiptoes through spinneys of murdering herbs, agony dancing in his crucibles, and mixes especially for Mrs Pugh a venomous porridge unknown to toxicologists which will scald and viper through her until her ears fall off like figs, her toes grow big and black as balloons, and steam comes screaming out of her navel . . .

Thomas can indulge in his phantasy here, because he feels safety in such a relationship in the conception of which he has totally given himself up to the joys of hating. No ambivalence troubles his picture of the Pughs, in whom normal feelings and values are so inverted that no-one is going to believe them possible: there is no attempt to enlist our assent to their ruthlessness. We laugh *at* them.

Thus, Dylan Thomas is at his best when his material is given over entirely to absurd phantasy. Falsity creeps in when he has the double purpose of trying to convince us that moral inversions can be real and valid. This he tries to do disastrously with Waldo and Polly Garter—'Saint Polly Garter' as Mrs Pugh calls her:

. . . She was martyred again last night. Mrs Organ Morgan saw her with Waldo.

MRS ORGAN MORGAN

And when they saw me they pretended they were looking for nests . . . But you don't go nesting in long combinations, I said to myself, like Mr Waldo was wearing, and your dress over your head like Polly Garter's. Oh, they didn't fool me.

SECOND VOICE

One big bird gulp, and the flounder's gone. She licks her lips and goes stabbing again.

MRS ORGAN MORGAN

And when you think of all those babies she's got, then all I can say is she'd better give up birdnesting that's all I can say, it isn't the right kind of hobby at all for a woman that can't say No even to midgets . . . (p. 64)

Often Dylan Thomas shows that his view of sex is essentially that of a child: children's voices in courting games merge into the voices of Waldo and a woman, towards whom he is evidently making Thomas-like advances:

LITTLE BOY

Give us a kiss, Matti Richards

LITTLE GIRL

Give us a penny then.

MR WALDO

I only got a halfpenny

FIRST WOMAN

Lips is a penny . . .

From this childs-eye view, Thomas reveals under the surface the kind of fear a child has of sex which seems full of threat and dangers (as a form of 'eating'):

PREACHER

Will you take this woman Matti Richards

SECOND WOMAN

Dulcie Prothero

THIRD WOMAN
Effie Bevan
FOURTH WOMAN
Lil the Gluepot
FIFTH WOMAN
Mrs Flusher
WIFE
Blodwen Bowen
PREACHER
To be your awful wedded wife
LITTLE BOY (*Screaming*)
No, no no!

Dylan Thomas conveys to us that Waldo's compulsive promiscuity (like his own) is a compensation for fear of woman—who
is a 'Gluepot' and 'awful'. In the reference to Mrs Organ Morgan
swallowing a fish (like a greedy heron) we have a clue to the
reason. Thomas is trying to suggest that in her gossiping hostility
there is a sadistic envy directed at the sexual act between Waldo
and Polly. Mrs Organ Morgan at that moment is the castrating
mother, whom Thomas fears in every woman. The way to escape
her is by seeking a kind of 'object' that can be controlled. He finds
her in Polly—a child-woman who is unreal enough to manifest
none of the dangers and demands of the adult woman, and who
can be dissociated from the consequences of sexual relationship.
She is a split-off libidinal object. It is thus possible to phantasy
parental intercourse without the dangers of mutual incorporation,
and in a depersonalised and sadistic way without involving harm
to oneself. Dylan Thomas's vision of Waldo having intercourse
with Polly while he is drunk is a phantasy of the primal scene.
Into this scene he phantasies his own infantile wishes—which are
that the father's embraces should not 'matter' to the mother—who
really wants the son. Thus Waldo is nothing to Polly Garter, who
remains nostalgic for 'Little Willy Wee'—the infant Thomas, who
seeks in regression to return to 'cuddle up' to her.

FIRST VOICE
. . . Mr Waldo drunk in the dusky wood hugs his lovely Polly
Garter under the eyes of the neighbours and the birds, and he
does not care. He smacks his live red lips . . . (p. 85)
But this Oedipus dream is combined with the schizoid feeling

that the libidinal ego which the mother would prefer, to match
her as libidinal object, is *dead*:

> But it is not *his* name that Polly Garter whispers as she lies under
> the oak and loves him back. Six feet deep that name sings in the
> cold earth.
>> But I always think as we tumble into bed
>> Of Little Willy Wee who is dead, dead, dead.

Furthermore, we can say, I believe, that little Willy Wee is the
dead sibling, the 'other' who was confused with him, whom the
mother seemed to be loving when she should have been loving
Dylan. So, he is himself in Waldo's predicament, in a sense.

So, Polly Garter is the epitome of, and the vindication of, all the
women to whom Dylan has 'cuddled up' in his strange combination of primitive hatred and fear and infantile need. The
presentation of her is inevitably hushed and religiose. But at the
same time her libidinousness is a vengeance on the wives, as is the
protagonist's in *Lament*:

> CAPTAIN CAT
> . . . Hully, Polly, who's there?
> POLLY GARTER (*off*)
> Me, love.
> CAPTAIN CAT
> *That's* Polly Garter. (*Softly*) Hullo, Polly my love, can you
> hear the dumb goose-hiss of the wives as they huddle and peck
> or flounce at a waddle away? Who cuddled you when? Which
> of their gandering hubbies moaned in Milk Wood for your
> naughty mothering arms and body like a wardrobe, love . . .
>> (p. 43)

'Men are brutes on the quiet': sex is sadistic and like eating. The
'Garter' is a partial object: taking is all there is to love. She is only
a *wardrobe*: a depersonalised protector of identities (clothes), a
space to be entered, and who can enclose protectively. But also
need feel no responsibility to her as to a person: and she likes it
like that.

With a characteristic schizoid sense of futility, Dylan Thomas
can find no-one in the Place of Love who can represent mature
love: the (adult) wives are capable of only envy and malice. They
receive from him only the contempt of 'schizoid superiority':

Scrub the floors of the Welfare Hall for the Mothers' Union Social Dance, you're one mother won't wriggle her roly poly bum or pat her fat little buttery feet in that wedding-ringed holy tonight . . . (p. 43)

Thomas is able to see, to some extent, that Waldo's sexual rampages are a false solution to identity. But he betrays this falsity by the phrase about Polly, 'she loves him back', while dreaming of Willy Wee. Failure to merge one's apprehensions of the object with the person one is relating to sexually is seen by Laing and Guntrip as a schizoid problem—and, of course, it was Dylan Thomas's. Polly Garter's nymphomania is endorsed with all his advocacy—almost devoutly. But she is also a dehumanised libidinal object, best pleased in her turn by partial-objects: she virtually reduces her lovers to mere phalluses to fill her inner space:

I loved a man whose name was Tom
He was strong as a bear and two yards long
I loved a man whose name was Dick
He was big as a barrel and two feet thick . . . (p. 54)

Little Willy Wee is 'six feet deep': he is in the grave but (by the obscene *double entendre* here) he is also buried in the womb, and in Polly's vagina, which is a monstrous grave or wardrobe. Little Wille Wee 'downed and died' in the act of sex which is an incorporative act and can threaten loss of identity in giving.

Polly's lovers are 'good bad boys', and, as I pointed out in *Llareggub Revisited*, her soliloquy on her predicament, like the stage directions for the Cherry Owens, manifests what Dylan Thomas *wanted* to believe. He wants to believe that there is no hate in depersonalised and irresponsible sexual activity any more than in alcoholism:

POLLY GARTER

Me, Polly Garter, under the washing line, giving the breast in the garden to my bonny new baby. Nothing grows in our garden, only washing. And babies. And where's their fathers live, my love? Over the hills and far away. You're looking up at me now. I know what you are thinking, you poor little milky creature. You're thinking, you're no better than you should be, Polly, and that's good enough for me. Oh, isn't life a terrible thing, thank God.

(*Single long high chord on strings*) (p. 31)

The chord (which is the heaven-revealing 'lost chord' of the sentimental song) is a religiose endorsement of behaviour the real consequences of which Thomas wishes to deny. He himself had suffered an environmental failure in infancy and his identity was deeply flawed by the impingement of a not-good-enough mothering. He was not reflected either ('you're looking up at me now'). This left him with a hungry regressed libidinal ego—the child in him. As we have seen, in the poems there is an under-current of hatred directed at infants, since they evoke the 'unborn' hungry weakness in him and the female element which he so fears. But this is because he himself has an infantile incorporative need which he directs at Pollies—and he knows, in truth, that this kind of urge is likely to reproduce its own suffering. ('Poor little bugger, he doesn't deserve this . . .') So, he idealises the libidinal Polly, and tries to insist that all is really well and that sex without responsibility to the person is to be seen as acceptable—she is still untroubled, free, happy, and joyful.

At about this time Thomas wrote the ballad for *Under Milk Wood*:

> O it's my turn now said Flossie Snail
> To take the baby from the milking pail
> It's my turn now said Johnnie Crack
> To smack it on the head and put it back
>
> . . . One would put it back and one would pull it out
> And all it had to drink was ale and stout
> For Johnnie Crack and Flossie Snail
> Always used to say that stout and ale
> Was *good* for a baby in a milking pail . . . (p. 51)

There is something bewildered behind this, about his capacity to 'find' the baby, the child, and something even more disturbing. And about this time also Thomas received a prize for his poetry and spent the money on an abortion for his wife. The symbolism is obvious ('milking pail' in folksong has a double meaning for female sex organ).

> Well, anyway: I won a prize, for the book of the year, of £250, which put paid to baby . . .

Thomas was evidently struggling with his own guilt at acting out in reality the feelings he expressed in '*If my head hurt a hair's foot*', and the picture he gives of Polly Garter is one by which he tries to keep attitudes to sexual creativity and meaning as superficial as possible, to avoid the pains of his own anguish about his own sexual capacities, and their consequences, which he felt to be full of dread.

So, *Under Milk Wood* is a mixture of the highly moral and the highly immoral, of impish realism, self-delusory phantasy, sympathy and hate. And despite Thomas's avowal, there may be some awareness of the human predicament—but there is little that can be called 'love'. Thomas's original intentions for the piece are made plain in a letter to Madame Caetani, in October 1951.

As the piece goes on two voices will be predominant: that of the preacher, who talks only in verse, and that of the anonymous exhibitor and chronicler called, simply, 1st Voice. And the 1st Voice is really a kind of conscience, a guardian angel.

(*Letters*, p. 365)

This 'conscience' or guardian angel, however, is concerned to penetrate beyond conventional morality, to deeper existential questions. This voice presents the material from a point of view by which all human 'eccentricities' are seen as a symbolism of 'strategies of survival'. But in consequence, at times, schizoid behaviour is offered by Dylan Thomas as itself 'simple and ordinary'—as acceptable. Thus there is both a 'moral and an immoral motive' behind the work. By the moral motive he seeks to tell us what madness feels like—it is a way of symbolising one's predicament: it is the only way in which one can deal with the world of such people. The intention here is to generate compassion for predicaments, which are everyone's to some degree. The immoral motive is to vindicate the kind of behaviour which implies—'since the joys of loving are barred to me I may as well give myself over to the joys of hating'. By this motive Thomas seeks to have falsities endorsed by 'a guardian angel'. There is thus a mixture of compassion and defiant acceptance of false solutions. Compassion as, for example,

. . . the old woman who every morning shouts her age to the heavens; she believes the town is the chosen land, & and little river Dewi the River of Jordan; she is not all mad; she merely believes in heaven on earth. And so will all of them, all the eccentrics whose eccentricities, in these first pages, are but

briefly & impressionistically noticed: all, by their own rights
are ordinary & good; & the 1st Voice, & the poet preacher,
never judge nor condemn but explain and make strangely
simple & simply strange. (*Letters*, p. 365)
But there is also a concern to endorse in a subtle way a mode which
withholds itself from commitment, which 'once it is made clear'
can be seen as 'most natural':

Mr Edwards the draper, and Miss Price, the sempstress, & their
odd and, once it is made clear, most natural love . . . all their
lives they have known of each other's existence, and of their
mutual love . . . easily they could have been together, married,
had children: but that is not the life for them: their passionate
love, at just this distance, is all they need. (ibid., p. 365)

Other forms of relationship are presented as 'enjoyable' which
could never be so:

Dai Bread, the baker, who has two wives: one is loving &
mothering, sacklike & jolly; the other is gypsy slatternly and,
all in love, hating: *all three enjoy it* . . . (ibid., my italics)

This is both a compassionate statement of how some individuals
find themselves in a 'cycle of hate': but also an attempt to make us
believe it would be possible for such a *ménage à trois* to be successful. Again, Thomas is trying to seduce us into believing his own
delusions about 'false solutions', in a 'came to a bad end—very
enjoyable' mood. In the same mood he wrote to Mme Caetani:

And Polly Garter has many illegitimate babies because she loves
babies but does not want only one man's . . . (ibid.)

Over Polly Garter he indulges in an absurd romanticised view
of irresponsible promiscuity. It suggests that unconsciously he
cannot tolerate the role of the husband in providing support for
the woman, by taking care of the external world so that she can
'be' for her child. It is as if he cannot reconcile (as most people do)
object-constancy with the need to provide a 'facilitating environment' for the 'maturational processes'. There may be women who
can love babies but are not yet capable of loving one man: but
Thomas's flippancy diverts our attention from the inevitable
anguish, for mother and child, in this 'strategy of survival', as it
is in life.

But, of course, his most energetic apologies are for alcoholism:

And Cherry Owen the soak, who likes getting drunk every

night: and his wife *who likes living with two men, one sober in the day and one drunk at night* . . . (ibid., my italics)

Thomas wishes it were possible for others to enjoy living with a divided self—as he knew it is not. And yet he knew too that for some it *was* also necessary to live with a schizoid individual, in order to match, in that curious way, their own needs with the needs of others. The attitudes to human nature and existence behind *Under Milk Wood* are therefore inevitably contradictory and falsified: the bawdiness (perhaps most people don't see how bawdy it is) hides despair. Thomas manages on the one hand to evoke our compassion for the 'false solution' strategies, in those who cannot find love and a sense of being real in normal ways. On the other hand he seeks to involve us in a belief that schizoid solutions are superior to normal ones, *that there is no hate in them*, and that there are no other solutions. Yet as we know—those of us who are the 'manic-depressive people we call normal' as Winnicott put it—there are solutions which belong to love and reparation. Such ways of finding meaning are not, however, at a premium in our culture. If we accept such an attitude as Thomas's we are in danger of becoming involved in his own disastrous delusions, and his impulse to dehumanise himself and others. Yet we can find a great deal of amusement, as we can with Swift, in a comedy rooted in such bitter despair about ever feeling fully human.

16

The Poet and the Point of Living

Does my attempt at a 'schizoid diagnosis' help us to understand and place Dylan Thomas's poetry? In its light even his most chaotic and destructive manifestations, in life or work, can be seen to belong to a 'strategy of survival', and as a means to hold a self together by 'pseudo-male doing' and 'bad thinking'. His verbal inchoateness is a defence against being 'found'. His visceral imagery is a way of not being drawn back into the womb. His alcoholism is an attempt at cure. All can be seen as strange manifestations of the desire to find himself, and to find point in existence. He wanted to live: but, despite his heroism, his anti-libidinal ego and his false self turned to destructiveness and sought to carry out all that his parents unconsciously intended for him—which was to deny his independent existence. In the end they succeeded. The terrible truth of Dylan Thomas then is that we have a 'liveliness' that asserts life—but which also conceals death and destruction. We cannot respond to the poetry as creative art without discriminating against this undercurrent in which the man turns against his own humanness.

What is often taken for his vitality, seems often something like 'manic denial'. His compulsive hedonism was in fact a manifestation of 'deterioration', marking the increasing collapse of the capacity to deal with reality. Fairbairn sees compulsive pleasure-seeking as deteriorative (a truth recognised by Thomas when he spoke of his London bouts as his 'capital punishment'):

With the child's inexperience goes a tendency on his part to be more emotional and impulsive, and to be less tolerant of the many frustrations which he encounters. These various factors must all be taken into account; and it is only in so far as conditions of adaptation become too difficult for the child that the reality principle gives place to the pleasure principle as a secondary, and deteriorative (as against regressive) principle of behaviour calculated to relieve tension and provide compensatory satisfaction. (*Psychoanalytical Studies*, p. 157)

Thomas was, of course, a man, not a child, though he was imprisoned in limitations on his capacities for finding reality, because, it would seem, certain processes of personal development which are normally completed in infancy, were not in him completed. But this is true of most of us and we all tend to burst out into compensatory behaviour when tension mounts, as we try to solve our existence problems. The important thing for us to see in trying to understand someone like Dylan Thomas, however, is that what seems to be the natural expression of a 'pleasure-principle' turned out to be the expression of a desperate attempt to overcome inner fear and anxiety. If those around him at the time had understood this, they might have helped him more—helped him, that is, more towards survival, rather than, as it were, to more drink ('What will you have?' 'Too much!').

This raises the whole question of the effect of the prevalent ethos of the *avant-garde* on poets and other creative individuals suffering from existential anguish. It is surely ridiculous to say that Dylan Thomas was 'killed by the Income tax': but it might be less absurd to say that he was helped towards his death by the fashionable literary atmosphere of contemporary America, and a schizoid society. The trouble is that, from a certain point of view, such manifestations as Dylan Thomas's libidinous behaviour in America looks like the expression of a larger than normal libido and an assertion of 'life'. There is evidently a dangerous split between the reader's envious fascination with this legend and the desperate truth of the man's false attempt to deal with 'bad objects' which threatened from within until he became encapsulated in a circuit of self-hate, from which escape becomes increasingly impossible:

It is also to a massive return of repressed bad objects that we must look for the explanation of the phenomenon which Freud described as 'the repetitious compulsion'—a concept which loses much of its explanatory value once it is recognised that it is not so much a case of compulsively repeating traumatic situations as of being haunted by bad objects against the return of which all defences have broken down and from which there is no longer any escape (except in death). (ibid., p. 166)

In the light of more recent existentialist theories we may, I believe, see the struggle against 'bad objects' within as being, at greater depth, a struggle against the fear of loss of meaning in life. The unborn regressed libidinal ego within cries out ferociously to be born into a meaningful existence—but is hated because of its voracity. The anti-libidinal ego turns energetically and sadistically upon it. At the same time a conformist, pseudo-male, false self, or pattern of confused selves, is turned outwards to deal with the world. In all these there are energetic oral elements, which are expressed both in the poetry and the alcoholism of Dylan Thomas. Both drink and poetry were attempts at self-cure: both were forms of 'masculine protest' and falsification, combined with an aggressive nihilism which turns against the self. Such energies can be employed to create that chaos which holds others at harm's length who could love one, and to forestall the understanding that is also desperately sought for.

So, Dylan Thomas's 'capital punishment' has its counterpart in his work, as Sylvia Plath's libidinal attachment to self-destruction has its expression in hers. Both poets developed a need to cling to bad internal objects, which they could not rid themselves of, and round which they constructed a kind of identity based on hate. This collection of bad objects is Sylvia Plath's 'Daddy', and Dylan Thomas's 'old ram rod'. Ted Hughes writes a ballad to this element in himself, *Song for a Phallus*. All three poems reveal that this 'bad object' self is constructed around the father's stolen penis: as Fairbairn indicates, the schizoid individual, deprived in infancy of normal love through giving and meeting, had had to 'steal' love, and can only do so by stealing parts of objects and internalising them. Because these part-objects have been stolen, the individual is guilty about his possession of them, but also endows them with intense libidinal attention. These internal bad objects are thus the focus of both devotion and rejection—a 'sulking, skulking, coal black soul'. In her poem *Daddy* Sylvia Plath tries to reject her bad object, as a 'black telephone', 'cut off at the root'— this particular way of relating can be dispensed with, she declares —but very soon after commits suicide. Dylan Thomas's old ram-rod is dying in *Lament* and 'is a man no more no more', as he gives

himself up to the joys of hating and cries 'Good be thou my evil',
in final rejection and despair,

And all the deadly virtues plague my death!

In such poems we may see how the individual becomes, in final
hopelessness, 'identified with the aggressor' against the self. As
Peter Lomas says:

> it would perhaps be least confusing to restrict the term 'false'
> to behaviour designed, for whatever reason, to conceal the
> existence of the true self and therefore to deny meaning. The
> reasons for this kind of aim would include the avoidance of a
> real experience of life that was too awful to contemplate, the
> preservation (as Winnicott has shown) of a hidden but intact
> true self, and the attainment of some kind of meaning and satis-
> faction from the spurious personality which is erected. Although
> some satisfaction may be gained in this way, true meaning
> cannot. In such a state the person is 'depersonalised': his identity
> is based on delusion and parasitism, dependent on the use of
> mechanisms known to psychoanalysts by such terms as intro-
> jection, identification, narcissism, masochism, etc.: he has
> become a quisling, and has, in Anna Freud's phrase 'identified
> with the aggressor', the latter being, in this context, the world
> which has prevented him from becoming himself . . . Actual
> behaviour, will necessarily be a function of both the true and
> the false. (*Psychoanalysis Observed*, ed. Rycroft, p. 137)

There are many phrases in this discussion of what we mean by
'false' and 'true' in such terms as 'false self' and 'true self' that illuminate the dreadful predicament of Dylan Thomas. In turning
on himself, he was, in a sense, identifying with the world which
he felt had prevented him from becoming himself. What seems to
me unfortunate is that the literary sphere in which he moved often
tended, on the whole, to encourage and endorse this identification,
and so to hasten those processes by which he came in the end to
destroy both true and false self together. This is not necessarily to
say, however, that anyone could ever have rescued Dylan Thomas
from his terrible plight.

It is very difficult here to keep a clear discrimination between
the man and the poetry, and between art and the utterance of
schizophrenic patients, such as those Laing discusses, who could
not deal with the world at all because instead of an identity they

had only a fragmentary set of false systems. But Dylan Thomas *has* the capacity to communicate, at times eminently, as in his letters. It is only at a certain depth in the personality and at certain times that we encounter fragmentation.

This fragmentation at the core was however a continual threat to the integral self which dealt with the world. Dylan Thomas reveals himself as perpetually afraid of internal sabotage, and (whatever attempts his critics make to gloss over the truth) his life was continually sabotaged from within. He expresses his fear with clarity to Marguerite Caetani:

> I can't explain why I didn't write to explain why I couldn't finish the piece. (No, I can't explain. When I try to explain my fear, the confused symbols grow leaden and a woolly rust creeps over the words. How can I say it? I can't. I can say: One instinct of fear is to try to make oneself as little, as unnoticeable, as possible, to cower, as one thinks, unseen and anonymous until the hunt is past. My fearful instinct is to bloat myself like a frog, magnify my unimportance, to ring a bell for a name, so that, as I bluster and loom twice my size, the hunt, seeing me monstrous, bays by after different & humbler prey. But that is not what I mean: the symbols have wet-brain, the words have swallowed their tongues. (*Letters*, p. 381)

The fear was justified, because episodically he himself, driven by false elements in his make-up, would wreck his own world—as we see from the confused and dissociated apologia for the events which largely destroyed his relationship with Pamela Hansford Johnson and represent from the beginning his catastrophic incapacity for object-constancy.

> ? 26th May 1934
> Sunday morning
> Bed
>
> I'm in a dreadful mess now. I can hardly hold the pencil or hold the paper. This has been coming for weeks. And the last four days have completed it. I'm absolutely at the point of breaking now . . . As well as I can I'll tell you the honest honest truth. I never want to lie to you. You'll be terribly angry with me I know and you'll never write to me again perhaps. But darling you want me to tell you the truth don't you . . . I slept with her that night & for the next three nights. We were

terribly drunk day and night. Now I can see all sorts of things.
I think I've got them.

Oh darling, it hurts me to tell you this but I've got to tell you
because I always want to tell you the truth about me . . . I love
you Pamela always & always. But she's a pain on the nerves.
. . . I see bits of you in her all the time & tack on to those bits . . .
I've got to be drunk to tack on to them . . . Don't be too cross
or too angry. What the hell am I to do? And what the hell are
you going to say to me? Darling I love you & think of you
all the time . . .

XXXX Darling. Darling oh (*Letters*, pp. 132–3)

Despite all his attempts to dispel normal moral reactions to
Dylan Thomas, by pleading a special allowance for the world of
the *avant-garde*, Constantine Fitzgibbon is yet forced to admit that
Dylan Thomas's attachment to his own 'death circuit', and his
childishness, undermined his whole life in such ways. The confusion of object-constancy is already plain here. In the phrase 'I see
bits of you in her' we have the attitude 'they're all Caitlin really'
in embryo: and the man shows a strange incapacity for insight in
not seeing how much worse this admission would make it. We
find the same syndrome years later when Thomas said to Brinnin
in bewilderment, 'I'm in love with Sarah, and I'm in love with
my wife. I don't know what to do' (*Dylan Thomas in America*,
p. 93).

Even Fitzgibbon sees that to Thomas, as to Laing's schizoid
patients, to accept the reality of the world, self, others and time
seemed to involve an impossible sacrifice of freedom. He even
glimpses the death-circuit element in *Lament* of which I have
written above:

. . . in his later poems, which he once defined to a journalist
as 'statements on the way to the grave', this emotion is of far
greater complexity, and nostalgia itself becomes an inadequate
word with which to define it.

He had never lost his conviction that his would be a short life.
Nor was this a pose, as his 'T.B.' had perhaps once been, for he
was far too sensitive and sensible to play-act in front of Caitlin.
To her, too, he said repeatedly that he would not live till forty.
Though two stone heavier, thanks largely to the beer he had

drunk, and no longer a thin and sickly boy, he was convinced
that time was ticking away against him. All the more reason,
then, to come to terms, poetical terms, with his own past. As he
had put it some years before:

> The ball I threw while playing in the park
> Has not yet reached the ground.

When it does reach the ground, he must no longer be there,
and thus all he can hope truly to comprehend is its upward
flight, the first stage of its parabola. And from such compre-
hension much can be understood about the only vital problem,
that of the relationship between birth and death. For even when
he was young and easy under the apple boughs

> Time held me green and dying
> Though I sang in my chains like the sea.

And now the imminence and soon the reality of war made the
eternal and infinite omnipresence of death even more real to
Dylan than before. It is by no means coincidental that the two
victims of that war whom he should have mourned in poems
were a girl child and an old man aged one hundred. And again,
in one of his last poems, 'Lament', he completes the circle from
his infancy to his own coming death and his own children's
infancy, with the obvious implication that the circle must again
be completed in their brief lives. (*Life*, p. 258)

He sees that Thomas's attachment to his regressed libidinal ego
meant both an inadequacy in dealing with the real world, but
also was the impulse in his heroic pursuit of the 'point of life':

There is the question of what I have called Dylan's own regressive character, his frequently infantile behaviour. This is perhaps in some ways a matter more for a psychologist than a biographer. But certainly Dylan found it extremely difficult to
deal with an adult's problems, with laundry, money and civil
servants. Certainly, too, he preserved infantile habits into early
middle age, asking his friends to sing him to sleep, sucking at
his bottle or his cigarette, eating sweets and reading trash or
watching science fiction films goggle-eyed. Much of this must
be accountable to the early, perhaps the earliest, days at No. 5
Cwmdonkin Drive, but it can also be explained in part by the
fact that his very powerful brain was devoted, not quite exclusively but almost so, to his work. The trivia of life bored him,

his failures to deal with them distressed him, his own dishonesty and partial compromise with the outside world disgusted him, and therefore he looked back to the golden age before women and publishers and tax gatherers, when birth and a child's vision of fresh beauty and death were the realities. Certainly it was there that he found his purest and deepest inspiration.

(Life, p. 259)

Thomas often speaks of his poetry as a means by which he sought to lay the devils which plagued his personal life. ' . . . I always call it the invoking of devils. And, mark my grisly words, invoke the devils too much, and by God they will come' *(Letters,* p. 84). Yet the contest is not with the problems of coping with life, but rather with some nameless fear:

> . . . I received a rather disquieting note from Richard Rees of the Adelphi, who, last week, asked me to send him some recent poems. He compliments me upon the high standard & the great originality exhibited & said my technique was amazing (One Up for Formal Me), but accused me—not in quite so many words—of being in the grip of devils. 'The poems have an unsubstantiality, a dream-like quality', he writes, 'which non-plussed me.' He then goes on to say that the poems, as a whole, reminded him of automatic or trance-writing.
>
> Automatic writing is worthless as literature, however interesting it may be to the psychologist & pathologist. So perhaps, after all I am nothing but a literary oddity, a little freak of nature whose madness runs into print rather than into ravings and illusions. It may be, too, an illusion that keeps me writing, the illusion of myself as some misunderstood poet of talent. The note has depressed me more than the usual adverse criticism. It shows not dislike, or mere incomprehension, but confession of bewilderment, & almost fear, at the method by which I write my poetry.
>
> But he is wrong, I swear it. My facility, as he calls it, is, in reality, tremendously hard work. I write at the speed of two lines an hour. I have written hundreds of poems, & each one has taken me a great many painful, brain-racking and sweaty hours. *(Letters,* p. 62)

The work seems to him impelled as necessary, to attack some (bad) part of himself:

. . . I can't help what I write. It is part of me, however unpleasant a part it may be, and however necessary it should be to cauterize and castrate that part (*Letters*, p. 62).

And yet to construct something, but as if out of dead material:

A new poem accompanies this. I suppose it's my usual stuff again, and even a little more death-struck. But don't be put off by my anatomical imagery, which I explained months ago. Because I so often write in terms of the body, of the death, disease, and breaking of the body, it doesn't necessarily mean that my Muse (*not* one of my favourite words) is a sadist. For the time at least, I believe in the writing of poetry from the flesh, and, generally, from the dead flesh. So many modern poets take the *living* flesh as their object, and, by their clever dissecting, turn it into a carcase. I prefer to take the *dead* flesh, and, by any positivity of faith and belief that is in me, build up a *living* flesh from it. (*Letters*, p. 74)

These quotations would seem to confirm that Thomas's poetry was an attempt to overcome 'bad internal objects' and in this to lay reality bare and to find truth, and to discover a new sense of being through resurrection of some kind. In part of himself Thomas had a creative honesty which denied all obligations except the existential one with which the schizoid individual is necessarily concerned:

. . . There is no necessity for the artist to do anything. There is no necessity. He is a law unto himself, and his greatness or smallness rises or falls by that. He has only one limitation, and that is the widest of all: the limitation of form. Poetry finds its own form; form should never be superimposed; the structure should rise out of the words and the expression of them. I do not want to express only what other people have felt; I want to rip something away and show what they have never seen.
(*Letters*, p. 24)

Yet the sense of being has to be forged out of hate—'burning hell in its own flames':

I want to forget all that I have ever written and start again, informed with a new wonder, empty of all my old dreariness, and rid of the sophistication which is a disease. How can I ever lie on my belly on the floor, turning a narrow thought over and over again on the tip of my tongue, crying in my wordy wilderness, mean of spirit, brooding over the death of my finger which lies straight in front of me? How can I, when I have news to scream up to heaven, and when heaven has news to scream down to me? I want to read the headlines in the sky: birth of a star, death of a comet. I want to believe, to believe for ever, that heaven is *being*, a state of being, and the only hell is the hell of myself. I want to burn hell with its own flames.

(*Letters*, p. 84)

'Only the Devil can eat the Devil out', was Sylvia Plath's conclusion, and we have seen how this turning of hate on the hate within becomes a delusion, which is that of schizoid suicide. The harrowing of hell is the harrowing of the false self, towards resurrection. In the *Letters* Thomas speaks of his daily contemplation of suicide, and in the letter quoted above he goes on:

'The universe is wild and full of marvels.' In the shape of a boy, and a funny boy at that, I have only a very short time to learn how mad and marvellous it is; I think in cells; one day I may think in rains. All round us, now and forever, a spirit is bearing and killing and resurrecting a body; I care not a damn for Christ, but only for his symbol, the symbol of death. But suicide is wrong; a man who commits suicide is like a man who longs for a gate to be opened and who cuts his throat before he reaches the gate. (*Letters*, pp. 84–5)

The elements in his cultural efforts which belong to the death-circuit, however, ultimately triumphed—as if he strove to eliminate a minus quantity in himself by minus quantities, hate by hate, burning hell with its own flames, resurrecting a dead body (i.e. a self in the psychic tissue which had never been born). And this attempt to establish an identity based on false male doing by further false male doing had its counterpart in his work, as when he confesses that he sought to 'take all the life out' of words. Somehow, he seems to have come to feel, in his efforts to find rebirth, *life* itself has to be eliminated, because living as a human being inevitably entails all the risks of *being* which he had experienced disastrously in primary stages.

The 'anatomical imagery' of his quest to be reborn, his 'dead flesh', has its own significance in the symbolism of the regressed ego. As Guntrip says in 'Phantasies of the breast, and of anal and incestuous genital relations with the mother of post-natal exist-

ence, are expressions of a struggle by a different part of the personality to "stay born"' (*Schizoid Phenomena*, p. 53).

Dylan Thomas's 'flesh' imagery can therefore be seen as expressing a desire to stay in existence. The fear we have noted at the
heart of his personality is, in terms of Guntrip's diagnosis from
clinical experience, a fear of the danger of being 'drawn back
inside', because of a flight from life. Yet by his withdrawal the
schizoid person 'risks the total loss of all objects, and therewith
the loss of his own ego as well' (ibid., p. 56). The 'anatomical'
poems are thus to be regarded in the same sense as phantasies of
a contest with elements in his 'world of internalised objects' in an
attempt to overcome his fear of 'loss of all objects' and loss of his ego.

This kind of need distorts his poems in their 'outwardness' too.
For some individuals, and for all of us at times, it is necessary, in
order to feel real and alive, to challenge everything upon which we
have based our sense of the point of life, and to reject what comes to
seem to us a false way of conforming to a world that inhibits us.
But this creation of chaos can either be creative, or wildly disruptive merely. As we have seen, there is sometimes a wild degree
of exaggeration in Dylan Thomas's attitudes to the world because
of an excessive (and untrue) paranoid feeling of oppression. So, his
attitude to society tends to become a caricature:

> ... Of course you don't like his [Kipling's] flagflapping, for
> you know as well as I do that patriotism is a publicity ramp
> organised by holders of excess armament shares; you know that
> the Union Jack is only a national loin-cloth to hide the decaying
> organs of a diseased social system; you know that the Great War
> was purposely protracted in order for financiers to make more
> money; that had it not been for the shares in armament firms
> the War would have ended in three weeks; that at one period
> of the War French and German were shelling each other with
> ammunition provided by the same firm, a firm in which
> English clergymen and politicians, French ambassadors and
> German business men all had a great deal of money invested;
> that Kipling, rejected by the army because of weak physique,
> is nevertheless a 'I gave my son' militarist; that the country
> which he lauds and eulogises is a country that supports a system
> by which men are starved, and fish, wheat and coffee are burnt
> by the hundreds of tons; a system by which men are not allowed

to work, to marry, to have children; by which they are driven mad daily; by which children are brought into the world scrofulous; by which the church is allowed to prevent the prevention of sexual diseases . . . (*Letters*, p. 31)

In this there are some valid criticisms of the horrors of hypocrisy and self-deception in our world, and the way we accept these as 'normal'. From the point of view of the schizoid individual who must continually challenge the nature of existence, he is trying to explode the whole fabric of conventional 'normality'. But because this impulse emerges from his own lack of confidence in his ability to find reality, it becomes grotesque—and sounds like some of the crudest of 'protest' or 'underground' polemics.

The exaggeration is surely that of a paranoid-schizoid view of the world, coloured by Thomas's need to project over 'society' his own internal anxieties and fears, and to throw over the world his own 'bad object' problem? He identifies some self-destructive part of himself with 'the world', an aggressor who has suppressed his capacity to become what he feels he should be. So, the world is to be blamed for immense destructiveness and waste. Despite the truths, the emotional pressure generates distortions which make the protest irrational and wild.

This imposition of the inner world on the outer is found in a more intense form in the poetry, as we have seen, and yet some of his best poems spring from the consequent dichotomy in apprehension. Elsewhere, where the problem of 'finding' a real world in which it is possible to live becomes too acute, Thomas withdraws, behind a screen of depersonalised mechanical activity with words, or behind deliberate chaos, so that one has the sense of being up against some kind of false system rather than a person—the real individual having shrunk back inside himself, out of touch. Yet he speaks of this anguish, too.

Turning from biographical history to the poems as art, we cannot avoid seeing that in the mechanical activity with words to which he resorted at times there is some denial of 'inner necessity', and a denial that it is necessary to come to terms with the world at all—which involves him in a denial of being human. In selecting words from Roget by chance Thomas worked like a machine, programmed to sort out synonyms, without any 'giving' in communication: 'I kill the life in them'. He becomes an automaton shuffling dead or frozen clichés, in order, in Balint's terms, to keep a pattern of identity based on that primitive hate which does not develop or grow, as contrasted with one based on love which is 'capable of growth'. Such poetry is language used at the uttermost extreme from creative metaphor, and from language which is shared: it is 'the code of night', composed of words 'picked of their live associations'.

This failure to engage, through the 'three-term' processes of symbolism, between the self and the world, marks a schizoid failure of communication, and when we encounter it we may feel that Thomas was trying to restore a primitive stage in development, or to regress to it. Yet for an adult, of course, this is impossible, because he is inevitably being presented continually with evidence that the world is not all 'him', that he cannot control it by phantasy, and that it is indifferent to him. Yet to accept this separateness involves recognition of his own vulnerability, his own mortality, his own 'nothingness' on the one hand, and the imperfectness and dreadfulness of the outside world itself. These problems are such as are gradually grasped and dealt with by the infant in what Melanie Klein calls the 'paranoid-schizoid position' the first stages of growth of the identity. If ontological security is not found in dealing with them at that stage, they torment the adult ever after.

Since it is impossible for the schizoid individual to accept these realities of self and world, because of his deep ontological insecurity, in his emptiness at the core, with his inability to find the universe benign, he may try to survive by becoming paranoid, by adopting a posture of 'masculine protest', or by seeking to take flight into further withdrawal. Yet none of these courses really solves the problem—tending rather to thrust reality further away, or to bring the terrors of the possible loss of all objects.

From such problems arise the kind of bafflement we have examined in Dylan Thomas, and, as I have tried to suggest, these dreadful problems have their roots in the original combination of maternal inadequacy with compensatory over-protectiveness. The mother has never 'disillusioned' the subject, and 'let him go', into his own independent existence. For him 'weaning has no meaning' and he cannot tolerate independence. He has never found the mother as 'objective object' and so cannot 'find' the world as object, or himself as real and autonomous over against it. An inability to experience separation from the object involves an inability to accept the whole self, dependent on another whole being, recognised as a separate entity in her own right, 'out there', or to accept a world-as-object in which an integrated subject lives, meaningfully. From this complex state of affairs develops forms of splitting: those aspects of reality which impinge are felt to be persecutory, because they disturb the defences by which ambivalence and ego-weakness are denied within the self. I believe all these problems can be found expressed in Thomas's poetry.

The confusions of language and creativity go with the problems. Thomas wants to create, but cannot tolerate the insights which creation brings. He wants to be in touch with himself, but yet fears nothing more. He wants to find the world, but cannot bear the pain: the beauty of *Fern Hill* is wrung out of this perplexity. To such a person the Eden perfection of the phantasy world which he managed to create when he was 'prince of the appletowns' is spoilt by the very urges which drive him to explore and develop his growing sense of perception as an adult. The conflict generates a life-tiredness, and this in its turn is reflected in his work, which also goes lifeless. A mechanical substitute is then resorted to, while in life the individual resorts to 'false male doing', frenetic meaningless activities in mere sexuality and other forms of 'capital punishment'—unto self-destruction.

The self-punitive element in this, despite its curative aspects, turns inward. Meanwhile, reality cannot be made other than it is, while inner reality turns out to be as stubborn. There seems to be less and less chance of being able to release the 'formative principle' of the true self, or to become what one wants to become. The consequence is an increasing hopelessness: as Sylvia Plath cried, 'I am incapable of more knowledge', and as Dylan Thomas wrote, albeit in bitter fun, 'I am a man no more, no more . . .', but later said, 'I don't know how to help myself any more'. The desire to love and be loved was still there ('I love you . . . but I'm alone', Brinnin, p. 272) but the defences of the false self took over increasingly and Dylan Thomas, even aware of 'the gates of hell', gave himself up more and more, in futility, to the joys of hating. For this he was acclaimed as a 'broily boy' by the world of cultural fashion—and urged on relentlessly to his doom.

Out of this chaos, with one like Dylan Thomas, whose problems focused in the mouth, there comes a strange mixture of
intense need and intense aggresion and fear, in various oral
manifestations, including the poetry. At times his chaos is a
creative chaos: at other times a denying and hiding chaos. This
is, in other terms, a strange mixture of female-element-being and
male-element-doing. Where there is creative failure, in the background is the father's willed wish that his son should be the poet
he never managed to become. Where there is genuine creativity,
it is often limited by the failure to escape from the mother's possessive will, and her failure to 'wean', psychically speaking. All these
terrible features of his 'psychic tissue' conspired against Dylan
Thomas's quest for a true self to express, and to find a meaning
in his life.

Yet, out of all this anguish, and despite all the terrifying forces
which ensnared him in contradictions and confusion and which
eventually destroyed him, Dylan Thomas managed to achieve
art, with great heroism. When he is questioning the validity of
his existence among the herons, fishes, and cycles of life and time
in the River Towy, we have a genuine preoccupation with the
meaning of life, from a true poetic self, though from the heart of a
man who disastrously lacked confidence in being. Out of the
death and chaos in himself he created some human moments in
drama and prose which are profoundly comic, and left a few
poems which touch on our deepest existential problems. They
illuminate our world with a vision which, as things go on—as
writing goes on—seems ever rarer.

From my psychological investigation I hope the reader may
be able to return to the poetry and respond to it with a new understanding. The reader alone can decide whether this is the effect of
this 'study in the psychology of culture'. In a review of a book by
Gaston Bachelard (the philosopher of surrealism) François Bott
wrote recently that 'Bachelard's criticism of conventional psychoanalysis helps us to explain the nature of his own approach'
(which was phenomenological).

He did not believe that the truth of a text could be reached by
studying the biography or even the subconscious mind of its
author.

Poetry in fact ushers in a new truth and a new reality . . .

poetry does not seek to express the inexpressible; it gives expression to something which cannot have been experienced in real life and which cannot exist outside words . . . 'language is above all a mystical experience.' . . . Bachelard was less concerned with the relationship between the author and his work than with the work and the reader. For him reading was a transference in the psychoanalytical sense of the word. We cannot enter a poem and it cannot enter us unless we open ourselves completely to the adventure embodied in it.

(*Le Monde*, 27 January 1971)

The reviewer quotes Hölderlin, 'Man lives poetically on this earth'. I have tried to emphasise the way in which we need to give priority to the poetic in our whole approach to man and his needs and to accept that what matters most about a poem is what it contributes to the inner dynamics of the reader in his living, and his quest for meaning, now. But, I believe, we cannot 'enter' many of Dylan Thomas's poems until we have done some phenomenological and psychoanalytical work on them, in some kind of 'transference' situation—as when, above, I found myself writing mad interpretations of mad poems.

In this kind of approach to poetry I believe there are many parallels with what is happening in psychoanalysis itself, in its concentration on 'creative reflection', and on bringing out of the patient what it is the patient has within himself to fulfil. In terms of literary criticism I believe we should aim at a reflection of what it is the artist has brought, and the articulation of this, so that others may share 'the adventure' better. By experiencing the critic's reflecting response, they can be brought towards a more dynamic engagement with the poetry itself.

To do such critical work is not, I hope, to be an 'outsider'. I have admitted 'mothering' Thomas, and my work here has changed my attitudes a great deal. Bachelard was afraid that to intellectualise was to 'decline profundity': as Mary Ann Caws says,

The psychoanalyst who intellectualises and translates . . . takes the position of an outsider, and 'l'attitude objective refuse la profoundeur.' . . . Bachelard leaves psychoanalysis for what Jean Hyppolite calls a *psycho-synthesis*, in which the image resulting from the unsatisfied desire is considered of equal importance to the desire itself. The psychoanalyst explains the flower by the fertiliser; Jung warns that the interest of the analyst moves away from the work of art itself. But poetry, says Bachelard, has its own happiness, no matter what drama it illustrates . . . Bachelard developed a 'phenomenology of the imagination' which was an 'ontologie directe', concentrating wholly on the poetics of the image, in which there are no 'pleas for scientific abstraction'.

But in my approach there has been, I hope, no 'scientific abstraction'. I have not treated the poetry as the expression of 'unsatisfied desires'. This approach, belonging to conventional psychoanalysis, of explaining away the quest for meaning in terms of the sublimation of some 'other', more real, physical drive, has been rejected. Man's primary needs are now seen as the fulfilment of the 'will-to-meaning'. And here there is no clash between awareness of the meaning and our response to it: we can still enjoy Humpty-Dumpty, although we recognise that as an egg he represents the fragility of the tegument of the identity. We need not, however, be always reducing the primacy of the symbol by explicitness and over-interpretation—a tendency now recognised in psychoanalytical technique as a danger. Yet, with someone like Dylan Thomas one often cannot *begin* until one does begin to interpret.

Exploration of the meaning of poetic symbolism 'phenomenologically', as a manifestation of consciousness in the here and now can, I believe, deepen and extend our response to creativity. In this we are no mere 'outsiders', but draw gladly on the 'psychosynthesis' offered by the poetry itself. In this we can find gratitude in outselves for the immense efforts a poet has made, not least in the face of desperate life-problems. Such an approach recognises that his efforts have contributed to our capacity to find our own deeper potentialities, and our own sense of meaning, by the symbolic energy he has managed to exert and develop between separation and union, in the sharing between man and man that we call culture.

Bibliography

BOOKS BY DYLAN THOMAS

18 Poems, London: The Sunday Referee and the Parton Press, 1934.
Twenty-five Poems, London: J. M. Dent, 1936.
The Map of Love, London: J. M. Dent, 1939.
The World I Breathe, Norfolk, Conn.: New Directions, 1939.
Portrait of the Artist as a Young Dog, London: J. M. Dent, 1940.
New Poems, Norfolk, Conn.: New Directions, 1943.
Deaths and Entrances, London: J. M. Dent, 1946.
Selected Writings of Dylan Thomas, New York: New Directions, 1946.
Twenty-six Poems, London: J. M. Dent, 1950.
In Country Sleep, New York: New Directions, 1952.
Collected Poems, 1934–52, London: J. M. Dent, 1952; paperback edition, 1971.
The Doctor and the Devils (film scenario), London: J. M. Dent, 1954.
Under Milk Wood, London: J. M. Dent, 1954.
Quite Early One Morning (broadcasts), London: J. M. Dent, 1954.
Adventures in the Skin Trade, London: Putnam, 1955.
A Prospect of the Sea, London: J. M. Dent, 1955.
A Child's Christmas in Wales, Norfolk, Conn.: New Directions, 1955.
Letters to Vernon Watkins, London: J. M. Dent and Faber & Faber, 1957.
The Beach of Falesà, New York: Stein & Day, 1963.
Letters of Dylan Thomas, ed. Constantine Fitzgerald, London: J. M. Dent, 1966.
Twenty Years a-Growing (film script), London: J. M. Dent, 1964.
The Burning Baby (short stories), *unpublished*.

BOOKS ABOUT DYLAN THOMAS

Ackerman, John, *Dylan Thomas, His Life and Work*, London: Oxford University Press, 1964.
Bokanowski, Helene, and Alyn, Marc, *Dylan Thomas*, Paris: Seghers, 1962.
Brinnin, John Malcolm, *Dylan Thomas in America*, Boston: Little, Brown, 1955.
— (ed.), *A Casebook on Dylan Thomas*, New York: Crowell, 1960.
Cox, C. B., *Dylan Thomas, A Collection of Critical Essays*, Englewood Cliffs: Prentice Hall, 1966.
Davies, Aneirin T., *Dylan: Druid of the Broken Body*, London: J. M. Dent, 1964.

Davies, Walford (ed.), *Essays on Dylan Thomas*, London: J. M. Dent, 1971.

Emery, Clark M., *The World of Dylan Thomas*, Coral Gables, Fla.: University of Miami Press, 1962.

Firmage, George J., and Williams, Oscar (eds.), *A Garland for Dylan Thomas*, New York: Clarke and Way, 1963.

Fraser, G. S., *Dylan Thomas*, London: Longmans, Green, 1957.

Heppenstall, Rayner, *Four Absentees*, London: Barrie and Rockliff, 1960.

Holbrook, David, *Llareggub Revisited: Dylan Thomas and the State of Modern Poetry*, London: Bowes and Bowes, 1962. Published in U.S.A. as *Dylan Thomas and Poetic Dissociation*, Carbondale: University of Southern Illinois Press, 1964.

Hornick, Lita R., *The Intricate Image: A Study of Dylan Thomas*, Ann Arbor, Michigan: University Microfilms, 1958.

Jones, T. H., *Dylan Thomas*, Edinburgh: Oliver and Boyd, 1963.

Kappus, Dieter, *Die Dichterische Entwicklung von Dylan Thomas*, Freiburg: Albert Ludwigs University Dissertation, 1960.

Kleinman, Hyman H., *The Religious Sonnets of Dylan Thomas: A Study in Imagery and Meaning*, Berkeley: University of California Press, 1963.

Maud, Ralph, *Entrances to Dylan Thomas's Poetry*, Pittsburgh: University of Pittsburgh Press, 1963.

—, *Poet in the Making, The Notebooks of Dylan Thomas*, London: J. M. Dent, 1965.

—, and Davies, Aneirin T. (eds.), *The Colour of Saying: An Anthology of Verse Spoken by Dylan Thomas*, London: J. M. Dent, 1963.

Michaels, Sidney, *Dylan*, New York: Random House, 1964.

Moynihan, W. T., *The Poetry of Dylan Thomas: A Study of its Meaning and Unity*, Ann Arbor, Michigan; University Microfilms, 1962.

Murdy, Thelma L. B., *Sound and Meaning in Dylan Thomas's Poetry*, Ann Arbor, Michigan: University Microfilms, 1962.

Olson, Elder, *The Poetry of Dylan Thomas*, Chicago: University of Chicago Press, 1954.

Read, Bill, *The Days of Dylan Thomas*, with photographs by Rollie McKenna and others, London: Weidenfeld and Nicolson, 1965.

Rolph, J. Alexander, *Dylan Thomas: a Bibliography*, London: J. M. Dent, 1956.

Sanesi, Roberto, *Dylan Thomas*, Milan: Lerici Editori, 1960.

Stanford, Derek, *Dylan Thomas*, London: Neville Spearman, 1954.

Tedlock, E. W. (ed.), *Dylan Thomas: The Legend and the Poet*, London: Heinemann, 1960.

Thomas, Caitlin, *Leftover Life to Kill*, London: Putnam, 1957.

Tindall, W. Y., *A Reader's Guide to Dylan Thomas*, New York: Farrar, Strauss and Cudahy, 1962.

Treece, Henry, *Dylan Thomas: Dog Among the Fairies*, London: Lindsay Drummond, 1949; revised edition, London: Ernest Benn, 1959.

BOOKS CONTAINING ARTICLES AND CHAPTERS ON DYLAN THOMAS

Adams, Robert M., *Strains of Discord: Studies in Literary Openness*, Ithaca: Cornell University Press, 1958.

Bayley, John, *The Romantic Survival*, London: Constable, 1957.

Daiches, David, *Literary Essays*, Edinburgh: Oliver & Boyd 1956.

Nowottny, Winifred, *The Language Poets Use*, London: The Athlone Press, 1962.

Scarfe, Francis, *Auden and After*, London: Routledge, 1942.

Scully, James (ed.), *Modern Poets on Modern Poetry* (contains an essay by Thomas), London: Collins, 1965.

Shapiro, Karl, *In Defence of Ignorance*, New York: Random House, 1960.

OTHER RELEVANT LITERARY WORKS

Caws, Mary Ann, *Surrealism and the Literary Imagination*, Paris: Mouton & Cie, 1966.

Holbrook , David, *Sylvia Plath and the Problem of Existence*, London: The Athlone Press, 1972.

Hughes, Ted, *Crow*, London: Faber & Faber, 1971.

Plath, Sylvia, *Ariel*, London: Faber & Faber, 1965.

—, *The Colossus*, London: Faber & Faber, 1960 and 1967.

—, *Crossing The Water*, London: Faber & Faber, 1971.

—, *The Bell Jar* (novel), London: Faber & Faber, 1963.

Rickword, Edgell (ed.) *The Calendar of Modern Letters, 1925-1927*, reissued by Cass, London, 1966.

RELEVANT BOOKS ON PHILOSOPHY, PSYCHOLOGY, ETC.

Balint, Michael, *Primary Love and Psychoanalytical Technique*, London: Tavistock, 1952.

Bowlby, John, *Child Care and the Growth of Love*, London: Penguin, 1953.

Chaloner, Len, *Feeling and Perception in Young Children*, London: Tavistock, 1963.

Erikson, Erik, *Childhood and Society*, London: Penguin, 1966.

Fairbairn, W. R. D., *Psychoanalytical Studies of the Personality*, London: Tavistock, 1952.

Farber, Leslie H., *The Ways of the Will*, London: Constable, 1966.

Grene, Marjorie, *Approaches to a Philosophical Biology*, New York; Basic Books, 1968.

Guntrip, Harry, *Personality Structure and Human Interaction*, London: Hogarth, 1961.

—, *Schizoid Phenomena, Object-relations, and the Self*, London: Hogarth, 1968.

Henry, Jules, *Culture Against Man*, London: Tavistock, 1966.

Holbrook, David, *Human Hope and the Death Instinct*, Oxford: Pergamon, 1971.

—, *The Masks of Hate*, Oxford: Pergamon, 1972.

Kasanin, J. S. (ed.), *Language and Thought in Schizophrenia*, Berkeley: University of California Press, 1944.

Klein, Melanie, *Developments in Psychoanalysis*, London: Tavistock, 1952.

Laing, R. D., *The Divided Self*, London: Tavistock, 1960; available in Penguin Books.

Langer, Suzanne K., *Philosophy in a New Key*, Cambridge, Mass: Harvard University Press, 1963.

Levy, David M., *Maternal Overprotection*, Columbia: Columbia University Press, 1943.

Lomas, Peter, *The Predicament of the Family*, London: Hogarth, 1967.

May, Rollo (ed.), *Existence—a New Dimension in Psychiatry*, New York: Basic Books, 1958.

Menninger, Karl, *Man Against Himself*, New York: Harcourt Brace & World, 1938; available in Harvest Paperbacks by Rupert Hart-Davis, London, no date.

Rycroft, Charles (ed.), *Psychoanalysis Observed*, London: Constable, 1966.

Segal, Hannah, *Introduction to the Work of Melanie Klein*, London: Tavistock, 1964.

Schlipp, Paul Arthur, and Friedmann, Maurice, *The Philosophy of Martin Buber*, La Salle, Illinois: Open Court, 1967, Cambridge University Press, 1967.

Winnicott, D. W., *Collected Papers*, London: Tavistock, 1958.

—, *The Family and Individual Development*, London: Tavistock, 1965.

—, *The Maturational Processes and the Facilitating Environment*, London: Hogarth, 1966.

—, *Playing and Reality*, London: Tavistock, 1971 (contains his essay on 'Mirror Role of the Mother', and essays on male and female element in relation to creativity and the 'location of culture').

—, *The Child, the Family and the Outside World*, London: Penguin, 1964.

Index